THE REPENTANT JOB

A Ricoeurian Icon
for Biblical Theology

Thomas F. Dailey, O.S.F.S.

UNIVERSITY
PRESS OF
AMERICA

Lanham • New York • London

Copyright © 1994 by
University Press of America® Inc.
4720 Boston Way
Lanham, Maryland 20706

3 Henrietta Street
London WC2E 8LU England

Imprimi potest:

Most Rev. Roger Balducelli, O.S.F.S., S.S.L., S.T.D., L.H.D.
Superior General
Oblates of Saint Francis de Sales

24 January 1993 *(Feast of St. Francis de Sales)*

Library of Congress Cataloging-in-Publication Data

Dailey, Thomas F.
The repentant Job : a Ricoeurian icon for Biblical theology /
Thomas F. Dailey.
p.   cm.
Includes bibliographical references and index.
1. Bible. O.T. Job—Criticism, interpretation, etc.   2. Ricœur,
Paul—Contributions in hermeneutics.   3. Phenomenology.
I. Title.
BS1415.2.D35   1994   223'.106—dc20   94–21285 CIP

ISBN 0–8191–9589–8 (cloth : alk. paper)
ISBN 0–8191–9590–1 (pbk. : alk. paper)

 The paper used in this publication meets the minimum requirements of
American National Standard for Information Sciences—Permanence
of Paper for Printed Library Materials, ANSI Z39.48–1984.

TABLE OF CONTENTS

iii

ACKNOWLEDGMENTS

For a writing such as this to emerge as a fruitful endeavor, and not merely a test of perseverance, the beneficence of others is indispensable. And so, let me preface this book with a public expression of gratitude to those who have aided me in this particular quest.

Initially, this work appeared as a doctoral dissertation at the Pontifical Gregorian University (Rome, Italy). I am grateful to the **Rev. Prof. Dermot Cox, O.F.M.**, my director, and to the **Rev. Prof. Charles Conroy, M.S.C.**, for their assistance in the academic realm.

The writing of the dissertation took place primarily in the city of Rome, at the Generalate of the religious congregation of the Oblates of St. Francis de Sales. I am indebted to the **Most Rev. Roger Balducelli, O.S.F.S.**, my Superior General, for his scholarly encouragement and paternal advice. And I extend a word of thanks to all my Oblate confreres.

To complete this work, I was given a leave of absence from my teaching position at Allentown College of St. Francis de Sales. Gratefully, I acknowledge the support of the **Very Rev. Daniel G. Gambet, O.S.F.S.**, president of the college, and the **Very Rev. Bernard O'Connor, O.S.F.S.**, my department chairman. A special word of thanks goes to the staff of the Trexler Library at Allentown College, whose extensive research assistance has proven invaluable to the swift completion of this study.

Finally, I cannot fail to acknowledge my parents, **Thomas F. Dailey, Jr. (†)** and **Mary E. Dailey**, without whose loving dedication and prayerful support none of this would have come to fruition.

To these my many friends, I say *thank you* — you have given me infinitely more than did the "friends" of Job!

To facilitate the publication of this work by the University Press of America, several publishers have given permission to use their copyrighted material, which I hereby acknowledge:

"Toward a Hermeneutics of the Idea of Revelation," by PAUL RICOEUR. Originally published in the *Harvard Theological Review*, volume 70/1-2. © 1977 by the President and Fellows of Harvard College. Reprinted by permission.

The Rule of Metaphor: Multi-Disciplinary Studies of the Creation of Meaning in Language, by PAUL RICOEUR, translated by ROBERT CZERNY, with KATHLEEN MCLAUGHLIN and JOHN COSTELLO. © 1977 by the University of Toronto Press.

"The Hermeneutics of Testimony," by PAUL RICOEUR. Originally published in the *Anglican Theological Review*, volume 61/4. © 1979 by the Anglican Theological Review.

Time and Narrative (3 volumes), by PAUL RICOEUR, translated by KATHLEEN MCLAUGHLIN BLAMEY and DAVID PELLAUER. © 1984, 1985, 1988 by the University of Chicago. All rights reserved.

PAUL RICOEUR: Hermeneutics and the Human Sciences, edited and translated by JOHN B. THOMPSON. © 1981 by the Maison des Sciences de l'Homme and Cambridge University Press. Reprinted with the permission of Cambridge University Press.

Man's Anger and God's Silence: The Book of Job, by DERMOT COX. © 1990 by St. Paul Publications (UK).

Parts of this book I have included in articles that have appeared elsewhere. To the publishers of these scholarly journals, I also acknowledge my gratitude for permission to re-print material from the following:

"'Wondrously far from me' — The Wisdom of Job 42,2-3," in the *Biblische Zeitschrift*, volume 36, pages 261-264. © 1992 by Ferdinand Schöningh (Paderborn, Germany).

"The Aesthetics of Repentance: Re-Reading the Phenomenon of Job," in the *Biblical Theology Bulletin*, volume 23, pages 64-70. © 1993 by the Biblical Theology Bulletin, Inc.

ABBREVIATIONS

AB	Anchor Bible
ABR	*American Benedictine Review*
AF	*Archivio di filosofia*, Atti del Colloquio internazionale
AJSL	*American Journal of Semitic Languages & Literature*
ALUOS	Annual of the Leeds University Oriental Society
AnGreg	Analecta Gregoriana
AnHuss	Analecta Husserliana
Anton	*Antonianum*
ASB	Atti della settimana biblica
AsiaJT	*Asia Journal of Theology*
ATD	das Alte Testament Deutsch
ATR	*Anglican Theological Review*
AusCR	*Australian Catholic Record*
AusJBA	*Australian Journal of Biblical Archaeology*
BAP	Bibliothèque des archives de philosophie
BDB	BROWN, F., S.R. DRIVER, and C.A. BRIGGS. *A Hebrew and English Lexicon of the Old Testament.* Oxford: Clarendon, 1952.
BeO	*Bibbia e Oriente*
BETL	Bibliotheca ephemeridum theologicarum lovaniensum
Bib	*Biblica*
BibIll	*Bible Illustrator*
BibOr	Biblica et orientalia
BInt	*Biblical Interpretation*
BJRL	*Bulletin of the John Rylands University Library*
BKir	*Bibel und Kirche*
BLit	*Bibel und Liturgie*
BM	*Beth Mikra*
BN	*Biblische Notizen*
BR	*Biblical Research*
BRev	*Bible Review*
BSac	*Bibliotheca Sacra*
BTB	*Biblical Theology Bulletin*

BVC	*Bible et vie chrétienne*
BZ	*Biblische Zeitschrift*
BZAW	Beihefte zur *ZAW*
CAT	Commentaire de l'Ancien Testament
CBQ	*Catholic Biblical Quarterly*
CBQMS	*CBQ* Monograph Series
CISymb	*Cahiers internationaux de symbolisme*
CJT	*Canadian Journal of Theology*
ComViat	*Communio Viatorum*
ConJ	*Concordia Journal*
ConsJ	*Conservative Judaism*
ConTM	*Concordia Theological Monthly*
CNRS	Centre national de la recherche scientifique
CritInq	*Critical Inquiry*
CuadT	*Cuadernos de Teologia*
CurTM	*Currents in Theology and Mission*
DD	*Dor le Dor*
ÉBib	Études bibliques
EgT	*Eglise et théologie*
ÉPhén	*Études phénoménologiques*
ETR	*Études théologiques et religieuses*
EvQ	*Evangelical Quarterly*
EvT	*Evangelische Theologie*
ExpTim	*Expository Times*
FOTL	Forms of Old Testament Literature
FRLANT	Forschungen zur Religion/Literatur des Alten/Neuen Testaments
GBH	*A Grammar of Biblical Hebrew*, 2 volumes.
	JOÜON, Paul and T. MURAOKA. Roma: PIB, 1991.
GeistL	*Geist und Leben*
Greg	*Gregorianum*
HALAT	*Hebräisches und aramäisches Lexikon zum Alten*
	Testament, 5 volumes.
	W. BAUMGARTNER (ed.). Leiden: Brill, 1967-1990.
HAR	*Hebrew Annual Review*
HBT	*Horizons in Biblical Theology*
HDB	*Harvard Divinity Bulletin*
HebSt	*Hebrew Studies*

HistTod	*History Today*
Hor	*Horizons*, Journal of the College Theology Society
HTS	*Hervormde Teologiese Studies*
HUCA	*Hebrew Union College Annual*
IB	The *Interpreter's Bible*, 12 volumes. Edited by G.A. BUTTRICK. Nashville: Abingdon, 1951-57.
ICC	International Critical Commentary
IDB	The *Interpreter's Dictionary of the Bible*, 4 volumes. Edited by G.A. BUTTRICK. Nashville: Abingdon, 1962.
IDBSup	*IDB Supplementary Volume*. Edited by K. CRIM. Nashville: Abingdon, 1976.
IJT	*Indian Journal of Theology*
Int	*Interpretation*
IPQ	*International Philosophical Quarterly*
ITQ	*Irish Theological Quarterly*
ITS	*Indian Theological Studies*
JAAR	*Journal of the American Academy of Religion*
JAOS	*Journal of the American Oriental Society*
JBL	*Journal of Biblical Literature*
JBR	*Journal of Bible and Religion*
JBQ	*Jewish Bible Quarterly*
JGenEd	*Journal of General Education*
JP	*Journal of Philosophy*
JRel	*Journal of Religion*
JSOT	*Journal for the Study of the Old Testament*
JSOTSup	*JSOT* Supplement
KAT	Kommentar zum Alten Testament
LTP	*Laval théologique et philosophique*
LumVie	*Lumière et Vie*
ModT	*Modern Theology*
MTZ	*Münchener theologische Zeitschrift*
MW	*Man and World*
NB	*New Blackfriars*
NCent	New Century Bible
NedTTS	*Nederlands theologisch tijdschrift*
NICOT	New International Commentary on the Old Testament
NRT	*Nouvelle Revue Théologique*

OBT	Overtures to Biblical Theology
OTE	*Old Testament Essays*
OTL	Old Testament Library
OTM	Old Testament Message
OTS	Oudtestamentische Studiën
PACPA	Proceedings of the American Catholic Philosophical Association
ParSpV	*Parola, Spirito e Vita*
PE	*Philosophic Exchange*
PhänF	*Phänomenologische Forschungen*
PIB	Pontificio Istituto Biblico
PIBA	*Proceedings of the Irish Biblical Association*
PSC	*Philosophy and Social Criticism*
PT	*Philosophy Today*
PUG	Pontificia Universitatis Gregoriana
RB	*Revue biblique*
RCatalT	*Revista Catalana de Teología*
RelLit	*Religion and Literature*
RelSRev	*Religious Studies Review*
RelSt	*Religious Studies*
ResQ	*Restoration Quarterly*
RevExp	*Review and Expositor*
RevistB	*Revista bíblica*
RevScRel	*Revue des sciences religieuses*
RHPR	*Revue d'histoire et de philosophie religieuses*
RICP	*Revue de l'Institut Catholique de Paris*
RivB	*Rivista Biblica*
RP	*Research in Phenomenology*
RPFE	*Revue philosophique de la France et de l'Étranger*
RRel	*Review for Religious*
RSPT	*Revue des sciences philosophiques et théologiques*
RSR	*Recherches de science religieuse*
RTL	*Revue théologique de Louvain*
RTP	*Revue de théologie et de philosophie*
RUO	*Revue de l'université d'Ottawa*
SalTer	*Sal Terrae*
SBFLA	*Studii biblici Francescani Liber Annuus*
SBLDS	Society of Biblical Literature, Dissertation Series
SBLSS	Society of Biblical Literature, Semeia Studies
SBT	Studies in Biblical Theology
ScEs	*Science et Ésprit*

ScrC	*Scripture in Church*
SJT	*Scottish Journal of Theology*
SLJT	*St. Luke's Journal of Theology*
SpTod	*Spirituality Today*
SR	*Studies in Religion/Sciences religieuses*
StBib	Studia biblica
STK	*Svensk Teologisk Kvartalskrift*
StMiss	*Studia Missionalia*
StMyst	*Studia Mystica*
SubsBib	Subsidia Biblica

TBT	*The Bible Today*
TDig	*Theological Digest*
TF	*Tijdschrift voor Filosofie*
THAT	*Theologisches Handwörterbuch zum Alten Testament,*
	2 volumes. Edited by E. JENNI and C. WESTERMANN.
	Münich: Kaiser, 1971/1976.
TQ	*Theologische Quartalschrift*
TrinJ	*Trinity Journal*
TRu	*Theologische Rundschau*
TS	*Theological Studies*
TTod	*Theology Today*
TWAT	*Theologisches Wörterbuch zum Alten Testament.*
	Edited by J. BOTTERWECK and H. RINGGREN.
	Stuttgart: Kohlhammer, 1970-.
TynOTC	Tyndale Old Testament Commentary

USQR	*Union Seminary Quarterly Review*

VSpir	*Vie spirituelle*
VT	*Vetus Testamentum*
VTSup	Supplement to *VT*

WBC	Word Biblical Commentary
WMANT	Wissenschaftliche Monographien zum Alten & Neuen Testament
WTJ	*Westminster Theological Journal*
WW	*Word and World*

ZAW	*Zeitschrift für die alttestamentliche Wissenschaft*
ZBAT	Züricher Bibelkommentar Alten Testament
ZTK	*Zeitschrift für Theologie und Kirche*

If the book of Job holds the place it does in world literature, it is first of all because it provides us with a "classic" of this argumentative mode of wisdom. It is also because of the enigmatic and perhaps deliberately ambiguous character of its conclusion. The final theophany brings no direct answer to Job's personal suffering, and speculation is left to pursue more than one direction.

PAUL RICOEUR

"Evil, A Challenge to Philosophy and Theology"

INTRODUCTION

"The riddles of God are more satisfying than the solutions of man."
Such is the reflection of G.K. Chesterton nearly one hundred years ago
concerning any attempt to explain the Book of Job. A century later,
such exasperation is hardly nearer to being relieved. The full meaning
of this sacred text continues to invite investigation, yet it eludes the
grasp of even the most erudite scholars.

At the same time, though, its very mystery is what inspires its
never-ending appeal! Not only philosophers and theologians, but
playwrights and poets, psychologists and sociologists, even political
analysts — any and all persons who have struggled with the meaning
of human existence have, in turn, taken an interest in Job and proffered
a commentary of one form or another on this enigmatic text. It is amid
this plethora of studies that we wish to enter the theological discussion,
especially as it concerns the interpretation of Job's paradoxical
repentance.

Reading the Book of Job

Any attempt to offer a comprehensive explanation of the Book of
Job is hampered by the multiplicity of possible themes dealt with by its
author. Whatever be the "stuff" of Job, it seems that the tale as a
whole, and the final sections in particular, offer to readers both a
question and a teaching.

The question, ostensibly noted by exegetes and theologians alike, is
one of "theodicy" or the attempt to understand and explain the notion
of divine justice. Many "existentialist" commentators see in the Joban
drama an attempt to deal with the paradox of human suffering and

divine compassion. For them, the actions of Job offer a way to overcome this dilemma and provide a model for right conduct amid adversity.[1] Read in this light, Job's engagement with Yahweh in the whirlwind and his subsequent "repentance" reflect an encounter with the supernatural rather than an answer to a question. But this new-found awareness of the divine may serve only to obfuscate Job's rational dilemma.[2]

Beyond the particular context of human suffering, the tale of Job likewise questions the moral order of the universe. For Job, this entails an admission of humanity's essential finiteness and a recognition of his own personal bitterness,[3] the dual confession of which enables him to transcend both his individual suffering and the established absurdity of the world in which he lives.[4] As concerns the conduct of the God who supposedly founds the moral order of the world and the divine principles by which he governs it, the tale of Job clearly critiques the traditional doctrine of retribution. It dares to suggest that God simply may not be concerned about human affairs[5] or, even more

---

[1] J.E. HARTLEY, *The Book of Job* (NICOT; Grand Rapids 1988) 48: "... with an avowal of innocence he places his destiny in God's hands and demonstrates that a person's moral resolve can grow stronger even amid the worst adversity. Job thus stands as the prime example of how an upright person can maintain his own integrity even when overwhelmed, for no apparent reason, by the most painful suffering."

[2] H. KNIGHT, "Job (Considered as a Contribution to Hebrew Theology)," *SJT* 9 (1956) 65: "For the most remarkable thing about the whole poem is that it is not simply a philosophical discussion between friends, but that it is alive with a soul's tremendous sense of the overpowering majesty and greatness of God."

[3] J. LÉVÊQUE, *Job et son Dieu:* Essai d'exégèse et de théologie biblique (ÉBib; Paris 1970) 517: "Dieu ne se propose pas seulement de susciter chez Job une nouvelle capacité d'émerveillement devant ses oeuvres; Il veut le placer devant une triple limite: la limite de sa durée d'homme, celle de son savoir et celle de son pouvoir." Cf. J. WILCOX, *The Bitterness of Job:* A Philosophical Reading (Ann Arbor 1989), who argues that belief in a moral order to the world underlies Job's curse and subsequent bitterness.

[4] Cf. N.C. HABEL, *The Book of Job:* A Commentary (OTL; Philadelphia 1985) 69: "The design of God frees Job from a mechanical, blind submission to a moral law of retributive justice .... Job, like God, comes to transcend the moral order of his innocent suffering." D. COX, *The Triumph of Impotence:* Job and the Tradition of the Absurd (AnGreg, 212; Roma 1978) 26: "Man has, from the earliest times, faced the problem of meaningless suffering and injustice, and among the ways he has reacted has always been a recognition of the absurdity of human existence. Job was part of this tradition."

[5] N.H. SNAITH, *The Book of Job:* Its Origin and Purpose (SBT, n.s., 11; London 1968) 53.

strikingly, that God may not, after all, be truly omnipotent.[6] In fact, there may be no justice at all and, therefore, no basis for assuming a moral order in the first place![7]

Contrary to such pessimism, the tale of Job also teaches its readers something about the divine-human relationship as characterized by faith and knowledge.[8] Highlighting the fact that Job *does* encounter God, whether resulting in assurance or humiliation,[9] the author of this sacred book alludes to the reality of faith, whether as an epistemological limit or as an existential effusion.[10] In this sense, the faith that issues forth in Job's silence and surrender is the human counterpart to the divine as *mysterium tremendum et fascinans*.[11]

This faith response, in turn, seems to imply that human knowledge is inherently limited. Even after the supernatural encounter, the suffering of Job, as well as the mentality of his God, remain a mystery, both for the protagonist and for the reader. Yet, perhaps this non-answer of God *is* the answer![12] Perhaps the meaning of the book of

---

[6] A. BRENNER, "God's Answer to Job," *VT* 32 (1981) 133: "... God is in fact conceding that he cannot dispose of the wicked and of evil, at least no more than Job can. If so, God is not absolutely omnipotent: he rules the world he has created, but has little or not control over evil."

[7] M. TSEVAT, *The Meaning of the Book of Job and Other Biblical Studies:* Essays on the Literature and Religion of the Hebrew Bible (New York 1980) 31-37.

[8] J.G. JANZEN, *Job* (Interpretation; Atlanta 1985) 21: "... the Book of Job may be seen as contributing to a deepening of the bases, a re-casting of the nature, and a renewal of the viability of the divine-human covenant relation."

[9] Cf. E. JONES, *The Triumph of Job* (London 1966) 110-113, who suggests that the Theophany overcomes Job's lack of certainty regarding God, and H.W. HERTZBERG, "Der Aufbau des Büches Hiob," *Festschrift für A. Bertholet* (Tübingen 1950) 252, who argues that the magnificence of this encounter impels Job to total silence.

[10] Cf. M.H. POPE, *Job:* Introduction, Translation, and Notes (AB, 15; Garden City [3]1973) lxxxiii: "Job's journey from despair to faith is the way each mortal must go .... Only by faith can such seeming defeat be turned to victory ...." S. TERRIEN, *Job* (CAT; Neuchâtel 1963) 5: "Il offre la réponse de la foi pure à la grâce pure."

[11] D.E. GOWAN, "God's Answer to Job: How Is It an Answer?" *HBT* 8,2 (1986) 96: "... it (the Theophany) opened a window in that prison out on to the rest of the world, arousing a sense of wonder which brought something new that could make (Job) forget his pain for a time."

[12] M. BURROWS, "The Voice from the Whirlwind," *JBL* 47 (1928) 125: "Job finds no answer to his question, but he does find satisfaction in a profound religious experience."

Job is that an understanding of God is beyond the question of justice,[13] that the existence of a divine moral order is beyond human comprehension.[14] In the end, the tale of Job may simply teach us that our search for meaning is a quest for a God who is utterly "unfathomable."[15]

This multiplicity of viewpoints concerning the Book of Job indicates not only the complexity of the interpretive task itself but also the need to adopt a novel stance with regard to biblical studies. Such a position assumes and furthers the contemporary shift taking place in biblical studies, namely, that from historical criticism to hermeneutics.[16]

That historical-critical exegesis has been the preferred modality among biblical interpreters is clear from the proliferation and variety of studies based on this methodology.[17] The task of this interpretive enterprise centers on determining the textual meaning of the sacred writings in their original context, which is understood to be foundational and normative to any further theological explications. In this sense, the method of historical criticism proceeds within the ambiance of an historical positivism reminiscent of Romanticism,[18] and it contributes to the on-going theological reflection which constitutes sacred Tradition.[19]

---

[13] A. GELIN, "'Voir Dieu' dans l'Ancien Testament," *BVC* 23 (1958) 10: "Job après sa nuit obscure, a redécouvert son Dieu comme un mystère, au-delà des catégories morales dans lesquelles il le rangerait d'abord."

[14] C. KUHL, "Vom Hiobbuche und seinen Problemen," *TRu* 22 (1954) 281-283.

[15] L. ALONSO SCHÖKEL, *Job* (Los Libros Sagrados; Madrid 1971) 11.

[16] Cf. S. SCHNEIDERS, "From Exegesis to Hermeneutics: The Problem of the Contemporary Meaning of Scripture," *Horizons* 8,1 (1981) 23-39 and "Freedom: Response and Responsibility: The Vocation of the Biblical Scholar in the Church," *Wither Creativity, Freedom, Suffering?:* Humanity, Cosmos, God (Proceedings of the Theology Institute of Villanova University [ed. F.A. EIGO]; Villanova 1981) 25-52.

[17] Cf. T. DAILEY, "In Praise of God's Word: Biblical Studies Since Vatican II," in *The Church in the Nineties: Its Legacy, Its Future* (ed. P. HEGY) (Collegeville 1992) 50-62; J. WICKS, "Biblical Criticism Criticized," *Greg* 72 (1991) 117-128.

[18] R.M. GRANT, *A Short History of the Interpretation of the Bible*, rev. ed. (New York 1972) 186: "It would appear that the primary task of the modern interpreter is historical, in the sense that what he is endeavoring to discover is what the texts and contexts he is interpreting meant to their authors in their relationships with their readers."

[19] SCHNEIDERS, "From Exegesis to Hermeneutics," 31. Cf. K. STENDAHL, "Contemporary Biblical Theology," *IDB* 1:418-432.

Yet, although such "critical" methods should be preferred to previous theological enterprises such as proof-texting, nevertheless the adoption of this "scientific" method of investigation has not been without its critics. Because the nature of the sacred writings demands a value judgment on the part of the interpreter prior to any analysis of the text and subsequent to his/her findings, the "objectivity" of exegesis, and by consequence the adequacy of the historical-critical method as such, have come under question.[20] The contemporary crisis of meaning and relevance demands instead that the work of exegesis not be truncated by misguided critical presuppositions and that of theology not be stunted by unnecessary competition with exegesis.[21]

In response to this demand, biblical theology can profit from the resurgence of "hermeneutics," which enjoins a more open-ended process on the interpretive task. Benefitting from advances in the study of the nature of language, texts, and the act of understanding, biblical hermeneutics extends beyond historical-critical exegesis in three key areas.[22] It sees the biblical writings as literary texts of a religious rather than historical nature and, hence, employs multi-disciplinary methods in the search for their complete sense. It focuses on the present reality rather than past witness of the truth of Scripture and, hence, is less concerned with the production and transmission of the text. Finally, it situates the role of interpretation within the realm of process rather than methodology and, hence, emphasizes the necessity of a reader's engagement with the text itself.

Such a shift in the paradigm of biblical interpretation will allow readers of the Book of Job greater access to the depth of its meaning. Since this tale does not report the situation of a particular historical

---

[20] Cf. W. WINK, *The Bible in Human Transformation:* Toward a New Paradigm for Biblical Study (Philadelphia 1973), and P. STUHLMACHER, *Historical Criticism and Theological Interpretation of Scripture:* Towards a Hermeneutic of Consent (Philadelphia 1977).

[21] SCHNEIDERS highlights the factors undermining the paradigm of historical criticism ("Freedom: Response and Responsibility," 29-36) and concludes her study thus: "The day of positivistic historical criticism in which freedom has been defined solely in terms of responsibility to method is yielding to a time in which the true freedom of the biblical scholar will be rooted in response to the Word and expressed in responsibility for the Word in the assembly of believers" (p. 46).

[22] SCHNEIDERS, "Freedom: Response and Responsibility," 40.

figure, its religious meaning is applicable at all times to all peoples.
Since the various themes of this book are of perennial value, it conveys
a significant truth for present times. And since this truth value is of
tremendous relevance for contemporary readers, the story of Job can
be fully understood and appreciated only through a hermeneutical
engagement with the paradoxical factors inscribed in the tale. Such an
interpretive stance leads us now to consider the particular insights of
philosophical hermeneutics, especially as championed by Paul Ricoeur.

Interpreting with Paul Ricoeur [23]

Though neither an exegete nor a theologian in the strict sense,
Ricoeur has contributed so much to the horizon of biblical studies by
way of his various writings that "he deserves to be presented as the
most theologically sophisticated of the major theorists of interpretation."[24] His writings on the subject of hermeneutics constitute but one
development, albeit a significant one, along the way of elaborating a
philosophy of human volition.[25]

---

[23] Ricoeur offers an autobiographical survey of his career in an essay entitled "From
Existentialism to the Philosophy of Language," reprinted in his *The Rule of Metaphor:
Multi-Disciplinary Studies of the Creation of Meaning in Language* (Toronto 1977) 315-
322. He gives further indications of his philosophical journey in two "responses" to his
collected works: *Hermeneutics and the Human Sciences:* Essays on Language, Action
and Interpretation (ed. J.B. THOMPSON) (Cambridge 1981) 32-40, and *Essays in Biblical
Interpretation* (ed. L.S. MUDGE) (London 1981) 41-45. For other biographical
introductions, see R.D. SWEENEY and L. WETHERBEE PHELPS, "Rhetorical Themes in
the Work of Paul Ricoeur," *PreText* 4 (1983) 215-223, and M. GERHART, "Paul
Ricoeur," in *A Handbook of Christian Theologians*, enlarged edition (eds. M.E. MARTY
and D.G. PEERMAN) (Nashville 1984) 608-624.

[24] M. GERHART, "Paul Ricoeur's Hermeneutical Theory as Resource for Theological
Reflection," *Thomist* 39 (1975) 497.

[25] "A Response by Paul Ricoeur," in THOMPSON (ed.), *Hermeneutics and the Human
Sciences*, 32: "... each work responds to a determinate challenge, and what connects
it to its predecessors seems to me to be less the steady development of a unique project
than the acknowledgment of a residue left over by the previous work, a residue which
gives rise in turn to a new challenge."

The Ricoeurian itinerary, influenced by the thought of major thinkers past and present,[26] devolves from his over-arching concern for human existence and his perduring interest in human creativity. His first writings reflect the tutelage of Marcel, from whom Ricoeur understands the task of existential philosophy to be more the elucidation of a mystery than the resolution of a problem, and from Jaspers he delves into this mystery in terms of paradox (cf. his *Gabriel Marcel et Karl Jaspers* and *Karl Jaspers et la philosophie de l'existence*). With Husserl, Ricoeur sets out on the path toward "a second reflection," toward "the recovery of mystery in clear thought, in a rigorous consciousness — in brief, in discourse."[27] This Husserlian path he trods, in critical dialogue with Kant, by way of phenomenology, which for Ricoeur is nothing less than "a search for meaning" which proceeds by "an analysis of significations" through "the method of imaginative variation."[28] In all this, Ricoeur counters the traditionally pessimistic thought of existentialism with an optimistic humanism that seeks to transform consciousness by fashioning "a notion of being which is *act* rather than *form*, living affirmation, the power of existing and making exist."[29]

Ricoeur's early works form a trilogy on the philosophy of the will and personal ethics under the guise of finitude and culpability. In *Le volontaire et l'involontaire*, he posits the essential structure of the will

---

[26] GERHART, "Paul Ricoeur," 609: "In whatever else he has done, Ricoeur has demonstrated an ability to draw upon, to build upon, and to modify the entire Western philosophical tradition." Similarly, M. PHILIBERT, "The Philosophic Method of Paul Ricoeur," in *Studies in the Philosophy of Paul Ricoeur* (ed. C.E. REAGAN) (Athens, Ohio 1979) 134: "The trait that makes Paul Ricoeur unique in our time, and no less unique in the history of philosophy, lies in the way he combines an eager and humble attention to practically all previous philosophers with a feeling for our present situation and a modest but strong determination to speak his own mind on any problem he deals with."

[27] P. RICOEUR, "L'homme et son mystère," *Le mystère* (Semain des intellectuels Catholiques; Paris 1960) 120. Cf. his *Idées directrices, pour une phénoménologie d'Edmund Husserl*, traduction et présentation (Paris 1950).

[28] P. RICOEUR, "Philosophy of Will and Action," *Phenomenology of Will and Action* (The Second Lexington Conference on Pure and Applied Phenomenology [eds. E.W. STRAUS and R.M. GRIFFITH]; Pittsburgh 1967) 15. Cf. "From Existentialism to the Philosophy of Language," where RICOEUR describes phenomenology as the attempt "to extract from lived experience the essential meanings and structures of purpose, project, motive, wanting, trying, and so on" (p. 316).

[29] P. RICOEUR, *History and Truth* (Evanston [2]1965) 328.

in its volitional experience as being both free and bound. In *L'homme faillable*, he then elaborates upon the constitutional weakness of the will, "the disproportion between the intended meaning of freedom and the experience of finitude," by explaining how "fallibility" pertains to the actuality of willing, common to all persons, rather than to the particular make-up of the decision-making subject. Finally, in *La symbolique du mal*, Ricoeur grapples with this servility of the volitional consciousness by an analysis of three levels of symbols "wherein the avowal of fault was inscribed," namely, the experience of guilt, the myths of the origin of evil, and the rationalizations of the corresponding defect in the process of willing.

With this detour into the creative realm of cosmic and religious symbolism, Ricoeur begins to shift interests, entering into what he calls the "semiological challenge." This challenge is occasioned by a two-fold influence on the work of interpretation: that of Freud in the area of psychoanalysis and that of the French school of structuralism in the area of textual analysis.

In *De l'interprétation: essai sur Freud*, Ricoeur unearths in psychoanalysis the key role played by language, for the analysis of instinctual desires is, in fact, an interpretive discipline which seeks to discover the depth of meaning latent in the psyche. Yet Ricoeur moves beyond the reductive tendency in Freud's hermeneutic of suspicion toward a recollective hermeneutics of affirmation which restores meaning by amplifying the productive and projective character of symbols. In this way Ricoeur discovers the dynamism inherent in interpretation, which moves "from first *naivete* through critique toward ... a second *naivete*." In turn, this movement demonstrates "the necessity of the detour through indirect signs," and it highlights "the conflictual structure of hermeneutics and thus of self-knowledge."[30]

This archaeology and teleology of the subject in psychoanalytic interpretation leads Ricoeur to challenge and critique the advances of structural linguistics. As promoted by Lévi-Strauss and Propp, among others, the structural model of interpretation considers language to be a steady state of objective units whose constitutive parts are able to be analyzed in a scientific fashion. Ricoeur, however, rejects this purely semiological approach, for "(n)ot only the reference of the text to an external world, but also its connections to an author who *intended* it

---

[30] RICOEUR, "From Existentialism to the Philosophy of Language," 318.

and to a reader who *interprets* it are excluded by structuralism."[31]
In a series of articles collected under the rubric of *Le conflit des
interprétations*, and later in a more systematic treatment entitled
Interpretation Theory, Ricoeur advocates a more semantic approach to
interpretation, which recognizes the existential reality of language as
primarily a process of communication or discourse.

Hereby promoting the necessity of an interpretive "circle" in
response to the semiological challenge occasioned by psychoanalysis
and structuralism, Ricoeur enters head on into an exhaustive study of
hermeneutics, whose task is "to show that existence arrives at speech,
at sense, and at reflection only by proceeding to a continual exegesis
of all the significations that come to light in the world of culture."[32]
In dialogue with Schleiermacher and Dilthey, as well as with Gadamer
and Heidegger,[33] he proceeds by means of a "hermeneutic phenomenology," which is at once semantic (rooted in the multiple architecture
of sense in language), reflective (concerned with growth in self-understanding), and existential (implicating the self as an interpretant and a
being-intepreted).[34] He thus arrives at the conclusion that "there is no
self-understanding which is not *mediated* by signs, symbols and texts;
in the last resort understanding coincides with the interpretation given
to these mediating terms."[35] Critical to his hermeneutic phenomenology of the creative and mediating elements in language are his
monumental studies on metaphor (*La Métaphore vive*) and narrative
(*Temps et récit*). In these complementary works, Ricoeur analyzes the
meaning-effects which are engendered by semantic innovations; both

---

[31] RICOEUR, "From Existentialism to the Philosophy of Language," 319.

[32] P. RICOEUR, "Existence et herméneutique," *Le conflit des interprétations* (Essais
d'herméneutique; Paris, 1969) 26. In "The Creativity of Language," *Dialogues with
Contemporary Continental Thinkers* (ed. R. KEARNEY) (Manchester 1984), RICOEUR
acknowledges that "Language possesses deep resources which are not immediately
reducible to knowledge ... and my interest in hermeneutics ... has always been an
attempt to detect and describe these resources" (pp. 22-23).

[33] See especially P. RICOEUR, "The Task of Hermeneutics," in THOMPSON (ed.),
Hermeneutics and the Human Sciences, 43-62.

[34] Cf. RICOEUR, "Existence et herméneutique," 7-28 and *A l'école de la phénoménologie* (BAP; Paris 1986). On the historical context of hermeneutic phenomenology as
a philosophy of language, see his *Main Trends in Philosophy* (New York 1979) 243-
273.

[35] P. RICOEUR, "On Interpretation," in *Philosophy in France Today* (ed. A. MONTE-
FIORE) (London 1983) 191.

metaphor and narrative, he argues, issue from a productive imagination and aim at a novel intelligibility.[36]

In a variation on these hermeneutical investigations, Ricoeur has also endeavored to extend the horizon of interpretation. Previously he associated the thought necessary for significant historical work with the testimony which evidences this thought in a critique of civilization (*Histoire et vérité*), and he has continued this interpretive pedagogy in published works devoted to both history (*The Contribution of French Historiography to the Theory of History* and *The Reality of the Historical Past*) and to politics (*Political and Social Essays* and *Lectures on Ideology and Utopia*). He has also delved into the work of the social sciences (*Hermeneutics and the Human Sciences*) by drawing parallels between the interpretation of texts and that of actions (*Du texte à l'action*). Most recently, Ricoeur has begun to bring full circle his quest for a "poetics of the will," by interpreting the personal and existential implications of these previous studies (*Soi-même comme une autre*).

Throughout the long-winding route of his philosophical journey, Ricoeur has maintained as his goal the understanding of the self in the process of reflection, which is "the appropriation of our effort to exist and our desire to be through the works which testify to this effort and this desire."[37] This same process likewise frames his brief, though significant, forays into the realm of religious understanding (*Les incidences théologiques*). Here influenced by the work of Bultmann

---

[36] In his preface to the first volume of *Time and Narrative* (Chicago 1984), RICOEUR explains the complementarity of these two studies: "Understanding, in the first case, is grasping the dynamism in virtue of which a metaphorical utterance, a new semantic pertinence, emerges from the ruins of the semantic pertinence as it appears in a literal reading of the sentence. Understanding, in the second case, is grasping the operation that unifies into one whole and complete action the miscellany constituted by the circumstances, ends and means, initiatives and interactions, the reversals of fortune, and all the unintended consequences issuing from human action" (p. x).

[37] RICOEUR, "Existence et herméneutique," 21. Elsewhere, he elaborates: "A reflexive philosophy considers the most radical philosophical problems to be those which concern the possibility of *self-understanding* as the subject of the operations of knowing, willing, evaluating, etc. Reflexion is that act of turning back upon itself by which a subject grasps, in a moment of intellectual clarity and moral responsibility, the unifying principle of the operations among which it is dispersed and forgets itself as subject" ("On Interpretation," p. 188).

and Barth,[38] Ricoeur applies his general theories of hermeneutics to the field of biblical studies (*Essays on Biblical Interpretation*). For him, Scripture evidences a textuality akin to any written work; as "poetic" texts which express a confession of faith, the biblical writings reflect and promote the same existential issue with which Ricoeur is elsewhere concerned, namely, the possibility of being in the world. Yet, although he has treated the parables at great length and has commented on certain biblical passages,[39] Ricoeur has never directly applied his hermeneutic theory to an entire book of the Bible. It is this reflective and interpretive project upon which we now embark with regard to the Book of Job.

Understanding "The Repentant Job"

Our summary of Ricoeur's philosophical venture highlights his emergence as one of the major figures in the phenomenological movement. Of particular note for the work of biblical theology is the progress in his thought with regard to the understanding of what hermeneutics entails. In his early works on the philosophy of the will, Ricoeur conceives of hermeneutics in terms of symbols and defines it thus as "the art of deciphering indirect meanings." In his encounter with psychoanalysis, he opposes two trends of hermeneutics, "the first tending toward a reductive explanation, the second tending toward a recollection or a retrieval of the original meaning of the symbol." In contrast to the structural method, Ricoeur's hermeneutics seeks "to reach beyond the 'sense' — as the immanent content of the text — to its 'reference,' i.e., to what it says *about* the world." With his systematic

---

[38] GERHART, "Paul Ricoeur," 622: "In Bultmann, Ricoeur took seriously the need to mediate the understanding of sacred texts by means of a 'second naivete.' After Barth, Ricoeur preserved an emphasis on the initiative taken by God ('the Word from beyond') toward the human being."

[39] On the parables, see "Listening to the Parables of Jesus," *Criterion* 13 (1974) 18-22; "La Bible et l'imagination," *RHPR* 62 (1982) 339-360; and "From Proclamation to Narrative," *JRel* 64 (1984) 501-512. For the interpretation of particular texts, see "Sur l'éxègese de Genèse 1,1 - 2,4a," in *Exégèse et Herméneutique* (Parole de Dieu, 6; [ed. X. LÉON-DUFOUR] Paris 1971) 67-84; "La logique de Jésus: Romans 5," *ETR* 55 (1980) 420-425; "Le récit interprétif: exégèse et théologie dans les récits de la Passion," *RSR* 73 (1985) 17-38; and "Entre philosophie et théologie: le Regle d'Or en question," *RHPR* 69 (1989) 3-9.

investigation of the nature and functioning of discourse, Ricoeur relates hermeneutics to "the specific problems raised by the translation of the objective meaning of written language into the personal act of speaking" which he calls "appropriation."[40] Most recently he specifies that the task of hermeneutics is "to reconstruct the set of operations by which a work lifts itself above the opaque depths of living, acting, and suffering, to be given by an author to readers who receive it and thereby change their acting."[41]

Ultimately, Ricoeur attempts to graft the contours of hermeneutics onto a phenomenological foundation, one in which "*understanding* ceases to appear as a simple *mode of knowing* in order to become a *way of being* and a way of relating to beings and to being."[42] It remains to be seen how this general philosophical theory can be applied to the specific region of biblical interpretation. Thus we propose, in the first chapter, to expound upon the major tenets of Ricoeur's phenomenological hermeneutics, as these can be applied to biblical interpretation. His understanding of narrativity, poetics (symbol and metaphor), and appropriation will thus provide the philosophical background to our interpretation of the religious testimony revealed in Job's final words.

Following this theoretical presentation, we will localize our study in two brief sections. In chapter two, we will consider the Book of Job as a whole. Given its literary configuration and sapiential characterization, it will be suggested that the book be read as a "theo-novella" whose overall development provides the remote context for interpreting Job's final utterance. Among the diverse parts of the book, the encounter between Job and Yahweh provides the proximate context for our study. And so, in chapter three, we will study the significance of Job 38-41, with particular attention being given to the words in 38:1-3 by which Yahweh introduces the climactic sapiential dialogue.

In the central chapter that follows, we will deal directly and at length with the responses of Job to the speeches of Yahweh. First, we will suggest a reading of Job 40:4-5 which interprets the silence of the main character as a sapiential interiority, a deliberate stance on Job's part which contrasts with the verbalized contentiousness of the previous

---

[40] This summary is culled primarily from Ricoeur's own thoughts in "From Existentialism to the Philosophy of Language."

[41] RICOEUR, *Time and Narrative*, vol. I, p. 53.

[42] RICOEUR, "The Task of Hermeneutics," 44.

human diatribes. Then, after surveying commonly held interpretations, we will propose a novel translation of Job 42:2-6 which reads the "repentance" of Job as a poetic affirmation of his newfound wisdom.

Finally, in chapter five, we will argue that this repentant figure serves as an "icon" of what it means to be a sage. Read within the context of the wisdom literature of the Ancient Near East, the change of stance on Job's part may ultimately indicate that spiritual experience is not only valuable but necessary in the pursuit of wisdom. In conclusion, we will suggest that this message of "the repentant Job," interpreted via the hermeneutics of Ricoeur, concerns the duality of criticism and mysticism as these contribute to the integrity of biblical theology.

Chapter One

PHENOMENOLOGICAL HERMENEUTICS:

The Philosophy of Paul Ricoeur

Though vast in terms of its existential endeavor, the philosophy of Paul Ricoeur has focused primarily on the functioning of human language and, as a consequence, on the mediating process of interpretation. While first situating it within the realm of religious-cultural symbols and socio-political actions, Ricoeur most fully analyzes the phenomenon of interpretation in respect to the understanding of written works. Thus, in order subsequently to apply his philosophical thought to a reading of Job's final words, we will here delineate the major tenets of Ricoeur's hermeneutical theory.

To do so, we must explain three primary factors involved in literary interpretation — narrativity, poetics, and appropriation — and their implications for philosophical hermeneutics in general and biblical hermeneutics in particular. Following this presentation, we will set forth the specific issues which derive from this philosophy and which guide our interpretation of the final words of Job. First, however, a consideration of the phenomenological presuppositions which ground Ricoeur's hermeneutical reflection is necessary, for this philosophical starting point distinguishes his thought from other theories of interpretation.

PHENOMENOLOGICAL PRESUPPOSITIONS

By his own admission, that which occupies a place of predominance in Ricoeur's thought is a concern for language in its multiplicity of forms yet unity of function.[1] Approaching the subject by way of a phenomenological analysis, he posits as foundational to the process of human understanding the "eventfulness" of language and its subsequent transformation in writing. In this dynamic notion are to be found two distinctive presuppositions which underlie Ricoeur's theory of interpretation, namely, that interpretation is *possible* because of the discursive nature of communication in general, and that interpretation is *necessary* due to the specifically autonomous character of written works.

Language as Discourse

More enduring than the fleeting appearance of "speech,"[2] and less psychologically prejudicial than the model of "dialogue,"[3] Ricoeur's notion of "discourse" highlights the eventfulness of language in its

---

[1] P. RICOEUR, "Narrativité, Phénoménologie, et Herméneutique," in the *Encyclopédie philosophique universelle*, I: L'univers philosophique (dir. A. JACOB) (Paris 1989) 63-64. This same article offers a synthetic view of the position of hermeneutics within Ricoeur's overall philosophy (pp. 68-71).

[2] P. RICOEUR, "Explanation and Understanding: On Some Remarkable Connections Among the Theory of the Text, Theory of Action, and Theory of History," in *The Philosophy of Paul Ricoeur: An Anthology of His Work* (ed. C.E. REAGAN and D. STEWART) (Boston 1978) 153: "... it is discourse which calls for the ever more complicated process of exteriorization to itself; it begins with the separation of the act of speaking and what is said, is continued by alphabetic inscription, and culminates in the complex codifications of works of discourse, among which is that of the story."

[3] P. RICOEUR, "Événement et sens dans le discours," in *Paul Ricoeur où la liberté selon l'ésperance* (Philosophes de tous les temps, 72; [ed. M. PHILIBERT] Paris 1971) 177: "Je me propose ici de mettre en question les postulats de cette herméneutique au plan d'une *philosophie du discours*, afin de délivrer l'herméneutique de ses préjugés psychologisants et de son étroitesse existentielle; ces préjugés procèdent, à mon avis, d'une méconnaissance de la *dialectique de l'événement et du sens dans le discours*; cette méconnaissance, à son tour, conduit à assigner une tâche erronée à l'interprétation, tâche qu'exprime assez bien le fameux slogan: 'comprendre un auteur mieux qu'il ne s'est compris lui-même'."

movement from personal experience to reflective articulation.[4] Understood as "saying something to someone about something," language as discourse encompasses more than a signification of sense by means of established linguistic signs;[5] it refers instead to the uniquely human *creation* of meaning in and through the innovative uses of language.[6] Thus, discourse exhibits a dynamic character, with traits that distinguish it from the mere use of words.

In contrast to the virtual potentiality of words, discourse demands the *temporal actualization* of a message; one speaks, then, not of an a-temporal system but of a given "instance of discourse." As a predicative event, discourse necessarily involves a speaking subject; unlike the anonymity of a language system, the instance of discourse is, therefore, *self-referential.* Moreover, because such predication concerns the exchange of a message, discourse necessarily engages another person; more than merely a condition for the possibility of verbal intercourse, it actualizes communication by involving *another interlocutor* who contributes to the particularity of the message. Finally, this mutual exchange engages the speakers in a communication about something; far from confining itself to words bound to the interior of a linguistic system, discourse necessarily encompasses *reference to extra-linguistic reality* as it seeks to describe, express or represent the world of human existence.[7]

This inclusion of the self, the other, and the world in the event of discourse expands the horizon of hermeneutics beyond the empirical investigation proposed by structuralist approaches to interpretation.[8] More than the attempt to decode particular word-signs in opposition to

---

[4] RICOEUR, *Main Trends in Philosophy*, 253: "... it is in the medium of articulation and discourse which is characteristic of language that the unreflected comes to reflection."

[5] P. RICOEUR, "Philosophie et langage," *RPFE* 103 (1978) 456: "Nous touchons ici à la plus fondamentale implication de la distinction entre sémiotique et sémantique.... Le signe *diffère* du signe, le discours se *réfère* au monde...."

[6] RICOEUR, "The Creativity of Language," 19: "The creation of meaning in language comes from the specifically *human* production of new ways of expressing the objective paradigms and codes made available by language."

[7] Cf. RICOEUR, "Philosophie et langage," 453-458 and "Événement et sens dans le discours," 178-179.

[8] Cf. P. RICOEUR, "La structure, le mot, l'événement," *Le conflit des interprétations*, 80-97; "Structure et signification dans le langage," in *Pourquoi la philosophie?* (ed. G. LEROUX) (Montréal 1968) 101-120.

other word-signs within the closed system of an institutionalized language, a phenomenological hermeneutics concerns itself with the one who speaks, the other to whom one speaks, and the world about which one speaks. What requires interpretation, therefore, is not only the content of the words uttered but also the forceful attitude evidenced in them and the expected response elicited by them.[9]

Interpretation is thus rendered possible because of the dialectical mediation of event and sense at work in discourse. As a result, the general task of hermeneutics extends beyond the deciphering of signs to the discernment of experience. Yet, in the specific process of interpreting literary works, another factor must be considered, for the experiential dimension of discourse — the "something to say" which is the focus of interpretation — comes to be disclosed in a new and unique way in writing.

Writing as Distanciation

If discourse connotes the interplay of sense and event, writing exhibits what Ricoeur calls the "trans-eventfulness" of language, in that the text provides "the resource for all new actualizations" of the meaning of discourse.[10] Consequently, the interpretation of literary works must take into account the specific traits which distinguish written discourse from the spoken and which engender the autonomy of the text.

Ricoeur describes the phenomenological traits proper to written discourse in terms of its medium, message, reference, and audience. In writing, the otherwise fleeting event of speaking is purposefully fixed in a more *permanent mode*; the human factor fades into the background as what comes to the fore is not the event of saying but the

---

[9] Following Searle, RICOEUR speaks, respectively, of the locutionary proposition, the illocutionary force, and the perlocutionary action of discourse; cf. "The Hermeneutical Function of Distanciation," in *Hermeneutics and the Human Sciences*, 132-136.

[10] RICOEUR, "Événement et sens dans le discours," 186: "A cet égard l'écriture est la médiation exemplaire entre deux événements de parole; un événement de parole ne suscite un nouvel événement de parole que sous la condition de la suppression de l'événement dans la dimension du sens; seule cette universalité d'un type spécial, cette universalité du dit inscrit dans la lettre, peut engendrer de nouveaux événements de discours. L'étape trans-événementielle du sens est la resource de toutes les nouvelles actualisations."

meaning of what is said in and by the text.[11] In writing, therefore, the immediacy of understanding between speaker and listener is lacking; a *distance* is thereby established such that the author's intention in writing does not necessarily correspond to the reader's understanding of the message of the text.[12] Moreover, because the dialogic context of discourse is abolished, the ostensive constraints of the original situation are effaced by writing; as a result, a *new world of meaning* is projected with reference to new possibilities of existence derivable from the text.[13] Finally, since a person-to-person communication no longer takes place, the audience changes; it now becomes a *potentially universal audience*, comprised of those readers who render the text actual and significant.[14]

Hereby reflecting what Ricoeur calls "the spirituality of writing, (as) counterpart of its materiality and of the alienation which it imposes on

---

[11] P. RICOEUR, "The Model of the Text: Meaningful Action Considered as a Text," in *Hermeneutics and the Human Sciences*, 199: "Not the event of speaking, but the 'said' of speaking, where we understand by the 'said' of speaking that intentional exteriorisation constitutive of the aim of discourse thanks to which the *sagen* — saying — wants to become *Aus-sage* — the enunciation, the enunciated. In short, what we write, what we inscribe, is the *noema* of the speaking. It is the meaning of the speech event, not the event as event."

[12] RICOEUR, "The Model of the Text," 200-201: "With written discourse, the author's intention and the meaning of the text cease to coincide. This dissociation of the verbal meaning of the text and the mental intention is what is really at stake in the inscription of discourse. Not that we can conceive of a text without an author; the tie between the speaker and the discourse is not abolished, but distended and complicated.... What the text says now matters more than what the author meant to say, and every exegesis unfolds its procedures within the circumference of a meaning that has broken its moorings to the psychology of its author."

[13] For RICOEUR, this new world encompasses "the non-situational references which outlive the effacement of the first [dialogic situations] and which henceforth are offered as possible modes of being, as symbolic dimensions of our being-in-the-world" ("The Model of the Text," 202). Cf. "Événement et sens dans le discours," 182: "En ce sens Heidegger a raison de dire ... que ce que d'abord on comprend dans un discours, ce n'est pas un autrui, mais un projet, c'est-à-dire, l'esquisse d'un nouvel être-au-monde."

[14] RICOEUR, "The Model of the Text," 203: "In escaping the momentary character of the event, the bounds lived by the author, and the narrowness of ostensive reference, discourse escapes the limits of being face to face. It no longer has a visible auditor. An unknown, invisible reader has become the unprivileged addressee of the discourse."

discourse,"[15] the phenomenon of distanciation qualifies the interpretive process in ways that distinguish "hermeneutics" from "criticism." First, the fixation of discourse in a permanent form becomes a conditioning factor for hermeneutics in as much as the final form of the text takes precedence, not simply in terms of a contingent process to be studied historically but as the locus in which the inquiry into the sense of the text begins and through which it proceeds.[16] Moreover, the hermeneutical process must maintain an interpretive balance between an intentional fallacy, which entertains the romanticist illusion of a psychological congeniality between author and reader, and an objective fallacy, which promotes the positivist illusion of an hypostatized text as an absolute and self-contained entity.[17] Further, an acknowledgment of the "pro-ject" of written discourse, that aspect by which the "world" of the text transgresses the situational boundary of speaker and listener, provides for both the descriptive and non-descriptive potential of texts.[18] Finally, hermeneutics must take into account the influential role of the reader, who actualizes the meaning of a text by attending to

---

[15] RICOEUR, "Événement et sens dans le discours," 182: "Au lieu d'être seulement adressé à toi, seconde personne, l'écrit est adressé à l'audience qu'il se crée. Cela encore marque la spiritualité de l'écriture, contrepartie de sa matérialité et de l'aliénation qu'elle impose au discours."

[16] RICOEUR, "Événement et sens dans le discours," 180: "Ce qu'il faut donc montrer ici c'est que cette fixation n'est pas une aventure contingente, mais l'accomplissement plénier de ce que nous venons d'appeler la suppression de l'événement dans le sens; de cette façon, l'herméneutique procède tout entière de ce dépassement de l'événement dans le sens, sanctionné et consacré par le mouvement de la parole à l'écriture." On the importance of the final form of biblical texts, see B.S. CHILDS, "Die theologische Bedeutung der Endform eines Textes," *TQ* 167 (1987) 242-251.

[17] P. RICOEUR, *Interpretation Theory:* Discourse and the Surplus of Meaning (Fort Worth 1976) 30: "If the intentional fallacy overlooks the semantic autonomy of the text, the opposite fallacy forgets that a text remains a discourse told by somebody, said by someone to someone else about something." Cf. "Narrativité, phénoménologie et herméneutique," 70-71.

[18] RICOEUR, *Interpretation Theory*, 37: "For me, the world is the ensemble of references opened up by every kind of text, descriptive or poetic, that I have read, understood, and loved. And to understand a text is to interpolate among the predicates of our situation all the significations that make a *Welt* out of our *Umwelt*. It is this enlarging of our horizon of existence that permits us to speak of the references opened up by the text or of the world opened up by the referential claims of most texts."

its "itinerary of sense" and the destination of this sense in the situations of contemporary life.[19]

This two-fold movement of contextualization on the part of the reader responds to the necessity of interpretation with regard to written works. Respecting the uniqueness and autonomy of a text, the hermeneutical inquiry does not limit its focus to the analysis of words or the discovery of an author's intention; rather, it seeks comprehension of the truth of human experience signified in the event of discourse and transformed by the act of writing. To reach this comprehension, the first task of hermeneutics will be to reconstruct, through the dialectic of explanation and understanding, the dual work of the text, namely, the internal dynamic operative in narratives and the external projection therein of a poetic world of meaning.[20]

Toward a Hermeneutic of Narrativity

Distinct from a mere flight of fancy, as the popularized notion of the terms "story" and "fiction" might suggest, the phenomenon of narrativity concerns the authorial dynamics operative within a written

---

[19] RICOEUR, "La Bible et l'imagination," 340: "D'une part, je voudrais considérer l'acte de lecture comme une activité dynamique qui ne se borne pas à répéter des significations à tout jamais fixées, mais qui se place dans le prolongement d'*itinéraires de sens*, ouverts sur un travail d'interprétation. Par ce premier trait, l'acte de lecture convient à l'idée de productivité normée, dans la mesure où il se laisse guider par une imagination productrice à l'oeuvre dans le texte lui-même. En outre, je voudrais voir dans la lecture d'un texte comme la Bible une opération créatrice sans cesse employée à décontextualiser le sens et à le recontextualiser dans le *Sitz im Leben* d'aujourd'hui. Par ce second trait, l'acte de lecture réalise l'union de la fiction et de la redescription, caractéristique de l'imagination au sens le plus prégnant du terme."

[20] RICOEUR, "Narrativité, Phénoménologie, et Herméneutique," 70: "Une fois affranchie du primat de la subjectivité, quelle peut être la tâche première de l'herméneutique? Elle est, selon moi, de chercher dans le texte lui-même, d'une part la dynamique interne qui préside à la structuration de l'oeuvre, d'autre part la puissance de l'oeuvre de se projeter hors d'elle-même et d'engendrer un monde qui serait véritablement la 'chose' du texte. Dynamique interne et projection externe constituent ce que j'appelle le travail du texte. C'est la tâche de l'herméneutique de reconstruire ce double travail du texte."

mode of discourse.[21] In this respect, the message of any narrative
comes to be communicated through a particular form, within the
direction of thought of the story as a whole, and by means of a
singularly eventful style.[22] Hermeneutics must, therefore, take into
account both the artful "emplotment" of a narrative and its "imaginative" modality.

The Work of Emplotment

Adapting the thought of Aristotle, Ricoeur posits the notion of
"emplotment" (*muthos*) as both a foundational factor in the writing of
narratives and an elucidating element in the process of interpretation.[23] From the author's perspective, emplotment creates the
paradigmatic order which envelops a story's meaning. By providing an
actantial infrastructure, that is "a sequence of actions and experiences
of a certain number of characters, whether real or imaginary,"[24] the
author organizes the narrative from a particular point of view and
according to a definite progression. This ordering capacity, in turn,
generates intrigue and thereby contributes to the "followability" of a
narrative, which Ricoeur explains thus:

---

[21] In general, Ricoeur prefers the expression "mode of discourse" to that of "literary
genre" because the former maintains a sense of productivity while the latter is merely
a label of classification. Moreover, the term "narrativity" concerns, in the first place,
written discourse as a whole, and only later the bifurcation of historiography and
fictional literature.

[22] RICOEUR proposes these three features (codification, composition, and configuration) as distinctive of the "work" of discourse ("The Hermeneutical Function of
Distanciation," 136-138).

[23] In his *Poetics*, Aristotle speaks of *muthos*, which can be translated both as "fable"
(an imaginary story) and as "plot" (a well-ordered story). According to RICOEUR,
"Narrative and Hermeneutics," *Essays on Aesthetics* (FS. M. Beardsley; [ed. J. FISHER]
Philadelphia 1983) 152: "The context shows that both senses must be preserved in our
modern rendering of the term. What is at stake is the union of fiction and order within
one and the same operation." Thus "emplotment" is perhaps the best English equivalent
of Ricoeur's translation (*mise en intrigue*) of the term *muthos* because "the *Poetics* being
about the poesis of the poem — that is, its structuration rather than its structure — we
do justice to Aristotle's intention by using 'emplotment' or 'emplotting' to designate the
making of the fable as both fictional and ordered."

[24] P. RICOEUR, "The Narrative Function," in *Hermeneutics and the Human Sciences*,
277.

To follow a story is to proceed forward in the midst of contingencies and peripeties, under the thrust of an expectation that finds its fulfillment in the 'conclusion' of the story. But this conclusion is not the logical implication of some previous premises. It is the 'ending' that provides the vantage point from which the story may be seen as a whole. To understand the story is to understand how and why the successive episodes lead to this conclusion, which, even if it is not predictable, must be finally acceptable as fitting in with the episodes gathered by the story.[25]

It is this acceptability which allows the reader to integrate the parts of a narrative and bring the story being told to its fruition.

Thus, the emplotment of a narrative engenders a synthesizing judgment, for "(t)o narrate and to follow a story is already to 'reflect upon' events with the aim of encompassing them in successive totalities."[26] The accomplishment of this aim reflects the bi-dimensional character of any narrative. The first dimension encompasses chronologically the numerous *episodes* that take place within and affect the development of the story. When incorporated in a narrative, therefore, an event ceases to be a merely factual occurrence; instead, it comes to be known and defined as significant by its role in the progression of the story as a whole.[27] The second dimension concerns the *configuration* of these disparate events into a meaningful totality. The relative importance of a narrative's episodes thus pertains to the author's work of regulating the characters and their actions (i.e., all their thoughts, feelings, deeds, omissions, etc.).[28] It is in the combination of these episodic and configurational dimensions that the narrative receives its iterative form.

The grasping together which transforms contingent events into a meaningful succession that transpires within a specific beginning and

---

[25] RICOEUR, "Narrative and Hermeneutics," 153.

[26] RICOEUR, "The Narrative Function," 279.

[27] P. RICOEUR, "Contingence et rationalité dans le récit," *PhänF* 18 (1986) 13: "en distinguant l'événement de la simple occurrence et par sa contribution à la marche du récit, l'opération narrative transforme la contingence irrationnelle en une contingence réglée, signifiante, intelligible."

[28] RICOEUR, "Contingence et rationalité," 14-15: "Le 'prendre-ensemble' que nous avons d'abord appliqué aux événements, s'applique aussi à ces facteurs hétérogènes, faisant ainsi de la contingence sauvage caractéristique de la pure occurrence, une contingence réglée."

ending — this is the work of emplotment. And this ordering operation, which establishes and directs and frames the intrigue of a story, is what brings about the "miracle of narration."[29] In Ricoeur's phenomenological terms, this miracle is to be understood as the production of a "discordant concordance" or "synthesis of the heterogeneous."

For Ricoeur, the work of emplotment as a means of *concordance* issues from two corresponding perspectives. Seeing the story as a totality, emplotment is that which orders the singular events into the beginning, middle, and end of a complete story. Seeing the story in its parts, emplotment is that which confers "a contour, a limit and, consequently, a magnitude" on otherwise amorphous episodes.[30] Consequently, the interpretation of any part of a narrative unfolds only within the context of the story as a whole.

However, beyond this interconnectedness of parts and whole, the work of emplotment also incorporates a schema of *discordance*, and this on two levels.[31] First, on the level of emotions, emplotment engenders discord primarily by the inclusion of "fearful and pitiable incidents," whereby "(t)he spectator's emotional response is constructed in the drama, in the quality of the destructive or painful incidents suffered by the characters themselves." Added to these are elements of "surprise" or of "reversal" which also seek to move the affections. On a second level, that of reason, emplotment creates discord both in its typology of the characters ("whether the characters are good or evil, and whether their end is happy or unhappy") and in its presentation of the "tragic fault" as a conceptual anchor on which to support an explanation. As a result, the interpretation of meaning in a narrative

---

[29] RICOEUR, "Contingence et rationalité," 17: Mais — et c'est là le miracle de la narration — en même temps que la contingence est, comme je le disais en commençant, reconnue, magnifiée, honorée, elle est aussi, par la grâce du récit, mise au service du déroulement de l'histoire: la péripétie-hasard est incorporée à l'art de nouer et de dénouer ...."

[30] P. RICOEUR, "L'identité narrative," in *La narration: quand le récit devient communication* (Lieux théologiques, 12; [eds. P. BÜHLER et J.-F.HABERMACHER] Génève 1988) 291: "Par complétude, il faut entendre l'unité de composition qui exige que l'interprétation d'une partie soit subordonnée à celle de l'ensemble. ... Il en va de même de l'étendue: ce n'est que dans l'intrigue que l'action a un contour, une limite, et, en conséquence, une étendue ...."

[31] Ricoeur draws this analysis of discordant concordance from Aristotle's *Poetics* (*Time and Narrative*, vol. I, pp. 42-45).

requires the discernment of "the affecting within the intelligible" which a plot engenders.

Thus, in the space where paradigm and deviance clash, where discordance becomes concordance and a "synthesis of the heterogenous" is accomplished, the work of emplotment reveals the dynamic power of a narrative. Hermeneutics strives to discover this capacity to unite in a single experience both the intellectual and the affective, "a mixed intelligibility between what can be called the *thought* — the theme, or the topic of the story — and the intuitive presentation of circumstances, characters, episodes, changes of fortune, etc."[32] Most readily apparent in stories which center on a "crisis,"[33] the artful construction of a narrative elicits a reader's expectations and thereby generates an intellectual "interest."[34] Reading any story, the interpreter enters into an heroic quest; becoming enthralled with the intriguing development of events, he/she seeks to comprehend the response of the characters to the predicaments caused by changing situations.[35] To this end, hermeneutics focuses on the practical mediation which a narrative effects, "whether ... it attempts to restore an anterior order which is threatened or to project a new order which would be the promise of a hope for success."[36] To understand this mediation, this opening up of an order of being-in-the-world, is to appreciate a narrative's capacity to portray reality in an imaginative fashion.

---

[32] P. RICOEUR, "The Text as Dynamic Identity," in *The Identity of the Literary Text* (eds. M.J. VALDÉS and O. MILLER) (Toronto 1985) 178.

[33] With Frank Kermode, Ricoeur shares the conviction that "(c)risis, however, facile the conception, is unescapably a central element in our endeavours towards making sense of our world" (quoted in *Time and Narrative*, vol. II, p. 24, n. 38).

[34] RICOEUR, "Can Fictional Narratives Be True?", in *The Phenomenology of Man and the Human Condition*. Individualisation of Nature and the Human Being, I: Plotting the Territory for Interdisciplinary Communications (AnHuss, 14; [ed. A.-T. TYMIENIECKA] Dordrecht 1983) 15: "An interest is not simply a psychological factor. It concerns the goals which orient a cognitive activity."

[35] P. RICOEUR, *La Narrativité* (ed. D. TIFFENEAU) (Paris 1980) 41: "En ce sens, c'est la quête qui rend possible l'*intrigue*, c'est-à-dire la disposition des événements susceptibles d'êtres 'saisis ensemble'." Cf. *Time and Narrative*, vol. II, p. 19: "Literature as a whole may thus be globally characterized as a quest ...."

[36] RICOEUR, "Contingence et rationalité," 40: "Pour le dire autrement, la médiation opérée par le récit est essentiellement pratique, soit que, comme Greimas lui-même le suggère, elle vise à restaurer un ordre antérieur qui est menacé, soit qu'elle vise à projeter un nouvel ordre qui serait la promesse d'un salut."

The Role of Imagination

According to the phenomenology of Ricoeur, narratives demonstrate their heuristic capacity by virtue of a "creative imitation" (*mimesis*) which connects the figuring work of writing with the pleasure taken in reading.[37] Owing to the capabilities of the author's and the reader's imagination, fictional narratives communicate an innovative message, one whose existential intelligibility comes to light by way of an augmented notion of truth and reality.

This capacity of fictional narratives to augment truth derives from the power of a *productive* imagination. Understood in its narrative sense, imagination does not pertain to the limited psychological operation of perception.[38] Rather, it operates within a properly literary environment, where "the nothingness of the unreal concerns the referent of fiction" and where the mode of imagination appears to be creative rather than sensorial, productive rather than reproductive, for its aim is to "engender *novel* grids in order for reading experience."[39] Narratives thereby figure in a novel and inviting way the world of human life, a world which "can be called 'imaginary', in the sense that it is *represented* by writing in lieu of the world *presented* by speech."[40] A narrative creatively envisions this imaginary world not by duplicating historical events but by projecting the significance of human action "according to its essential and magnified traits." Ultimately, it is this magnification by way of imaginative variation that

---

[37] RICOEUR, *Time and Narrative*, vol. I, p. 31: "This second theme [creative imitation] is difficult to distinguish from the first one in Aristotle [the composing of the tragic poem], inasmuch as for him mimetic activity tends to be confused with emplotment."

[38] P. RICOEUR, "Imagination in Discourse and Action," in *The Human Being in Action* (AnHuss, 7; [ed. A.-T. TYMIENIECKA] Dordrecht 1978) 3-6.

[39] RICOEUR, *Narrativité*, 56: "... la fiction seule pose le problème de l'irréalité en tant que distincte de la simple absence. Tandis que le rien de l'absence ne concerne que les modes de donnée, le rien de l'iréel concerne le référent de la fiction. ... Parce que les fictions ne se réfèrent pas de manière reproductive à la réalité en tant que déjà donnée, elles se réfèrent à la réalité de manière productive en tant que prescrite par elles. ... Toutes [les systèmes symboliques] déploient ce pouvoir organisateur parce qu'elles ont une dimension signitive, parce qu'elles sont forgées par *travail* et savoir-faire et parce qu'elles engendrent de *nouvelles* grilles pour lire l'expérience."

[40] RICOEUR, "What Is a Text? Explanation and Understanding," in *Hermeneutics and the Human Sciences*, 149.

makes fiction "a sort of metaphor of reality" and that leads to a distinct view of the truth.[41]

Ricoeur theorizes that fictional narratives accomplish this imaginative variation in three successive stages. In the first (*prefiguration*), the activity of composition is grounded on the prior experience of the signifying power of human action, a "pre-understanding of the world of action, its meaningful structures, its symbolic resources and its temporal character" which passes into the narrative in terms of integration and actuality.[42] The second stage (*configuration*) encompasses the specific work of emplotment in its generation of "the kingdom of the *as if* " by which fiction is commonly identified.[43] The third and final stage (*refiguration*) occurs where the world of the text ("the world configured by the poem") and the world of the reader ("the world where real action occurs") intersect, so that "(w)hat is communicated, in the final analysis, is, beyond the sense of a work, the world it projects and that constitutes its horizon."[44]

This fictional world devolves from the properly poetic character by which narratives build on the ability of the imagination to see reality as something different from what the everyday interests of ordinary language propose or what the prejudices of scientific certitude declare to be. Borrowing from the language of art, Ricoeur describes this creative power in terms of a "paradox of iconic augmentation," whereby

---

[41] RICOEUR, *Narrativité*, 55: "La *mimésis* tragique réctive la réalité, c'est-à-dire ici l'action humaine, mais selon ses traits essentiels magnifiés. La *mimésis*, en ce sens, est une sorte de métaphore de la réalité. Comme la métaphore, elle met sous les yeux en 'signifiant la chose en acte'."

[42] RICOEUR, *Time and Narrative*, vol. I, pp. 56-57: "In passing from the paradigmatic order of action to the syntagmatic order of narrative, the terms of the semantics of action acquire integration and actuality. Actuality, because the terms, which had only a virtual signification in the paradigmatic order, that is, a pure capacity to be used, receive an actual [*effective*] signification thanks to the sequential interconnections the plot confers on the agents, their deeds, and their sufferings. Integration, because terms as heterogeneous as agents, motives, and circumstances are rendered compatible and work together in actual temporal wholes."

[43] RICOEUR, *Time and Narrative*, vol. I, p. 66.

[44] RICOEUR, *Time and Narrative*, vol. I, pp. 76-77.

The more imagination deviates from that which is called reality in ordinary language and vision, the more it approaches the heart of the reality which is no longer the world of manipulable objects, but the world into which we have been thrown by birth and within which we try to orient ourselves by projecting our innermost possibilities upon it, in order that we *dwell* there, in the strongest sense of that word.[45]

By means of this extraordinary "second-order reference,"[46] the poetic re-description of human existence is ultimately inclined to the universal and essential aspects of what is "real" and "true."[47] In order to discern fully this properly narrative vision of truth and reality, one must understand the specific functioning of poetic language.

IN THE POWER OF THE POETIC

Explanation of the poetic dimension of written discourse requires an understanding of the symbolic and metaphorical power with which such language is invested. The phenomenon intended here by "symbolic" reflects a specific way of thought and mode of expression relative to the domain of experience, while that intended by "metaphorical" refers to the masterful process by which language is empowered to incorpo-

---

[45] P. RICOEUR, "The Function of Fiction in Shaping Reality," *MW* 12,2 (1979) 139. He borrows the notion of "iconic augmentation" from François Dagognet "in order to characterize the power of the image to condense, spell out, and develop reality" (p. 136).

[46] RICOEUR, *Narrativité*, 57: "Comme toute oeuvre poétique la fiction narrative procède d'une *épochè* du monde ordinaire de l'action humaine et des descriptions de ce monde ordinaire dans le discours ordinaire. ... ou, pour le dire en d'autres termes, la suppression d'une référence de premier ordre — que nous avons appelée par convention la 'description' du monde — est la condition de possibilité d'une référence de second ordre que nous appelons ici la redescription du monde. Une oeuvre littéraire, me semble-t-il, n'est pas une oeuvre sans référence, mais un oeuvre avec une référence dédoublée, c'est-à-dire une oeuvre dont l'ultime référence a pour condition une suspension de la référence du langage conventionnel."

[47] RICOEUR, *Narrativité*, 66: "Aristote, se référant encore à la tragédie grecque, dit de manière paradoxale que la poésie est plus philosophique ... que l'histoire.' Il veut dire par là que, dans la mesure où l'histoire s'attache au contingent, elle manque l'essentiel, tandis que la poésie, n'étant pas l'esclave de l'événement réel, peut se porter directement à l'universel, c'est-à-dire à ce qu'une certaine sorte de personnes dirait ou ferait probablement ou nécessairement."

rate and express a unique type of cognition, imagination, and feeling. Understood primarily on a semantic level, the symbolic and metaphorical dimensions nevertheless contribute to and benefit from the development of the narrative as a complex whole.

The Domain of Symbolism

The phenomenological import of symbolism lies in the link it provides between experience and expression. Here, "the symbol becomes more than a key to modes of human experience; it is a key to human depth, because it brings out the point of articulation between the historical and the ontological ...."[48] The symbolic pertains to the domain of hermeneutics when this depth-experience is incorporated into a narrative frame. This is especially clear in the narration of myths, whose tripartite function is to universalize the depth-experience, to introduce a tension into this experience, and to explore the progressions and digressions of this tensive existence.[49] In particular, the power of symbolic language is activated in the narration of tragic myths, whose purpose is to force the question of one's moral consciousness. According to Ricoeur, "tragic symbols speak in the silence of the humiliated ethical. They speak of a 'mystery of iniquity' that man cannot entirely handle, that freedom cannot give reasons for, seeing that it already finds it within itself."[50] Hence, the full power of poetic symbols resides in their ability to transcend both imaginative intuition and reflective speculation.

To appreciate this poetic power, the phenomenon of symbolism must be considered in terms of its linguistic bearing. To this end Ricoeur posits a four-fold criteriology in the hermeneutics of symbols.[51] In the first place, they function according to a *double intentionality*, whereby both a literal and a non-literal meaning are simultaneously communicated. The relation between these two meanings can best

---

[48] P. RICOEUR, "The Symbol ... Food for Thought," *PT* 4 (1960) 206.

[49] P. RICOEUR, *The Symbolism of Evil* (Religious Perspectives; New York 1967) 161-164.

[50] P. RICOEUR, "The Hermeneutics of Symbols and Philosophical Reflection," in *The Philosophy of Paul Ricoeur*, 56.

[51] RICOEUR, "The Symbol ... Food for Thought," 199-201; cf. his "Poétique et symbolique," in *Initiation à la pratique de la théologie*, vol. I: Introduction (eds. B. LAURENT and F. REFOULE) (Paris 1982) 40-44.

be described as *donative* in that the properly symbolic meaning is given only in and by the literal meaning. Moreover, the symbol acts in an *evocative* manner, for unlike the translation of meaning at work in allegory, the sense of a symbol remains transparent. Finally, the linguistic import of symbols is necessarily *bound* to the narrative context; the meaning evoked and given by way of the symbol is determinable only in light of the situation in which it is deployed. Thus, by virtue of these essential characteristics, "the symbol gives rise to thought" and furnishes to hermeneutics the possible conjunction of criticism and belief.

At this epistemological juncture, a phenomenological hermeneutics recognizes that the language of symbols operates in a manner that differs significantly from other forms of communication. Unlike ordinary language, which proffers a description of the external world, poetic language is directed "towards an interior, an interior which is nothing other than the 'mood' — the state of soul — structured by the poem."[52] Unlike the language of science, which "seeks systematically to eliminate ambiguity," poetic language seeks "to preserve ambiguity, in order to have it express rare, new, unique and therefore — in the proper sense of the word — unpublished [*inédites*] experiences."[53] And unlike the language of rhetoric, whose goal is to persuade by means of the elaboration of arguments, poetic language seeks to move the reader toward a "catharsis" by means of a creative and imaginative reconstruction of human action.[54] It is from these uniquely "poetic" dimensions that the language of symbols obtains its driving force.

---

[52] P. RICOEUR, "Parole et symbole," *RevScRel* 49 (1975) 153: "... il est permis de dire, avec Northrop Frye, que le langage poétique, à l'inverse du langage didactique ordinaire, n'est pas dirigé vers le dehors mais vers le dedans, un dedans qui n'est pas autre chose que le 'mood' — l'état d'âme — structuré par le poème."

[53] P. RICOEUR, "The Power of Speech: Science and Poetry," *PT* 29 (1985) 63.

[54] P. RICOEUR, "Rhétorique - poétique - herméneutique," in *De la métaphysique à la rhétorique* (FS. Ch. Perelman; [ed. M. MEYER] Brussels 1986) 149. On the notion of poetic catharsis, see further his "Contingence et rationalité," 17: "Celle-ci consiste en effet en ce que des passions violentes telles que la frayeur et la pitié sont excitées pour être en même temps purifiées. Or cette purification ne consiste pas en autre chose que dans la clarification que la compréhension de l'intrigue exerce à l'encontre du trouble passionnel suscité par la péripétie, surtout lorsque celle-ci prend la form d'incidents effroyables et pitoyables, voire d'effets de violence, qui donnent au renversement de fortune une forme exacerbée."

Ultimately, the existential efficacity of symbolic language finds its coherence in the "poetic symbol" of a metaphorical network of significations, for

> Through symbolism, metaphor, as the gift of discourse, comes to structure within language the profound and cosmic being of man. But, in return, it is always by means of a strategy of language, of which metaphor is the most remarkable process, that the mythico-poetic depths of man can be evoked.[55]

To interpret the poetic symbolism of narratives, therefore, we must come to understand the particular functioning of the metaphorical strategy of language.

The Rule of Metaphor

As the semantic core of symbolism, the metaphorical process also operates within that poetic context which shapes and forms the material of language. In any metaphorical statement, an apparently absurd signification couples with a literal one to provoke a linguistic enigma. The context then serves "to transform (this) absurdity which destroys itself into *an absurdity that over-signifies* ...."[56] To understand how this transformation takes place, the metaphorical process must be considered in terms of the semantic modality of discourse rather than in the lexical domain of rhetoric.[57] In this framework, metaphor appears as a phenomenon of predication, where "it is not necessary to speak of a word employed metaphorically, but of a metaphorical utterance. The metaphor proceeds from the *tension* between all the terms in a metaphorical utterance."[58] More than simply a deviation of meaning, metaphor in this predicative context proceeds from the conflict occasioned by the impertinence of terms taken in their literal sense in order to produce "the reduction of this syntagmatic deviance

---

[55] RICOEUR, "The Power of Speech," 68.

[56] RICOEUR, "The Power of Speech," 66.

[57] Summarized in RICOEUR, "Parole et symbole," 144-145. For a more detailed analysis, see *The Rule of Metaphor*, where Ricoeur examines the Aristotelian tradition (study #1) and the subsequent decline of rhetoric in tropology (study #2).

[58] RICOEUR, "Parole et symbole," 146.

by the establishment of a new semantic pertinence."[59]   Such a semantic innovation emphasizes not so much the potential resemblance of terms, but the dynamics at work in an interactive rapprochement. As a result, "(t)he *new* pertinence or congruence proper to a meaningful metaphoric utterance proceeds from the kind of semantic proximity which suddenly obtains between terms *in spite of* their distance."[60]

By virtue of this semantic proximity, the metaphorical statement does not provide a substitution of meaning; rather, it engenders something novel.   Surrounded by a clash of interpretations, the meaning of a metaphorical utterance arises as "*a veritable creation of sense* ... in which a new extension of (the) sense of the words replies to a discordance in the phrase."[61]   Thus, unlike the purely ornamental or figurative usage of metaphor in rhetoric, the semantic process of metaphorization arouses and sustains the emergence of *new* significations:

> In other words, metaphorical meaning does not merely consist of a semantic clash but of the *new* predicative meaning which emerges from the collapse of the literal meaning, that is, from the collapse of the meaning which obtains if we rely only on the common or usual lexical values of our words. The metaphor is not the enigma but the solution of the enigma.[62]

Understood in this way, the metaphorical process gives evidence of a unique *mode of cognition*, one intimately connected with the knowledge given by human experience. Its "instructive and informative functions (are) linked to a bringing-together of terms that first surprises, then bewilders, and finally uncovers a relationship hidden beneath the paradox."[63]   This ability to cogitate beneath and beyond

---

[59] P. RICOEUR, "The Metaphorical Process as Cognition, Imagination, and Feeling," in *On Metaphor* (ed. S. SACKS) (Chicago 1979) 144.

[60] RICOEUR, "The Metaphorical Process," 145 (*emphasis added*).

[61] RICOEUR, "Parole et symbole," 147-148: "Dans la métaphore, en revanche, la tension entre les mots, ou plus précisément la tension entre deux interprétations, l'une littérale et l'autre métaphorique, au niveau de la phrase entière, suscite *une véritable création de sens* dont la rhétorique n'enregistre que le résultat.... Les véritables métaphores sont les métaphores d'invention dans lesquelles une nouvelle extension de sens des mots réplique à une discordance dans la phrase" (*emphasis added*).

[62] RICOEUR, "The Metaphorical Process," 144.

[63] RICOEUR, *The Rule of Metaphor*, 27.

paradox issues from two phenomenological modalities on which the semantics of a metaphorical relation depends:

> In effect, the expression first functions *literally*. It is ... a rule for pinpointing an object or situation. Subsequently, it functions *iconically*, by indirectly designating another, similar situation. Precisely because the iconic representation is not an image, it can point towards original resemblances, whether of quality, structure or locality, of situation or, finally, of feeling. In every case, the thing in focus is thought of as what the icon describes. Thus, the iconic representation harbours the power to elaborate, to extend the parallel structure.[64]

The elaborative power with which the metaphorical process resolves a cognitive enigma derives, in turn, from the *creative imagination* with which poetic language is infused. Here, again, the notion of imagination ranges far beyond the psychologisms of arbitrary evocation or contrived illusion; it accords rather with the "iconic" moment in which thought comes to speech. In this creative context,

> metaphor is established as the schematism in which the metaphorical attribution is produced. This schematism turns imagination into the place where the figurative meaning emerges in the interplay of identity and difference. And metaphor is that place in discourse where this schematism is visible, because the identity and the difference do not melt together but confront each other.[65]

This metaphorical confrontation capitalizes on a properly imaginative vision of the world, a "seeing as" which gives sense to poetic language:

> Half thought, half experience, 'seeing as' is the intuitive relationship that holds sense and image together. ... (T)hanks to its character as half thought and half experience, it joins the light of sense with the fullness of the image. In this way, the non-verbal and the verbal are firmly united at the core of the image-ing function of language.[66]

The vision articulated in this imaginative variation generates, in turn, a *feeling-response* on the part of the reader. More than simply

---

[64] RICOEUR, *The Rule of Metaphor*, 189 (*emphasis added*).

[65] RICOEUR, *The Rule of Metaphor*, 199.

[66] RICOEUR, *The Rule of Metaphor*, 213.

a subjective sensation or an emotional representation, the "feeling" or "mood" evoked in the metaphorical process is a "state of soul" which "creates or induces a new manner of finding oneself, of feeling oneself living in the world."[67] It supports the assimilation of existential cognition, affects the presentation of iconic understanding, and contributes to the split reference of poetic discourse by suspending, and then transforming, the literal emotions of everyday life.[68] In all this, feeling accompanies and completes the work of the imagination in giving heuristic force to the metaphorical process.

Through this transformation of feelings, the metaphorical process attunes the reader to the everyday world in an extra-ordinary way. Through the productivity of the imagination, metaphorical language bespeaks a unique manner of seeing, expressing and engendering human living. Through the innovative understanding provided by the metaphor's cognitive pertinence, poetic discourse expands our existential knowledge.   Consequently, the rule of metaphor holds a central place in the hermeneutics of poetic texts, for it both reflects the work of narrativity and contributes to it.

On the one hand, an understanding of the functioning of poetic texts contributes to the interpretation of single utterances. That which a fictional narrative projects is a "metaphorical" world, a world which transcends the historical situation and which opens itself up through the text "as possible modes of being, as possible symbolic dimensions of our being-in-the-world."[69] To appraise us of this world, poetic discourse tends toward the suspension of descriptive denotation in favor of a fictional re-description. In this transposition it envelops the tensional conflict of the metaphorical function, for "(j)ust as the metaphorical statement captures its sense as metaphorical midst the ruins of the literal sense, it also achieves its reference upon the ruins of what might be called (in symmetrical fashion) its literal reference."[70] The fictional narrative likewise displays an affinity with the creative mechanism of metaphorical language, for just as *mimesis* "makes human actions appear higher than they are in reality," so "the

---

[67] RICOEUR, "The Power of Speech," 69. Cf. *The Rule of Metaphor*, 246.

[68] RICOEUR, "The Metaphorical Process," 154-155.

[69] P. RICOEUR, "Metaphor and the Central Problem of Hermeneutics," in *Hermeneutics and the Human Sciences*, 177.

[70] RICOEUR, *The Rule of Metaphor*, 221.

function of metaphor is to transpose the meanings of ordinary language by way of unusual uses."[71] Hence, the poetic text provides the narrative environment within which the nascent or emerging character of the metaphorical process comes to be interpreted.

On the other hand, an understanding of this metaphorical process contributes to the explanation of poetic narratives as a whole. In as much as it concerns the construction of meaning, the metaphorical process prefigures the text "in miniature" by producing a particular understanding which would otherwise, in ordinary language, be lacking in cognitive, imaginative or emotional content. As metaphorical utterances focus the power to inform and enlighten on "a momentary creation of language, a semantic innovation which does not have a status in the language as something already established, whether as a designation or as a connotation,"[72] so fictional narratives individuate a pertinent message through their novel configurations. And it is from this innovative production, in the metaphorical "twist" and in the narrative emplotment, that meaning emerges.[73] Hence, metaphorization founds both the process of creation, on the side of the author, and the process of interpretation, on the side of the reader.

Thus, the mutual relation between the functioning of the metaphorical process and the creativity of fictional narratives highlights the hermeneutical notion of a poetic world — "another world that corresponds to other possibilities of existence, to possibilities that would be most deeply our own".[74] It is the potential meaningfulness of this narrative "world" that interpretation ultimately seeks to grasp. In doing so, by way of "appropriation," the hermeneutical process reaches its culminating stage.

FOR THE APPROPRIATION OF TRUTH

The interpretive inquiry championed by Ricoeur comes to its completion when the twofold movement of understanding narrative texts and explaining poetic language coalesces in the reception of the work

---

[71] RICOEUR, "Metaphor and the Central Problem of Hermeneutics," 181.

[72] RICOEUR, "Metaphor and the Central Problem of Hermeneutics," 174.

[73] RICOEUR, *The Rule of Metaphor*, 98-99.

[74] RICOEUR, *The Rule of Metaphor*, 229.

by the one who reads it. In other words, hermeneutics proceeds from the discovery of the sense and reference which constitute the "world of the text" to the confrontation of this message with the "world of the reader." In this fusion of the possible and the actual, the literary text serves to mediate a renewed understanding of one's existence in the world.

The World of the Text

Devolving from the semantic autonomy and creative liberty of the text, the uniquely literary world with which hermeneutics must grapple is one that transcends the bounds of everyday language. As Ricoeur explains, this fictional world imaginatively projects a redescription of the depths of human potentiality:

> The world of the text is therefore not the world of everyday language. In this sense, it constitutes a new sort of distanciation which could be called a distanciation of the real from itself. It is this distanciation which fiction introduces into our apprehension of reality. ... Through fiction and poetry, new possibilities of being-in-the-world are opened up within everyday reality. Fiction and poetry intend being, not under the modality of being-given, but under the modality of power-to-be. Everyday reality is thereby metamorphised by what could be called the imaginative variations which literature carries out on the real.[75]

This poetic variation extends the notion of meaning from the "sense" of a text to that of its "reference" and thereby transposes our comprehension of reality. In terms of the *sense* of an utterance, what needs to be interpreted is "the semantic dynamism by virtue of which, in a metaphorical statement, a new semantic relevance emerges from the ruins of the semantic non-relevance as this appears in a literal reading of the sentence."[76] Applied by extension to the interpretation of entire texts, this same explanatory effort seeks to understand the meaning of given sentences as they are read in light of the written work as a whole.

In terms of the *reference* of a written work, what requires interpretation is the englobing perspective which is projected in and through the

---

[75] RICOEUR, "The Hermeneutical Function of Distanciation," 142.

[76] RICOEUR, "On Interpretation," 184.

text. Here, the mimetic power of a narrative results from the combination of the semantic complexity of individual utterances within the text and the reader's viewpoint beyond the language of the text. As Ricoeur concludes,

> Narrative fiction ... 'imitates' human action, not only in that, before referring to the text, it refers to our own pre-understanding of the meaningful structures of and of its temporal dimensions, but also in that it contributes, beyond the text, to reshaping these structures and dimensions in accordance with the imaginary configuration of the plot.[77]

Thus, a phenomenological hermeneutics must take into account not only the literary features of the text but its existential value as well. Its ultimate goal is the actualization of a text's potential to engage our understanding and, by consequence, to transform our lives.

This potential for transformation issues from the metaphorical strategy of fictional texts. By means of its poetic power, the language of a narrative eclipses the limits of descriptive denotation and enigmatically "invents" meaning.[78] Especially evident in works of tragedy, the world of such an inventive discourse is formed by the conjunction of emplotment and creative imitation

> because, on the one hand, the *muthos* takes the form of a 'story' and the metaphoricity is attached to the plot of the tale, and because, on the other hand, the referent consists in human action which, due to its motivational course, has a certain affinity to the structure of the story.[79]

---

[77] RICOEUR, "On Interpretation," 185.

[78] RICOEUR, *The Rule of Metaphor*, 239: "It would seem that the enigma of metaphorical discourse is that it 'invents' in both sense of the word: what it creates, it discovers; and what it finds, it invents."

[79] RICOEUR, *The Rule of Metaphor*, 245.

In this way, fictional narratives lead to a "metaphorical" concept of truth and reality whereby "to see something as ... is to render manifest the *being-as* of the thing."[80]

In order to explain this metaphorical truth, hermeneutics proceeds by way of a dialectical mediation between guess and validation. Due to the semantic autonomy of the text, the interpreter must initially *guess* what it means, for "to understand is not merely to repeat the speech event in a similar event, it is to generate a new event beginning from the text in which the initial event has been objectified."[81] What has to be guessed in this event of explanation is, first of all, the architecture of the text; here the interpreter gives a judgment of importance relative to a hierarchy of topics displayed in the text as a whole. In addition, the explanatory guess involves the individualization of the text; here the interpreter proffers a judgment of taste relative to the form and structure localized in the particular perspective of the work. Finally, the genius of guessing requires a delineation of the potential horizons of meaning in a text; here the interpreter offers a judgment of value relative to the concrete actualization of the symbolic and metaphorical expressiveness of a given text.

These "guesses" relative to thematic importance, formal style, and existential value must, in turn, be submitted to a procedure of *validation* which, due to the nature of poetic discourse, pertains more to logical probability than to empirical verification. By means of this procedure, hermeneutics reins in the "circle" of subjectivity and objectivity. It thereby avoids both dogmatism and skepticism, for "(i)t is always possible to argue for or against an interpretation, to confront

---

[80] RICOEUR, "Narrativité, phénoménologie, et herméneutique," 71: "D'une part, en effet, c'est sous le signe de ce que je viens d'appeler la véhémence ontologique dans la théorie du langage que je m'emploie à donner une portée ontologique à la prétention référentielle des énoncés métaphoriques: ainsi je me risque à dire que voir quelque chose comme ... c'est rendre manifeste l'*être-comme* de la chose. Je mets le 'comme' en position d'exposant du verbe être et je fais du 'être-comme' le rérérent ultime de l'énoncé métaphorique. ... Mais, d'autre part, l'attestation de l'*être-comme* ... ne saurait, selon moi, être séparée d'une étude détaillée des modes référentiels du discours et requiert un traitement proprement analytique de la référence indirecte, sur la base du concept de '*split reference*' reçu de Roman Jakobson. Ma thèse sure la *mimesis* de l'oeuvre narrative et ma distinction des trois stades de la *mimesis* — préfiguration, configuration, transfiguration du monde de l'action par la poème — expriment la même souci de joindre la précision de l'analyse à l'attestation ontologique."

[81] RICOEUR, *Interpretation Theory*, 75.

interpretations, to arbitrate between them and to seek agreement, even if this agreement remains beyond our immediate reach."[82]

Thus, the hermeneutical task according to Ricoeur undertakes first an explanation of the "world of the text" by proposing a hypothetical explication of the possible meanings proposed in and by the sentences which make up a written work. From this encounter with the textual world, interpretation then turns its attention to another "world" — that of reality today — where the understanding of the text can engender new significance for its readers.

The World of the Reader

The intersection of the world of the text and that of today takes place in and through the act of reading. There the horizon of the possible projected in the poetic language of a narrative comes to be actualized in the real world of contemporary human living. This actualization becomes the corollary, on the reader's side, of the dynamism of emplotment on the part of the author.

In writing, the work of emplotment gives imaginative form to the experience being communicated by an author; in reading, the eventfulness of this experience is reproduced as meaning. According to Ricoeur, this transposition occurs due to a certain mutuality inherent in the reading of a narrative:

> On the one hand, received paradigms provide structure to the *expectations* of the reader and help him or her to acknowledge and identify the formal rule, the genre, or the type exemplified by the story told. ... On the other hand, it is the act of reading which, as it were, 'accompanies' the configuration of the narrative and actualizes its followability.[83]

Reading, then, functions as "the *vector* of the transfiguration of the world of action under the auspices of fiction" in the sense that "the effect caused by the text on its recipients is an intrinsic component of the actual meaning of the text."[84] As that which brings a text to its

---

[82] RICOEUR, *Interpretation Theory*, 79.

[83] RICOEUR, "The Text as Dynamic Identity," 184.

[84] RICOEUR, "The Text as Dynamic Identity," 185.

fulfillment in the here and now, the act of reading thus plays a key role in the hermeneutical process.

The role ascribed to the act of reading has been highlighted by Ricoeur in terms of "appropriation," whereby "the interpretation of a text culminates in the self-interpretation of a subject who thenceforth understands himself better, understands himself differently, or simply begins to understand himself." Linked to the distanciation of writing and to the objectification of a narrative work, this appropriation is an event of interpretation correlative to that of communication in discourse: "In this sense, interpretation 'brings together', 'equalises', renders 'contemporary and similar', thus genuinely making one's *own* what was initially *alien*." Appropriation thus emphasizes the ever *present* character of interpretation and demonstrates that any text is not an end in itself nor an entity with a significance that remains fixed forever. Rather, through the ongoing process of reading and interpreting, hermeneutical reflection renders contemporaneous the constitution of meaning and the constitution of the self.[85]

Such a reflective hermeneutics does not, however, portend the wandering illusions of subjectivism. To appropriate a text is not synonymous with a search for the intention of the original author or for the understanding of an original audience addressed by the text. As Ricoeur explains,

> what is 'made our own' is not something mental, not the intention of another subject, nor some design supposedly hidden behind the text; rather, it is the projection of a world, the proposal of a mode of being-in-the-world, which the text discloses in front of itself by means of its non-ostensive references.

Moreover, appropriation does not limit itself to the subjective input of a given reader's capacity to understand:

> If the reference of a text is the projection of a world, then it is not in the first instance the reader who projects himself. The reader is rather broadened in his capacity to project himself by receiving a new mode of being from the text itself.[86]

---

[85] RICOEUR, "What Is a Text?", 157-164.

[86] P. RICOEUR, "Appropriation," in *Hermeneutics and the Human Sciences*, 192.

In this way, the process of appropriation, as that of hermeneutics as a whole, is continually oriented toward the text itself and the message conveyed therein for those who read it.

Appropriation thus integrates the roles of the author, the text, and the reader. The imaginative variations incorporated through the emplotting work of an author, the metamorphosis effectuated through the three-fold figuration of a narrative, one's own imagination and congeniality with the issue of the text — all are brought into "play" as contributing to the dynamic, ongoing process of interpretation demanded by human understanding.[87] As the culminating moment of hermeneutics, therefore, appropriation serves to bridge the distance between narrative and life.[88]

To receive the meaning of a text by way of life's experience and as a contribution to the fulfillment of human action — this is the ultimate goal and greatest value of a phenomenological hermeneutics. It is all the more significant in the interpretation of biblical works, whose discourse seeks to communicate the meaning of religious experience. To understand and explain the texts of Sacred Scripture, therefore, we must now consider the specific character by which these writings form a particular region within the general field of hermeneutics.

BIBLICAL HERMENEUTICS

In the movement from a philosophy of hermeneutics to the interpretation of biblical texts, we cross the threshold from literature to

---

[87] On the notion of "play" as the mode of being of appropriation, see RICOEUR, "Appropriation," 185-190.

[88] For RICOEUR the connection between narrative and life is bi-directional, as he explains in "Life: A Story in Search of a Narrator," in *Facts and Values:* Philosophical Perspectives from Western and Non-Western Traditions (eds. M.C. DOESER and J.N. KRAAY) (Dordrecht 1986) 121-132. On the one hand, narrative leads to life because "the process of composition, of configuration, does not realize itself in the text but in the reader, and under this condition configuration makes possible reconfiguration of a life by way of the narrative" (p. 126). On the other hand, an existential dimension complements narrative understanding in that "our life, enveloped in one single glance, appears to us as the field of a constructive activity, deriving from the narrative intelligence through which we attempt to recover (rather than impose from without) *the narrative identity which constitutes us*" (p. 131).

Scripture, from linguistic phenomenology to biblical theology. Because
the itinerary of sense remains bound to the words of a text, biblical
hermeneutics still focuses on written works, but it must also take into
account the poetic dimensions of a specifically religious language.
Moreover, the texts of Sacred Scripture demonstrate a unique bearing
in that they give transcendent expression to spiritual experience; hence,
the understanding of their meaning unfolds within a hermeneutic of
revelation.   Finally, the existential reflection and reflexive existence
expressed in the works of the Bible project a new world of religious
being and living; thus, biblical interpretation is fully realized within a
hermeneutic of testimony.

The Specificity of Religious Language

The mutual relationship between philosophical and biblical
hermeneutics derives from common phenomenological presuppositions.
On the one hand, both are concerned with interpreting the meaning of
experience as it comes to be identified in and through language.[89]
Because this religious faith is expressed in writing, the phenomenological notions of distanciated discourse, narrative objectification, poetic
creativity, and personal appropriation may be brought to bear upon the
interpretation of biblical texts. On the other hand, the religious experience communicated in these written works exhibits a unique meaningfulness and has a particular sense, at least for those who "believe."
For this reason, Scriptural texts display a foundational value for the
believer's own existence, and it is this special claim relative to the truth
of the text which distinguishes biblical hermeneutics from a purely
literary analysis.

Among the principles of Ricoeur's phenomenological hermeneutics,
the biblical interpreter must first account for the element of *distanciation*. Thanks to this character of written discourse, the religious speech
of biblical texts "reaches all the way to us and touches us through its
'meaning' and its 'sense' which is at stake in it, although no longer

---

[89] P. RICOEUR, "Philosophy and Religious Language," *JRel* 54 (1974) 71:
"Whatever ultimately may be the nature of the so-called religious experience, it comes
to language, it is articulated in a language, and the most appropriate place to interpret
it on its own terms is to inquire into its linguistic expression."

through the 'voice' of its proclaimer."[90]   Consequently, the focus of attention in biblical hermeneutics is not the static conceptualization of a theological doctrine localized in sacred statements but the participative appreciation in a spiritual experience conveyed by poetic language.

Moreover, like any structured work of language, religious texts encode a faith experience by means of a particular style, genre, and plot.   As a result, Ricoeur's notion of *narrativity* constitutes an essential parameter in biblical hermeneutics, for "(t)he 'confession of faith' which is expressed in the biblical documents is inseparable from the *forms* of discourse" in which it is expressed.[91]   In addition, biblical hermeneutics must also consider the theological tension which is sustained by the inclusion of diverse, and potentially contrasting, forms of theological meaning within a unified corpus of writings.[92]

Because narrative modes of discourse display a particular referential claim upon reality, the *poetic* creativity at work in the text also functions as a controlling factor in biblical hermeneutics.   In the writings of Sacred Scripture, a uniquely literary world is proposed by the imaginative variations of an author and generated by the second-order dynamism of symbolic and metaphorical language.   From this it follows that the biblical texts project a world of meaning unlike that in everyday reality.   As Ricoeur ponders it:

> Is not the new being projected and proposed by the Bible a case *par excellence* of this trait?   Does not the new being make its journey through the world of ordinary experience and in spite of the closedness of this experience?   Is not the force of this projected world a force of rupture and of opening?   If this is not so, must we not accord to this

---

[90] P. RICOEUR, *Philosophical Hermeneutics and Theological Hermeneutics:* Ideology, Utopia, and Faith (Protocol of the 17th Colloquy; [ed. W. WUELLNER] Berkeley 1975) 7.

[91] RICOEUR, "Philosophy and Religious Language," 75.   Regarding this connection, Ricoeur concludes thus: "... the finished work which we call the Bible is a limited space for interpretation in which theological significations are correlatives of *forms of discourse*. It is no longer possible to interpret the *significations* without making the long detour through a structural explication of the *forms*" (p. 78).

[92] RICOEUR, *Philosophical Hermeneutics and Theological Hermeneutics*, 11: "Throughout these discourses God appears differently each time: sometimes as the Hero of the saving act, sometimes as wrathful or compassionate, sometimes as he to whom one can speak in an I-Thou relation, or sometimes as he whom I meet only in a cosmic order which ignores me."

projected world the poetic dimension, in the strong sense of the word, the poetic dimension which we have acknowledged as the issue of the text?[93]

The scope of biblical hermeneutics, then, is to comprehend this poetic dimension, which not only brings us into contact with what is real but opens up for us the way to what is possible.

In the projection of this new religious world, the act of *reading* serves not only to discern the meaning encoded in a text and generated by it, but further to respond to the message of the written word in such a way that the reader is re-formed by the text. In the particularity of biblical hermeneutics, this final act of appropriation concerns directly the reality of faith, for as Ricoeur claims, "it must be said that what, in theological language, is called faith, is constituted in the strongest sense of the term, by the new being which is the 'thing' of the text."[94] As necessarily bound to the progress of interpretation, such a biblical faith is both suspiciously critical and imaginatively transcendent.[95]

As a consequence, religious faith acts as *the* limit to hermeneutics. Whether as "ultimate concern" or as "feeling of absolute dependence" or as "unconditional trust," faith both precedes linguistic articulation and extends beyond it. Nevertheless, this faith also complements linguistic phenomenology as "the nonhermeneutical origin of all interpretation," for "(it) is the attitude of one who accepts being interpreted at the same time that he interprets the world of the text."[96] Connected to this attitude of faith are "revelation," in the world of the text, and "testimony," in that of the reader.

---

[93] RICOEUR, *Philosophical Hermeneutics and Theological Hermeneutics*, 14.

[94] RICOEUR, *Philosophical Hermeneutics and Theological Hermeneutics*, 18.

[95] RICOEUR, *Philosophical Hermeneutics and Theological Hermeneutics*: "Today a 'hermeneutics of suspicion' is an integral part of all appropriation of meaning. And with it follows the 'de-construction' of prejudgments which impede our letting the world of the text be" (p. 19). "Imagination is that dimension of subjectivity which responds to the text as *poem*. When the distantiation of imagination responds to the distantiation which the 'issues' of the text unfolds in the heart of reality, a poetics of existence responds to a poetics of discourse" (p. 20).

[96] RICOEUR, "Philosophy and Religious Language," 84.

The Hermeneutics of Revelation

With regard to biblical interpretation, the hermeneutical problem is aggravated by the properly religious import of the texts, in as much as they act as a vehicle of revelation. In biblical language, the experience of faith comes to expression not so much in the form of propositional assertions as in that of "poetic" discourse. From this linguistic modality follow two complementary implications for biblical hermeneutics.

In the first place, the *textual character* of revelation remains paramount. Consequently, the meaning and significance of the biblical writings are made contemporaneous in the act of interpretive reading, for as Ricoeur notes,

> ... the reading which we practice begins from the fact that the sense of the events recounted or of the institutions proclaimed has been detached by writing from its original *Sitz-im-Leben* and that writing has substituted for it what could be called a *Sitz-im-Wort*. Our reading begins there, with the *Sitz-im-Wort* of events, of actions, of institutions which have lost their first roots and which, consequently, have only a *textual* existence.[97]

Secondly, this situation in the word of the text is effected in diverse ways, according to varying *literary genres*. Whether narrative, prophetic, prescriptive, hymnic or sapiential, the modes of biblical discourse "do not constitute a rhetorical facade which it would be possible to pull down in order to reveal some thought content that is indifferent to its literary vehicle."[98] As a result, scriptural revelation can be apprehended only by way of its imaginative configurations.

In particular, the interpretive situation in the "Wisdom" mode of Scripture is distinct by virtue of its trans-historical character.[99]

---

[97] P. RICOEUR, "Temps biblique," *AF* 53,1 (1985) 26.

[98] P. RICOEUR, "Toward a Hermeneutic of the Idea of Revelation," in *Essays on Biblical Interpretation*, 91.

[99] RICOEUR, "Temps biblique," 32: "Les commentateurs n'ont pas manqué en effet de souligner l'indépendance de la Sagesse par rapport à tout récit. ... A la faveur de ce nouveau contraste entre des écrits qui sont tous, d'une manière ou d'une autre, marqués par une histoire passée ou à venir, *les écrits de Sagesse se désintéressent de l'histoire, mais non point du temps.*"

Beyond giving instruction in "the art of living well," the Wisdom
literature proffers "a reflection on existence that aims at the individual
behind the people of the Covenant, and through him, every human
being."[100] In these writings, what comes to be revealed is the
possible junction of *ethos* and *cosmos*, the potential sense of human life
in a divinely created world.

In their revelation of the potentiality of human existence, the
Wisdom texts focus on the experience and expression of "limits," which
Ricoeur explains as

> those situations — including solitude, the fault, suffering, and death —
> where the misery and the grandeur of human beings confront each
> other. Hebraic wisdom interprets these situations as the annihilation of
> humans and the incomprehensibility of God — as the silence and
> absence of God. If the question of retribution is so acute here, it is so
> to the extent that the discordance between justice and happiness, so
> cruelly emphasized by the triumph of the wicked, brings to light the
> overwhelming question of the sense or nonsense of existence.[101]

In their depiction of these limit-situations, the Wisdom texts engender
a confrontation between God and humans. At the crux of this clash,
wisdom becomes "a struggle for sense in spite of non-sense."[102] In
this sapiential quest, the biblical writings provide the opportunity and
means for transforming human existence. By engaging the limit-
situations of human life, Wisdom literature attempts to explicate the
religiosity of ordinary human experience:

> The human condition as such includes experiences which baffle
> discourse and *praxis*. ... But it is not just experiences of distress that
> have this power of rupture; culminatory experiences — "peak experi-
> ences" — especially experiences of creation and joy ... are no less
> extreme than are the experiences of catastrophe. Nor are they less
> baffling. They even have a greater capacity to reorient life, in a way

---

[100] RICOEUR, "Toward a Hermeneutic of the Idea of Revelation," 85.

[101] RICOEUR, "Toward a Hermeneutic of the Idea of Revelation," 86.

[102] P. RICOEUR, "Nommer Dieu," in *Theolinguistics* (ed. J.-P. VAN NOPPEN)
(Brussels 1981) 356: "Elle s'adresse directement au sens et au non-sens de l'existence.
Elle est une lutte pour le sens en dépit de non-sens."

that no plan or rational project could equal or exhaust, than to break it.[103]

Thus, as the on-going promotion of the world of the "possible," the Wisdom mode of biblical discourse exhibits a revealed character that is at once enigmatic, perduring, and universal.[104]

In order to promote the possibility of an existential re-orientation, however, ordinary language does not suffice. Instead, the biblical texts reveal a radically re-described vision of the world by means of limit-expressions. Corresponding to the limit-experiences to which they refer, these expressions alone can combine the "odd personal discernment" and "total commitment" and "universal significance" of religious language.[105] Hence, biblical hermeneutics must also engage the phenomenon of the poetic, which furnishes limit-expressions that speak of paradox from the perspective of metaphorical extravagance.

Paradox functions as an interpretive element here due to its character as an "intensification" of experience. It "dissuades the hearer in some way from forming a coherent project and from making of his/her own existence a continuous totality." In this way it "contrasts the realism of history and the extravagance of the denouement" of the Wisdom tale.[106] This extravagance disrupts the normal orientation of a narrative and transgresses the logic of rational thought by invoking, in metaphorical fashion, the "extraordinary in the ordinary."

---

[103] P. RICOEUR, "Biblical Hermeneutics," *Semeia* 4 (1975) 128.

[104] RICOEUR, "Temps biblique," 33: "Aussi changeant que puisse être l'homme, les situations-limites ont quelque chose d'immuable, or, pour mieux dire, de perdurable et de sempiternel. C'est pourquoi le discours qui débat de ces énigmes est lui-même sans âge. D'une façon, tout, ici, a dès toujours été dit. C'est ce trait qui rend ce discours étranger à tout récit. Le récit fondait l'identité narrative d'un peuple. La sagesse s'adresse à la condition humaine dans son caractère universel."

[105] RICOEUR, "Biblical Hermeneutics," 124: "The discernment that religious language brings about is 'odd' *because* the commitment is 'total.' It is total in the twofold sense that it engages the whole of my life and because as religious language it intends the whole of human life." (Here Ricoeur is commenting on the terminology of Ian Ramsey.)

[106] RICOEUR, "Nommer Dieu," 359: "paradoxes et hyperboles dissuadent en quelque sorte l'auditeur de former un projet cohérent et de faire de sa propre existence une totalité continue.... C'est alors le contraste entre le réalisme de l'histoire et l'extravagance du dénouement qui suscite l'espèce de dérive par laquelle l'intrigue et sa pointe sont soudain déportés vers le Tout-Autre." (Ricoeur is here adopting the vocabulary and viewpoint of W.A. Beardslee.)

Yet it is only by means of this disorientation that a true re-orientation can be revealed.

This metaphorical dialectic of the "extraordinary in the ordinary" preserves the tension "between the objective claim of knowledge and the poetic presentation of the Unconditioned."[107] Underlying the comprehension of human existence at its limits, this *tension* becomes characteristic of the Wisdom mode of discourse. The revelatory value of these writings lies, therefore, in the imaginative narration of figures who exemplify authentic human action.

Accordingly, the task of interpreting Wisdom texts in light of Ricoeur's hermeneutics will be

> to coordinate the experience articulated by the Biblical text with human experience at large and as a whole ... (because) this polarity is required by the very nature of religious experience and discourse, inasmuch as it claims to describe — or redescribe! — the whole experience of man and the experience of all men.[108]

For biblical hermeneutics it is this re-described experience which constitutes revelation and which, in turn, engenders a novel experience of the divine for the interpretive reader.

The Hermeneutics of Testimony

As has been noted, the objective meaning of textual truth dwells in the "world" configured by the work of writing. As Ricoeur explains with respect to biblical texts,

> truth no longer means verification, but manifestation, i.e., letting what shows itself be. What shows itself is in each instance a proposed world, a world I may inhabit and wherein I can project my ownmost possibilities. It is in this sense of manifestation that language in its poetic function is a vehicle of revelation.[109]

This poetic revelation conveys meaning in a way that is often more pictorial than conceptual, and through this "figurative" language biblical

---

[107] RICOEUR, "Biblical Hermeneutics," 143.

[108] RICOEUR, "Biblical Hermeneutics," 130-131.

[109] RICOEUR, "Toward a Hermeneutic of the Idea of Revelation," 102.

texts mediate the thoughtfulness of religious representations and make possible its subsequent appropriation.[110]

Nevertheless, such a figurative world is not fully accessible through the limited means of rational criticism. To understand its meaning requires, in addition, a spiritual intelligence which would correspond to the metaphorical character of religious language. Hence, biblical hermeneutics in the Ricoeurian vein acknowledges that "the function of poetic discourse is to bring about (the) emergence of a depth-structure of belonging-to amid the ruins of descriptive discourse."[111] The historical possibility of this belonging-to is the testimony which the biblical text offers and which, in turn, it inspires.

Biblical testimony about human existence draws on the revelational character of divine manifestation. In this respect,

> (t)he absolute declares itself here and now. In testimony there is an immediacy of the absolute without which there would be nothing to interpret. ... This is a hard saying for philosophy to understand. For the self-manifestation of the absolute here and now indicates the end of the infinite regress of reflection. The absolute shows itself. In this shortcut of the absolute and its presence is constituted an experience of the absolute. It is only about this that testimony testifies.[112]

Conversely, the manifestation to which the biblical text refers demands interpretation, and this for several reasons. First, the event experienced in the text "is both apparent and hidden: hidden to the extent that it is apparent." Moreover, the meaning of this dialectical event of testimony comes to the fore in and through its written form:

---

[110] See P. RICOEUR, "The Status of *Vorstellung* in Hegel's Philosophy of Religion," in *Meaning, Truth and God* (ed. L.S. ROUNER) (Notre Dame 1982) 85-87.

[111] RICOEUR, "Toward a Hermeneutic of the Idea of Revelation," 101. In "Phénoménologie et herméneutique," in *Phänomenologische Forschungen, 1: Phänomenologie heute: Grundlagen und Methodenprobleme* (ed. E.W. ORTH) (Münich 1975), Ricoeur elaborates upon this notion, which he borrows from Gadamer: "Hermeneutic's declaration is, so to speak, that the problematic of objectivity presupposes as prior to itself an inclusive relation which englobes the allegedly autonomous subject and the allegedly adverse object. It is this inclusive or englobing relation that I call participation or belonging-to (*appartenance*)" (p. 38; cited in *Essays on Biblical Interpretation*, 107).

[112] P. RICOEUR, "The Hermeneutics of Testimony," in *Essays on Biblical Interpretation*, 144.

"concerning things seen (it) only reaches judgment through a story, that is, by means of things said." Finally, the understanding of this narrative testimony entails an open-ended and reciprocal process, because "(t)he witness testifies about something or someone which goes beyond him."[113]

This transcendent "meaning" becomes existential "signification" when it is reflected upon and appropriated by an interpreting reader. Hereby historicizing the world of the biblical text in the world of the here and now, the mediation of self-understanding does not seek "to impose one's own finite capacity of understanding on it (the text), but to expose oneself to receive from it a larger self which would be the proposed way of existing that most appropriately responds to the proposed world of the text."[114] Appropriation thereby constitutes a subjective testimony to the affirmation of faith objectively configured in the text.

This subjective side of testimony acknowledges the hermeneutical convergence of the person who interprets with the work being interpreted. At this juncture, interpretation gives birth to a commitment born of reflection. For biblical hermeneutics, however, the truth of this reflection remains bound to that which is manifested in the text; from there it becomes transparent in the contemporary world by way of a reader's divestment and affirmation.

How revelation leads reflection toward *divestment* depends upon the experience of the absolute which the text communicates. This divestment, as explained by Jean Nabert, incorporates the historical world of the text and the personal world of the reader:

> For the apprehension of the divine, the divestment (*dépouillement*) essential for mystical experience and the link of the divine to a historic manifestation are mutually complementary. Thanks to the first, the grasping of the divine tends to be confounded with the advance of reflection by means of the lonely asceticism of philosophic consciousness. By the second, the divine is written in history by a testimony, the meaning of which consciousness never exhausts.[115]

---

[113] RICOEUR, "The Hermeneutics of Testimony," 144-147.

[114] RICOEUR, "Toward a Hermeneutic of the Idea of Revelation," 108.

[115] J. NABERT, *Le désir de Dieu*, book III: "Métaphysique de témoignage et herméneutique de l'absolu" (Paris 1966) 267 (cited with agreement by Ricoeur in *Essays on Biblical Interpretation*, 148).

Such a divestment allies the proper character of the perception of the divine and the finitude of a human consciousness in which absolute knowledge is unattainable.[116]   It thereby allows for the novel event of an *originary affirmation*.

The signification of such an affirmation lies in its capacity to transform one's thinking, acting, and feeling. At this level of spiritual experience, it renders the failure of pure speculation productive in that it enables a meaningful response to a situation otherwise devoid of sense. Coupled with this practical transformation, and as a necessary complement to it, is a catharsis of the emotions, which renders positive the otherwise negative connotations of divestment. In this way, the originary affirmation of faith, revealed in and engendered by the biblical texts, becomes for the one who shares in it a newfound testimony to salvific truth.

To summarize, Ricoeur's phenomenological analysis suggests that the relationship among religious language, revelation, and testimony can act as an interpretive locus for biblical hermeneutics. Respecting the presuppositions relative to any textual discourse, biblical hermeneutics engages the poetic dimensions of specifically religious language:

> By its narrative structure it recalls the altogether first rooting of the language of faith in the narrative. By its metaphorical process it renders manifest the poetic character ... of the language of faith in its entirety. Finally, in joining metaphor and limit-expression, it furnishes the very matrix of theological language, in as much as this joins analogy and negation in the path of eminence ....[117]

Biblical hermeneutics is further qualified by a uniquely revelational dimension, which constrains the interpreter to admit that absolute knowledge with regard to these texts is impossible:

> The confession that God is infinitely above human thoughts and speech, that he guides us without our comprehending his ways, that the fact that human beings are an enigma to themselves even obscures the clarity that God communicates to them — this confession belongs to the

---

[116] RICOEUR, "The Hermeneutics of Testimony," 148-149.

[117] RICOEUR, "Nommer Dieu," 360.

idea of revelation. The one who reveals himself is also the one who conceals himself.[118]

Hence, beyond "explaining" and "understanding," the predominant factor in biblical interpretation is "living" and its dominant concern that existential "testimony" which the originary affirmation of the text reflects.

This last dimension brings a phenomenological hermeneutics full circle, for "testimony, understood as the testimony of a life, is the equivalent of verification for any spiritual experience." As such, "the category of testimony rules the articulation between the religious scope of the work and its philosophical nucleus."[119] And in the process of this articulation, biblical hermeneutics comes to an unsurpassable limit, namely, that "(t)he mutual promotion of reason and faith, in their difference, is the last word for a finite consciousness."[120]

With this last word of Ricoeur, we conclude our presentation of the key factors which constitute his phenomenological hermeneutics. The question now arises as to how this philosophical theory can contribute to our understanding of the Book of Job.

To begin, what influence do Ricoeur's phenomenological presuppositions have on the approach to be taken in this study? From his emphasis on communication as *discourse*, it follows that an investigation into the meaning of Job's "repentance" cannot be limited to a lexical or structuralist analysis; rather, an explanation of Job's final utterance must capture the eventfulness of his change of stance in light of the tale as a whole. And in this consideration of the tale as a whole, Ricoeur's notion of *distanciation* focuses our attention on the final form of the text; prescinding from both an historical analysis of the cultural milieu in which the text was written and a diachronic analysis of the redactional stages of the text, we will begin our study from the vantage point of the story of Job as we read it today.

Thus, in the chapter that follows, our concern will be the narrative intelligibility of the Book of Job as a whole. Two critical questions will be treated there. First, what is the *work of emplotment* operative

---

[118] RICOEUR, "Toward a Hermeneutic of the Idea of Revelation," 93.

[119] RICOEUR, "Reply to Lewis S. Mudge," in *Essays on Biblical Interpretation*, 42.

[120] RICOEUR, "The Hermeneutics of Testimony," 153.

in the Joban narrative? How are the apparently disparate "episodes" configured so as to exhibit a meaningful concordance? Second, what is the *role of imagination* in the unfolding of the tale? How does the author's creativity in characterizing the protagonist as successively righteous, rebellious, and repentant contribute to an understanding of reality?

As Ricoeur notes, this mimetic power of the narrative pertains to the properly poetic world of the biblical text, which will be the subject of chapters three and four of our study. In this literary worldview, what import does the *symbolic* advent of the divine in a "theophany" bear upon our understanding of Job's ultimate change of stance? Moreover, can Job's seemingly contradictory statements in response to the speeches of Yahweh be explained as *metaphorical*, an affirmation that is at once "absurd" within the progressive development of the narrative, yet "meaningful" in terms of a cognitive, imaginative and emotive resolution?

Assuming that Job's unexpected repentance does portend meaningfulness, our last chapter will explore a truth to be appropriated from the portrayal of Job as a theological "icon." In the sapiential *world of the text*, what particular contribution does the characterization of Job make in terms of what it means to be wise? In turn, what message does the repentant Job offer regarding wisdom in the *world of the reader* today?

Chapter Two

THE BOOK OF JOB:

A Theo-Novella

In light of the essential elements of Ricoeur's hermeneutics, our project of interpreting Job's "repentance" must first take into account the phenomenon of narrativity. In other words, the remote context for the present study is the tale of Job read as a whole. Here, in the heuristic emplotment by which the story progresses and through the imaginative variations with which its message appears, the Book of Job emerges as a created and creative work of biblical discourse.

To demonstrate how these narrative phenomena contextualize Job's final words, we will first consider the created configuration of the tale: how do the heterogeneous episodes contribute to the followability of the story, and how is their significance synthesized in the paradoxical conclusion? Then, with a view toward highlighting the productive imagination of the author, we will consider the creative characterization in the tale: how do the diverse modes of language indicate the theological theme being narrated, and how do the various figures of Job elucidate the sapiential import of this paradigmatic tale?

LITERARY CONFIGURATION

Notwithstanding the matter of redactional history, our analysis of the configuration of the Book of Job seeks to ascertain the elements of its literary structuration, namely, what its key episodes are and how these contribute to the progressive emplotment of the story. In particular, we must confront the apparent complications which arise at the points where these episodes are joined, for in the phenomenology of the narrative, these junctures portend meaningfulness. In particular, we contend that the juxtaposition of Job's repentance and Yahweh's affirmation of his speech (42:6,7) serves as a hermeneutical key for interpreting Job's repentance, for only in these verses do we encounter the narrative resolution which invests the episodes of the tale with a theological magnitude.

A Discordant Tale

The overall composition of the Book of Job centers on two unusual elements: the apparent interplay of prose and poetry and the use of extended dialogue to treat a given theme.[1] Between the legendary lore and the disputational diatribes, the story progresses dramatically, though not so much by successive actions as by the development of a thematic plot via language and characterization.[2] This progression is accomplished by the inclusion of several narrative twists which pose a question to or elicit a reaction from the reader.

In the prose Prologue, the reader is made privy to heavenly deliberations, where Yahweh repeatedly affirms his faithful servant over against the purported threat of malediction. Yet the picture of a divine-satanic discussion provokes wonder, and it lulls the reader into joining the debate — yes or no, will Job curse God under material or physical duress? [He does not.]

Moving into the poetic Dialogues, Job mounts a reasonable attack on the time-honored conception of "God." Through the subsequent give-and-take of interlocutors, the reader impulsively sides with the impassioned stance of the main character. But such support risks the danger of divine self-destruction — if the much sought after "trial"

---

[1] S.R. DRIVER and G.B. GRAY, *A Critical and Exegetical Commentary on the Book of Job* (ICC; Edinburgh 1921) xxii. They also suggest that the "sustained treatment of a single theme" may be distinctive (n. 4).

[2] L. ALONSO-SCHÖKEL, "Toward a Dramatic Reading of the Book of Job," *Semeia* 7 (1977) 46: "The Book of Job is a drama with little action and much passion; or better, with much intellectual action involving an impassioned debate and search."

between Job and God were to occur, can God lose, as expected, and still be God? [Hardly!]

In the poetic Theologue,[3] Yahweh does respond, with a whirlwind of natural images and rhetorical questions which challenge Job to uphold his dis-accreditation of the divine management of the cosmos. Although the protagonist now "repents," an uneasy question remains: without addressing directly the concerns raised by Job in the Dialogues, does the divine speech accomplish anything more than to lead Job on a trek through the valley of the absurd? [It seems not.]

Then follows the prose Epilogue, with the surprising affirmation by God that Job has spoken "rightly" (42:7,8) and the bountiful restitution with which the Lord offsets the former suffering of his faithful servant. A "happy ever after" ending thus draws the tale to its close — but can this evaluation and restoration offer a truly meaningful conclusion to what is by now a thoroughly convoluted presentation of myopic piety, critical judgment, and repentant reversal? [So it must!]

Among these major episodes, a consensus of scholarly opinion holds as most structurally significant the coming of Yahweh onto the scene and the ensuing poetic exchange between Yahweh and Job. Less appreciated, however, is the divine action in favor of Job in the concluding chapter.[4] Yet both of these narrative junctures contribute to the resolution of the enigmatic development of the tale and, as such, become a locus for hermeneutical inquiry. While the place and function of the Theologue remains to be examined in detail (in our next chapter), we must now consider the relationship between the Prologue/Epilogue frame and the dialogic speeches.

---

[3] While "Theophany" is the more common descriptor for this section (38:1 - 42:6), the term "Theologue" — understood as "speech by and about God" — includes both characters and furthers the narrative focus on the integrity of Job's language.

[4] One of the first to signal the importance of the Epilogue for interpreting the book was J. BARR, in his survey of "The Book of Job and Its Modern Interpreters," *BJRL* 54 (1971) 46: "It adds a whole new dimension which, if the verse [42:7] were not there, would be entirely absent. If it is not there, our final impression is of a God who overwhelms Job with his mighty speech .... But when it is there, we have yet one final paradox to come: the God who has done all this aligns himself in the last instance with Job and says that what Job had said of God was 'right' ...." More recently, see S.E. PORTER, "The Message of the Book of Job: Job 42:7b as Key to Interpretation?" *EvQ* 63 (1991) 291-304.

While the disparity between the framework and core sections of the tale is readily apparent,[5] commentators differ on whether the relationship between them is conjunctive or disjunctive. In the former view, the Prologue initiates the movement of the tale by introducing the thematic concern to be explored[6] or by exposing the conflictual situation to be transformed.[7] By means of various literary devices, a relation of thematic *continuity* is thus established between prose and poetry such that the thought of the tale is anticipated and developed through their mutual interaction.[8] In this way the apparent superficiality of the Prologue reveals not the naivety of literary shallowness but the subtleness of narrative artistry.[9]

The contrary position sees between prose and poetry a thematic *disjunction*. In this view, the evident exaggeration with which Job is portrayed in the Prologue initiates the ironic ploy by which the contrasting dialectic of the speeches comes to be emphasized.[10]

---

[5] POPE notes six differences concerning the characterization of Job, the doctrine of retribution, the sacrificial cultus, the names of God, the temper and mood, and the literary forms (*Job*, xxiii-xxvi). L. ALONSO SCHÖKEL, *Giobbe:* commento teologico e letterario (Roma 1985) 37-39, highlights the discrepancies between the originator of Job's suffering, the mention of Job's sickness, and the presence of the Satan figure. S. TERRIEN, "Job — Introduction and Exegesis," *IB*, 3:885-886, adds that Job's career is presented differently.

[6] According to D. COX, *Man's Anger and God's Silence:* The Book of Job (Middlegreen 1991) 11, the theme takes shape as a question: *"what kind of God* is it that allows the innocent to suffer, and indeed seems to cause that suffering?"

[7] In a three-fold structure, HABEL refers to the introduction of an existential "conflict" which will then be explored and resolved (*The Book of Job*, 27-29). W. VOGELS, "The Inner Development of Job: One More Look at Psychology and the Book of Job," *ScEs* 35 (1983) 227-230, focuses on the story of Job's psychological transformation.

[8] See HABEL, *The Book of Job*, 28-29. The unity between prose and poetry sections is also sustained by numerous linguistic affinities and stylistic traits; cf. TERRIEN, "Job," 887 and M. GREENBERG, "Job," in *The Literary Guide to the Bible* (eds. R. ALTER and F. KERMODE) (Cambridge, MA 1987) 285-286.

[9] Cf. D.J.A. CLINES, "False Naivety in the Prologue to Job," *HAR* 9 (1985) 127-136 and A. COOPER, "Reading and Misreading the Prologue to Job," *JSOT* 46 (1990) 67-79.

[10] A. BRENNER, " 'Job the Pious': The Characterization of Job in the Narrative Framework of the Book," *JSOT* 43 (1989) 37: "Stylistic, literary and linguistic considerations show that the portrait of Job in the frame story is an ironic exaggeration of the concept of conventional piety. Once this is understood, it is not surprising that a different but more credible Job is substituted in the poem for his 'unreal' counterpart of the narrative."

Between the facile, trite story of the patient believer and the poetically profound lament of the cursing sufferer there is no integration.[11] Instead, the prose/poetry dialectic creates tension and alienation.[12] As such, it constitutes the narrative basis for a thorough-going parody of wisdom in the name of holy skepticism.[13]

From the perspective of Ricoeur's hermeneutics, these viewpoints need not stand in total opposition. Instead, the narrative phenomenon of "discordant concordance" invites us to read the succession of apparently disconnected episodes as a coherent whole. In this sense, the disparity engendered by the prose/poetry junctures is actually constitutive of the intrigue of the tale. As a result, each of the successive sections of the story is invested with meaningfulness only in as much as it contributes to the overall schema of the tale.[14] What results is a structured movement that can be described in terms of orientation, disorientation, and re-orientation.[15]

In the first place, the opening scenes do connect directly with what follows in that they provide the reader with an *orientation* to the sapiential theme which will be developed throughout the tale. The Prologue introduces Job as a legendary figure and focuses the reader's attention on the question of how he will speak about God in reaction to what has befallen him.[16] To be noted is the narrator's insistence that

---

[11] R.D. MOORE, "The Integrity of Job," *CBQ* 45 (1983) 31: "The poet has denied integrity to his character, and we should deny thematic integrity to the book."

[12] Y. HOFFMAN, "The Relation between the Prologue and the Speech Cycles in Job: A Reconsideration," *VT* 31 (1983) 169: "by referring to the popular myth about Job the righteous, not only does the writer find a common denominator for most of his audiences, but also hides himself dialectically behind a legend that provides him with an ambivalent overview of presuppositions which he himself set down, but to which he is nevertheless not fully committed."

[13] The controlling presence of "parody" is promoted by both K. DELL, *The Book of Job as Sceptical Literature* (BZAW, 197; Berlin 1991) 109-157 and B. ZUCKERMAN, *Job the Silent:* A Study in Historical Counterpoint (Oxford 1991) 93-135.

[14] For RICOEUR, this reflects the bi-dimensionality of a narrative, where "a story is *made out* of events to the extent that plot *makes* events *into* a story" ("Narrative and Hermeneutics," 152).

[15] For RICOEUR, this sequence represents the heuristic power proper to a "disclosure model" of religious language ("Biblical Hermeneutics," 125-126).

[16] This focus on the "how" of Job's language, rather than on "what" is said, has recently been explored in C.A. NEWSOM, "Cultural Politics and the Reading of Job," *BInt* 1 (1993) 119-138.

Job's words, to this point, have remained within the theological bounds of covenantal piety and propriety (cf. 1:22; 2:10).

But the tale does not develop in a simply linear progression.[17] What Job has undergone at the hands of the heavenly debaters provokes in him more than rehearsed responses and mournful silence. Now we are struck with fermenting execration as the protagonist decides to "curse" his coming into this life[18] and subsequently decries traditional notions about God and the world which are incapable of corresponding to the reality he is experiencing. This maledictory transposition from Prologue to Dialogue jolts the narrative proceeding and renders a first *disorientation*. Another disorientation follows later, this one resulting from the tempestuous words of Yahweh, which call into question the conclusions deduced from the critical reasoning with which Job has pressed his position in the speeches of chapters 4-27: in response to the panoramic whirlwind of the divine counsel, the same Job whose imprecation was so reasonably conceived suddenly and unexpectedly cowers in silence and repentance.[19] Then, a final disorientation surfaces in the Epilogue: after having trounced Job's accusations of cosmic mismanagement, Yahweh shifts gears to affirm that all along Job had, in fact, spoken "correctly" (42:7,8).

As convoluted as these episodes may be, the relationship among them, in terms of narrative congifuration, is not necessarily disjunctive. Their juxtaposition need not be attributed to the subversive ploy of irony nor be relegated to the depths of skepticism, for both of these viewpoints fail to consider the surplus of meaning suggested by Job's repentant response in the Theologue. Instead, the diverse speech-events of the Book of Job come to be integrated by the final narrative juncture (42:6,7) which, as we shall suggest in greater detail below, provides the decisive *re-orientation* to the tale. Having followed the story to this point, the reader is here confronted with the last utterance of Job and the definitive affirmation of Yahweh, which, taken together, convey the ultimate significance of the story.

---

[17] ZUCKERMAN argues the case against a linear reading (*Job the Silent*, 25-33).

[18] On the active decision implicit in the editorial seam of 3:1, see M. WEISS, *The Story of Job's Beginning*, Job 1-2: A Literary Analysis (Jerusalem 1983) 78-79.

[19] Cf. D. PENCHANSKY, *The Betrayal of God*: Ideological Conflict in Job (Literary Currents in Biblical Interpretation; Louisville 1990) 54; this author describes the sense of dissonance narrated here in somewhat melodramatic terms of "the tearful recantation of Job's words" in contrast to "Yahweh's blistering attack."

Thus, the structured movement from orientation to disorientation to reorientation informs the literary configuration of the Book of Job. As such, it also reforms our hermeneutical inquiry. Far from being signs of a narrative (and theological) disjunction, the various twists and turns constitute the intrigue of the tale; they contribute to its followability as they connect with and lead toward the story's paradoxical conclusion. As a result, the unexpected ending acts as the pole of attraction for the entire narrative. The vantage point offered to the reader in the Epilogue substantiates and furthers the "discordant concordance" of Job's repentance. How this phenomenon synthesizes the message of the Book of Job must now be considered.

A Paradoxical Conclusion

Often read as an unfortunate capitulation to the supposed demands of literary convention[20] or theological tradition,[21] the Epilogue has too easily been dismissed as superficial, a "banal deactivation" of the previously powerful poetry.[22] Some accept the inclusion of this

---

[20] Some commentators speak of a dramatic or formal "rounding off" to the tale; cf. H. McKEATING, "The Central Issue of the Book of Job," *ExpTim* 82 (1970) 244-45 and D. Cox, "The Book of Job as Bi-Polar *Mašal*: Structure and Interpretation," *Anton* 62 (1987) 160. As explained by H.H. ROWLEY, "The Book of Job and Its Meaning," *From Moses to Qumran:* Studies in the Old Testament (London 1963) 160: "To have ended the book without the Epilogue would have been to leave it unfinished. ... It would have been intolerable to leave (Job) in the hands of the Satan. No longer would this have been the test of Job, but mere malice and vindictiveness."

[21] According to A. DI LELLA, "An Existential Interpretation of Job," *BTB* 15 (1985) 53, without the epilogue "the book would never have been accepted by the religious establishment." Similarly, TSEVAT claims that "the very radicalism of the book's answer, shattering a central biblical doctrine and a belief cherished in ancient Israel, would itself demand the protection of a veil" (*The Meaning of the Book of Job*, 34). N. GLATZER, *The Dimensions of Job:* A Study and Selected Readings (New York 1969) 11, envisions the entire prose frame as "an escape clause" adopted to "absorb the shock of the drama."

[22] B. LANG, "Ein Kranker sieht seinen Gott (Hiob 38-41)," *Wie Wird man Prophet in Israel?* Aufsätze zum AT (Düsseldorf 1980) 148: "Nur der oberflächliche Leser, der immer die letzte Seite zuerst liest, vermag den Schluss des Ijobbuchs zum glücklichen Romanende zu banalisieren und so das ganze Buch zu entschärfen."

"happy ending" as but the ultimate irony[23] or the final comic conclusion.[24] If it has any credibility,[25] it is only to shatter prior characterizations of the divine.[26]

Given the discord previously engendered — wherein the innocent sufferer rightly laments then repents — the affirmation, intercession, and restitution presented in the concluding section (42:7-17) do contribute to the narrative intrigue by apparently contravening all that has preceded it. However, these same verses provide a decisive, albeit paradoxical, resolution to the enigmatic development of the tale in as much as they validate the theological theme heretofore configured.[27]

Following immediately upon Job's admitted repentance before the voice from the whirlwind, the Epilogue commences with the solemn tone of a heavenly decree, in which Yahweh vehemently rebukes the Friends and affirms Job:

וַיֹּאמֶר יְהוָה אֶל־אֱלִיפַז הַתֵּימָנִי חָרָה אַפִּי בְךָ וּבִשְׁנֵי רֵעֶיךָ
כִּי לֹא דִבַּרְתֶּם אֵלַי נְכוֹנָה כְּעַבְדִּי אִיּוֹב:

---

[23] In an essay entitled "An Uncanny World," W. KAUFMANN calls it a "strange conclusion" that "underlines the weirdness of the ways of the world, which is nothing less than grotesque" (in GLATZER [ed.], *The Dimensions of Job*, 241). Cf. DELL, *The Book of Job as Sceptical Literature*, 209.

[24] J.W. WHEDBEE, "The Comedy of Job," *Semeia* 7 (1977) 30: "The restoration is not at all superfluous or surprising when one traces out the plot line of comedy, where catastrophe is typically followed by restoration, penance by festivity, and alienation from society by reintegration into society." Cf. the objections by MOORE, "The Integrity of Job," pp. 20-21, n. 12, and H. FISCH, *Poetry with a Purpose:* Biblical Poetics and Interpretation (Indiana Studies in Biblical Literature; Bloomington 1990) p. 38, n. 28.

[25] According to BRENNER, "The way the epilogue unfolds sabotages its own credibility" ("Job the Pious," 45). Similarly, COX states that "The Epilogue solves nothing. ... A final solution simply does not exist within the *Book of Job*" ("Job as Bi-Polar *Mašal*," 15).

[26] According to J. PRIEST, "Job and *J.B.*: The Goodness of God or the Godness of Good," *Hor* 12,2 (1985) 282: "The author/redactor ... is saying that God is a malevolent being, or at best a capricious one who can provide no center of meaning for human experience. Humanity must dismiss Him and go on unhelped and uncomforted."

[27] Cf. R. POLZIN, *Biblical Structuralism:* Method and Subjectivity in the Study of Ancient Texts (SBLSS; Philadelphia 1977) 58: "confrontation of inconsistencies appears to be as much a feature of the book's structure as of its content."

(42:7)   *Then Yahweh said to Eliphaz the Temanite, my anger burns against you and your two friends, because you have not spoken of me rightly as (has) my servant Job.*

Thus, in the divine judgment, Job and Job alone among the interlocutors has spoken rightly about God. The key term in this evaluation — נְכוֹנָ ה — is usually translated by a nominal clause: "what is right." Such a rendering, however, occasions a purely propositional reading which tends to limit the interpretive focus; it supposes the declaration of some intellectual "truth" in the right content of Job's speech. Read in this way, the insights of Job would be contrasted with the "errors" of the Friends as regards the issues of divine retribution,[28] justice,[29] or providence.[30]

However, given the verbal characteristic of the participle in reference to its agent,[31] and in light of the discursive context of the tale,[32] an adverbial translation ("rightly, correctly") seems more

---

[28] G. RAVASI, *Giobbe:* traduzione e commento (Roma [3]1991) 106: "Le ragioni della loro condanna sono due. Essi applicano la loro teologia personale e ufficiale come se fosse la stessa parola di Dio che interpreta il caso concreto di Giobbe. ... In secondo luogo aboliscono la storia che è l'incrocio della libertà imprevedibile di Dio e di quella dell'uomo e vi sostituiscono gli schemi rigidi dei loro meccanismi teologici necessitanti (la legge della retribuzione)."

[29] Claiming that all are culpable, TSEVAT states: "The error of Job and the friends lay in this that they permitted the societal aspect of the dichotomy [justice-injustice] to encroach on the extrasocietal one [non-justice]" (*The Meaning of the Book of Job*, 37).

[30] According to R. FORREST, "An Inquiry into Yahweh's Commendation of Job," *SR* 9 (1979) 166, the term נְכוֹנָה "contains important religious connotations which are indicative to the righteous believer of the existence of a necessary relationship between providence and creation."

[31] In its Niphal form, the participle can indicate the state of its subject which is denoted by the action to which the verbal root refers; being passive it connotes the completion of that action. It is in this sense that נְכוֹנָה is employed in Ps 5:10 ("being trusted") and נָכוֹן in 1 Sam 23:23 ("being definite"), both of which refer more to the person than to the content in question.

[32] Cf. the significant qualification, based on related uses in Job, given by E. GOOD, *In Turns of Tempest:* A Reading of Job, with a Translation (Stanford 1991) 381: "Such a galaxy of different meanings shows that the word does not signify 'truth' in the merely intellectual sense but bears on the satisfaction of what has been established."

appropriate.[33] In this sense, the narrative conclusion remains focused on the *act* of Job's speech;[34] it concerns the propriety with which his various modes of discourse reflect his integrity.[35] Thus, in contrast to the presumptuous "folly" of his hypocritical friends (13:7-8; cf. 12:20; 26:3),[36] Job has spoken with a brash yet honest openness that reflects the divestment of himself in search of his God.

The question arises, then, as to the particular reference of this concluding affirmation. Because Job's speech is contrasted with that of the Friends, the divine judgment cannot be limited to Job's responses in the Theologue[37] nor to his reactions in the Prologue.[38] Nevertheless, because Job does speak about God in both those sections, the

---

[33] Cf. W. VOGELS, "Job a parlé correctement -- une approche structurale du livre de Job," *NRT* 102 (1980) 840-841 and nn. 21-22; W.L. HUMPHREYS, *The Tragic Vision and the Hebrew Tradition* (OBT, 18; Philadelphia 1985) 118; and M. GUINAN, *Job* (Collegeville Bible Commentary, OT 19; Collegeville 1986) 82-83;.

[34] According to COX, Job "pushes his revolt to the limits of moral courage, and the fact that this rebellion is not condemned, but is given at least a limited approval as against the stereotype of the tradition (42:7), suggests that *the act of revolt itself* was the right reaction— for a prisoner of the Absurd" (*Man's Anger and God's Silence*, 126). A similar conclusion is drawn by J.G. WILLIAMS, "Deciphering the Unspoken: The Theophany of Job," *HUCA* 49 (1978) 72, but by claiming that "it is not a matter of saying that Job is right or wrong," he mistakenly discards the explicit affirmation of the Epilogue.

[35] As GUINAN explains: "... Job has spoken in a proper way. He has lamented; he has argued; he has prayed (something the friends never do); he has challenged. All this can be summed up in a phrase: in all his speaking, Job has strenuously maintained the integrity of his experience" (*Job*, 82).

[36] In the view of POPE: "If this verse [42:7] refers to the arguments of the Dialogue, it is as magnificent a vindication as Job could have hoped for, proving that God values the integrity of the impatient protester and abhors pious hypocrites who would heap accusations on a tormented soul to uphold their theological position" (*Job*, 350). Cf. N. HABEL, "'Only the jackal is my friend': On Friends and Redeemers in Job," *Int* 31 (1977) 227-236.

[37] G. FOHRER, *Das Buch Hiob* (KAT, 16; Gütersloh 1963) 539, claims that it refers only to the words of Job's response to the Theophany. PENCHANSKY abruptly claims the opposite: "It would be narratively absurd to interpret Yahweh's words as referring to Job's words of repentance" (*The Betrayal of God*, 55).

[38] E. KISSANE, *The Book of Job,* Translated from a Critically Revised Hebrew Text with Commentary (New York 1946) xxxv, suggests that it concerns only "Job's pious expression of resignation given in the Prologue." In a variant on this opinion, C. KUHL, "Neuere Literarkritik des Buches Hiob," *TRu* 21 (1953) 203, maintains that the divine judgment refers to an earlier tradition of the prose tale in which the Friends would have suggested, like Job's wife, that he curse God.

positive evaluation cannot refer only to his side of the disputation in the poetic Dialogues, whether in whole or in part.[39] Instead, given the conclusive position of this divine decree in the overall structure of the narrative, the "being right" with which Yahweh doubly commends Job concerns the modality of *all* his speech about God.

This verbal affirmation is then complemented by the divine restoration of Job's religious and social prominence. First, Job resumes his role as spiritual benefactor by interceding on behalf of his friends. Extending beyond familial concerns (cf. 1:5), and in paradoxical reversal from their coming to comfort him (cf. 2:11), Job now prays for those with whom he had disputed. Yet this petitionary effort is more than merely the ironic fulfillment of the Friends' previous suggestions (cf. 22:27-30). Instead, following upon and intertwined with the divine affirmation of his speech (42:8),[40] Job's prayer is accepted (42:9) as the efficacious intercession of one now steeped in a newfound wisdom.[41]

After this, Job's social status is restored (42:10-17). Akin to the traditional gesture of two-fold restitution,[42] Job receives from the hand of the Lord all that he had before and more. Yet his sudden abundance of possessions and progeny need not imply a back-handed confirmation of the theory of retribution; nor does it intimate a placat-

---

[39] H.L. GINSBERG, "Job the Patient and Job the Impatient," in *Congress Volume* (VTSup, 17; [ed. J.A. EMERTON] Leiden 1969) 93, submits that the affirmation is in reference to chapters 27-28, while L.W. BATTEN, "The Epilogue of the Book of Job," *ATR* 15 (1933) 125-128, interprets it in reference to Job's apologia in chapter 31. Others suggest the "truth" of particular aspects of Job's speeches (see the survey in LÉVÊQUE, *Job et son Dieu*, 124-126).

[40] The first word of 42:8, וְעַתָּה ("and now"), has a conclusive as well as temporal sense; further, this verse explicitly connects (כִּי) the friends' need of Job's intercession with their not having spoken correctly about God.

[41] Comparing Job to the intercessory figures of Abraham (Gen 18:22-32; 20:7), Moses (Num 21:7), Samuel (1 Sam 7:5; 12:19), Amos (7:2-6) and Jeremiah (11:14; 37:3), C. LARCHER, *Le livre de Job* (Bible de Jerusalem; Paris 1957) 168, suggests that "Son épreuve semble être l'une des raisons de l'efficacité de sa prière." In describing the aim of the Epilogue, HARTLEY states: "The fact that Yahweh has Job intercede for the comforters indicates that Job has gained spiritual authority for having endured undeserved suffering and then yielding his complaint to God" (*The Book of Job*, 544).

[42] Cf. R. GORDIS, *The Book of Job:* Commentary, New Translation and Special Studies (New York 1978) 576: "The doubling of his possessions, his male offspring, and his lifespan is in accordance with the ancient biblical law in Ex. 22:3, 11, which ordains double payment for a theft."

ing substitution on the part of a defeated divinity.[43]   Rather, such beneficence serves as the public validation of Job's comportment,[44] in correspondence to the private judgment given in God's word.[45] The goods with which Job is blessed thus become the concrete expression of the unlimited freedom of God in bestowing the "gift" of wisdom.[46]

Therefore, the so-called storybook ending should not be disregarded as if it were purely fabricated fiction, an embellished conclusion so replete with scriptural saccharine that it cannot possibly connect with the real world.[47]   Nor should it be relegated to the status of a merely formal closure, incidental to the argument that has preceded it.[48] Most of all, it should not be disdained as destructive of the meaning of the tale.[49]   Rather, the inclusion of the Epilogue in the narrative structure is *essential* to the theological emplotment of the book.   Far from being a "letdown" inconsistent with the daring dialogues that precede it, the paradoxical ending actually furthers the strategy of the

---

[43] Contrary to the view of PENCHANSKY: "In so doing, God disassembles his own arguments, and shows himself to be in competition with Job's friends for characterization as the least sympathetic figure in the narrative. God's feeble attempts to rebuild Job's shattered life seem by their very shallowness and insensitivity to prove the soundness of Job's accusations" (*The Betrayal of God*, 55).

[44] Contrary to the conclusion of H.H. ROWLEY, *Job* (NCent; London 1986) 11: "Job's prosperity is restored, not because he is righteous but because the test is ended." Cf. JANZEN, *Job*, 261: "Now in the epilogue the vision arrived at through the dialogues is brought into the community."

[45] In his structural explanation, POLZIN claims that "By restoring Job's fortunes twofold, God's act both confirms his word of 42:7-9 and confirms *by deed* what he had only asserted *by word* in 38-41: his omnipotent power" (*Biblical Structuralism*, 72).

[46] Cf. HUMPHREYS, *The Tragic Vision*, 121: "The restoration is unnecessary; Job has already been at once crushed and affirmed by the deity. Thus, this restoration is an act of grace, pure and simple."

[47] As opines BRENNER, "Job the Pious," 39: "In short, the traditional legend seems to be a somewhat naive exemplum of extraordinary human conduct."

[48] As suggests COX, *Man's Anger and God's Silence*, 137: "The reason for the Epilogue would seem to be the exigence of the dramatic art rather than the demands of the argument."   Cf. E. DHORME, *A Commentary on the Book of Job* (London 1967) lxiv: "The Monument which the author aims at creating is the poem. The Prologue and Epilogue are no more than its entrance and exit."

[49] As thinks R. GIRARD, *Job, the Victim of His People* (Stanford 1987) 142: "The prologue and the conclusion eliminate the essential and make the Dialogues unreadable, to transform the Book of Job into a ludicrous anecdote recited mechanically by everyone."

story by synthesizing the heterogeneous events of its narrative movement.[50]

In the emplotment of the Book of Job, the literary synthesis provided by the Epilogue also indicates and furthers the theological focus of the tale. The divine decree provides the decisive closure by which the earthly and heavenly conflicts are resolved as the speech of Job, in the togetherness of its multiple forms, is rightfully confirmed. And the restitution of Job's religious and social status demonstrates in practical terms the advance in understanding which the poet has sought to narrate in the fictional life of this servant of Yahweh.[51] Appreciated in this way, the Epilogue invites us to re-read the Book of Job in a new perspective, and this, in turn, will give the particular contour to our interpretation of Job's repentance.

THEOLOGICAL CHARACTERIZATION

With reference to the theme of the Book of Job, the paradoxical conclusion to the tale highlights the importance of correct speech about God.[52] The divine approbation of Job's God-talk thereby acts as a hermeneutical lens with which to re-read the previous speech-episodes in the story. What will come to light in this interpretive process is the instructive manner in which theological tradition and methodological innovation are juxtaposed in the various "languages" of the main character. This linguistic theme also comes to imaginative expression in the various "figures" by which the biblical hero is portrayed. Thus,

---

[50] According to FISCH, the "letdown" of the Epilogue following the poetic grandeur of the previous chapters "is part of the book's strategy. We touch the depths and heights, but life goes on. We do not remain in the world of myth or the world of art. ... In the end we confront not tragedy but something else" (*Poetry with a Purpose*, 41).

[51] POLZIN, *Biblical Structuralism*, 105: "What appears to invest Job's latter good fortune with ultimate significance is not precisely the fact that it is twofold but rather than (*sic!*) now this good fortune is possessed with insight (by Job and by the reader) whereas the course of the story has shown so graphically how Job's blessings at the beginning were without such insight."

[52] Cf. L.G. PERDUE, *Wisdom in Revolt:* Metaphorical Theology in the Book of Job (JSOTSup, 112; Sheffield 1991) 239: "Indeed it is language about God, not Job's integrity, that is the significant and important basis for judgment. This fact itself moves the direction of the meaning of the book away from the moral theory of retribution."

we suggest that in the narrative link between abstract theme and creative presentation, the Book of Job comes to life as a "theo-novella" — a fictional tale promoting the truth of wisdom in the paradigmatic figure of Job the sage.

On Theo-Linguistics [53]

Though often denounced as lacking the "action" proper to dramatic movement,[54] the tale of Job does give evidence of a literary progression in terms of language.[55] Impelled by the dynamism of poetic diction,[56] the various speech-events which make up this biblical story give voice to diverse modes of theological thought. The "zig zag debate" which takes place thereby makes "dialogue" the overarching "event" of the narrative.[57]

---

[53] Strictly speaking, "theo-linguistics" is a neologism used to designate "the pluridisciplinary field of investigations offered by the linguistic articulation of religious belief and thought" (VAN NOPPEN, *Theolinguistics*, 1). A less technical sense of the term is intended here, namely, as that which refers to the plurality of modes of discourse as these seek to convey the import of religious experience.

[54] In an essay entitled "Of the Poem of Job," R. LOWTH roundly denounces the attribution of drama to Job: "... the poem of Job contains no plot or action whatever, not even of the most simple kind ..." (in GLATZER, *The Dimensions of Job*, 135). Cf. BARR, "The Book of Job and Its Interpreters," 40-41.

[55] Expanding his earlier work, W. VOGELS, *Reading and Preaching the Bible:* A New Semiotic Approach (Wilmington 1986) 79-106, proposes a semiotic analysis of Job that focuses on variations in language as the underlying feature of the narrative sequence.

[56] COX, *Man's Anger and God's Silence*, 86: "... the only 'dramatic movement' ... lies in the intransigence of the dialogue. The words *are* the play, and they must be violent and unyielding to carry the play."

[57] "Dialogue" here is to be understood as the multiple speech-events of the characters rather than as a strictly person-to-person conversational exchange. As GREENBERG explains: "Spontaneous debate, too, is characterized by zigzag, repetitive, and spiral movement in which sequence is determined more by word and thought association than by linearity. ... Such passionate argument is precisely reflected in the poetry of Job, as each interlocutor links theme to theme without troubling to arrange them according to logical sequentiality, and by that very liberty enriching the connotations and multiplying the facets of the argument" ("Job," 303). On the unique dialogic structure of the Book of Job, see also Y. HOFFMAN, "Ancient Near Eastern Literary Conventions and the Restoration of the Book of Job," *ZAW* 103 (1990) 402-405.

In the Prologue (chapters 1-2), the debate about theo-linguistics is initiated by the heavenly interlocutors. Stimulated by an adversarial avowal,[58] the question arises as to whether (or how) Job will "bless" God.[59] The potential for divergence latent in this question becomes the catalyst for the narrative action.[60]

For his part the earthly protagonist upholds the reputation he enjoys in the heavenly chambers. To the loss of his extra-personal goods, Job responds with the stock phrases of religious resignation:

עָרֹם יָצָתִי מִבֶּטֶן אִמִּי   וְעָרֹם אָשׁוּב שָׁמָ ה
יְהוָה נָתַן וַיהוָה לָקָח   יְהִי שֵׁם יְהוָה מְבֹרָךְ:

(1:21)   *Naked I came forth from my mother's womb,*
         and naked I will go forth there;
         Yahweh gave and Yahweh has taken away;
         may the name of Yahweh be blessed.

As if these words of worship were not enough, the narrator closes this first scene with an insistent affirmation relative to Job's linguistic behavior:

בְּכָל־זֹאת לֹא־חָטָא אִיּוֹב וְלֹא־נָתַן תִּפְלָה לֵאלֹהִים

(1:22)   *In all this Job did not sin, and he did not charge wrong-*
         doing to God.

---

[58] Whether read as a colloquial prediction (CLINES, "False Naivety," 132) or a rhetorical declaration (WEISS, *The Story of Job's Beginning*, 46) or an oath of affirmation (DHORME, *Book of Job*, 8; ROWLEY, *Job*, 31), the conclusion to both discourses of the satan shifts the narrative focus decidedly to the matter of Job's speech (cf. 1:11; 2:5). As HOFFMAN points out, this becomes the sole criterion for understanding the personality of the protagonist ("The Relation between the Prologue and the Speech-Cycles in Job," 166).

[59] On the philological ambiguity of ברך ("bless" or "curse"), see DRIVER/GRAY, *Book of Job*, II:4-6 and D.J.A. CLINES, *Job 1-20* (WBC; Waco 1989) 3-4.

[60] D. ROBERTSON, "The Book of Job," *The Old Testament and the Literary Critic* (Philadelphia 1977) 35, rightly sees the potential for Job to curse as "the hinge of the dramatic action."

In succession, Job succumbs to the loss of his physical well-being with glum silence (2:7-8). Provoked by the impetuous concern of his wife, who urges him simply to "curse (בָּרֵךְ) God and die" (2:9), Job replies to her:

כְּדַבֵּר אַחַת הַנְּבָלוֹת תְּדַבֵּרִי
גַּם אֶת־הַטּוֹב נְקַבֵּל מֵאֵת הָאֱלֹהִים וְאֶת־הָרָע לֹא נְקַבֵּל

(2:10a) *Like one of the foolish ones indeed you like to talk; should we accept the good from God and not accept the trouble?*

Immediately the narrator again declares Job's innocence, though this time with less gumption:

בְּכָל־זֹאת לֹא־חָטָא אִיּוֹב בִּשְׂפָתָיו׃

(2:10b) *In all this Job did not sin in his sayings.*

With these initial responses, the durability of the language of covenantal faith appears to be established. By "blessing" God the provider and by not cursing God the tester, Job's language clearly remains within the bounds of propriety; he has indeed spoken correctly, as the narrator has twice noted, though indirectly. Nevertheless, chinks in Job's theo-linguistic armor begin to appear. The progression from declarative resignation to rhetorical assertion does confront the foolishness suggested to him; but it may also imply a lessening of resistance on Job's part. Similarly, the narrator's declarations are clear in their judgment, but the second is less insistent than the first and may bode future dissension.[61] In the ritual reflectiveness with which the Prologue ends, the narrative space is left open for the ensuing debate.

With a quantum theo-linguistic leap, the soliloquy of chapter three inaugurates the poetic controversies (chapters 4-27). Venting his

---

[61] While a change between 1:22 and 2:10 is evident (and therefore indicative of some development), it need not be affirmed, as do WEISS (*The Story of Job's Beginning*, 72) and PENCHANSKY (*The Betrayal of God*, 51), that Job sinned intentionally though not vocally.

seething rage,[62] Job now adopts the language of diatribe. He probes a universally human anxiety; he postulates an overwhelming cosmic absurdity; he predicates a surreptitiously divine mismanagement. All in all, Job's prolix speech has become an offensive self-defense as he disputes the religious explanations voiced by the three Friends.[63]

But Job does not take issue only with his human interlocutors. Because his God has been agonistically silent and distant, Job's words assume the character of a frenetic lament — he seeks the source of meaning but is barred by the divine aloofness from finding it. As his frustration increases, his doxology decreases; as his hope grows hopeless, his prayer grows pointless.[64]

The rhetoric of debate comes to an end with chapter 28. Whether to signal resistance or exasperation, the words of this poem hoist once again the religious standard of the inaccessibility of wisdom and re-iterate the perduring value of a righteous "fear of the Lord."[65] Yet the theo-linguistic development of the main character does not cease here. In chapters 29-31 Job gives voice to a carefully constructed oath of innocence, fortified by the imprecation with which he ultimately

---

[62] Cf. H. HOHENSTEIN, "Oh Blessed Rage," *CurTM* 10 (1983) 162-168, who argues that biblical languages of anger function as a confirmation of the ambiguous nature of faith and as a corrective to any "Romantic wishful thinking" relative to the divine-human relation.

[63] See the summary of their opinions given by D. CLINES, "The Arguments of Job's Three Friends," in *Art and Meaning:* Rhetoric in Biblical Literature (JSOTSup, 19; [eds. D.J.A. CLINES, D.M. GUNN, and A.J. HAUSER] Sheffield 1982) 199-214; his thesis is that, while sharing fundamental presuppositions, each Friend presents a coherent and distinct position vis-à-vis Job.

[64] D. PATRICK, "Job's Address of God," *ZAW* 91 (1979) 272: "Indeed, one can describe Job's action in these speeches as a struggle to confront God with his questions and receive an answer. Once he utters his questions and receives no answer from God, his address [of God] declines and ceases. It re-appears for one brief moment later, but again ceases at the critical moment."

[65] Often segregated as the narrator's veiled intervention in maintenance of an inevitable truth, the words of this "wisdom poem" enter the tale abruptly under the rubric of *Job's* speech. Whoever the speaker, this chapter aptly closes the inconclusive human debate on "wisdom in principle" as it has developed from the beginning of the tale. (With HABEL [*The Book of Job*, 46] we note here the "fear of the Lord" *inclusio* between 1:1 and 28:28.)

repudiates religious complacency and upholds his own righteousness.[66] Thus does he spur the dialogic action to new heights — those
of heaven, from where the accused divinity is now dramatically compelled to respond.

The response of Yahweh comes in the theophanic discourses from
the whirlwind (chapters 38:1-40:2 and 40:6-41:34). Yet, despite the
longed-for encounter, Job replies to the bombastic intervention of his
divine adversary with decidedly unusual terseness. In seeming stupor
he utters two concise confessions (40:3-5 and 42:2-6). Neither words
of amelioration nor capitulation, these laconic utterances can only
reflect a newfound spiritual apprehension. In them Job's theological
speech assumes a new, supra-rational quality, consonant with and
attesting to the revelation that he has here experienced.

Thus has the language of the main character passed from faithful
formality to disputational diatribe to awesome avowal — and in all this
Job has spoken "rightly" about God, as the divine voice itself attests
(42:7).[67] Thus, too, has the author's tale of theo-linguistics passed
through several stages, the succession of which invites comparative
analysis. Here, in the confrontation between the old and new of speech
about God, the Book of Job discloses its narrative strategy with regard
to the "tradition" of sapiential theology.[68]

In the Prologue, the ideal of covenantal integrity is promoted. With
remarkable deliberateness,[69] Job there utters what seem to be formal-
istic dogmatisms of his inherited faith. When trouble persists,
however, his wife counsels an emotional backlash; certainly an acceptable response given his plight, such an antithetical option also offers the
swiftest way out of his problematic situation. But Job abruptly

---

[66] D. Cox, "Structure and Function of the Final Challenge: Job 29-31," *PIBA* 5
(1981) 62: "... in chs. 29-31 Job's continued claim to 'righteousness' is not meant to be
a claim to absolute innocence — no one is totally innocent before God and he knows it
(14:4). It is a plea for reason."

[67] That the divine voice proclaims this judgment is a telling advancement from the
similar act of the (human) narrator in the Prologue.

[68] For RICOEUR, the notion of "tradition" intends "not the inert transmission of some
already dead deposit of material but the living transmission of an innovation always
capable of being reactivated by a return to the most creative moments of poetic activity"
(*Time and Narrative*, vol. I, p. 68).

[69] For CLINES, the reactions of Job are doubly remarkable: first, by attributing his
suffering to divine deprivation and, second, by speaking only after some deliberate
(ritual) behavior ("False Naivety," 128).

dismisses such reactionary talk as impious "folly"[70] and re-iterates his faithful adherence to his God. Nevertheless, it quickly becomes evident that such a-critical worship reaches a point beyond which it no longer sustains the embattled believer.

That point Job reaches when, upon further reflection, he can no longer make sense of his life.[71] His impassioned speeches in the Dialogues arise as a two-pronged intellectual reaction to his own situation and, by extension, to the fate of all human existence. Based on the concrete data gleaned from reality, Job interrogates the prevailing theological positions as to the sort of God capable of so arbitrarily afflicting his own creations.[72] Amid such evident atrocities, and impelled by his consummate drive to know, Job cannot settle for the placating platitudes of his friends' theology. Instead, with an openness characteristic of his unique intellectual integrity,[73] he takes up the art of rational thought and reasoned speech. By means of this "new" method, he pushes the existential question to its logical limit.[74]

---

[70] Such folly would be the opposite of wisdom; cf. A. PHILLIPS, "*Nebelah* — A Term for Serious Disorderly and Unruly Conduct," *VT* 25 (1975) 237-238: "The fool is unable to see the order in things, says the wrong thing at the wrong moment, and takes action which results in unruliness and disorder." To be noted is the divine assertion in 42:8 that Job's friends have likewise spoken foolishly.

[71] COX, "Structure and Function of the Final Challenge," 65: "Suffering could be accepted, and cheerfully, if there were a reason for it: either the reasons given by the friends, or a particular reason of God's. The contrast between the traditional 'Job' of the prologue, and the 'Job' of the dialogues — a contrast deliberately cultivated by the author — makes this clear. What alienates Job is the mental suffering of being unable to explain his intellectual estrangement from the traditional basis of his faith."

[72] For COX this "what kind of God" question is not only the focus of the Dialogues but the critical issue in the book as a whole (*Man's Anger and God's Silence*, 11). However, if Job, and not Yahweh, is seen as the main character of the tale, and if the Epilogue provides an interpretive clue to the story's theme, then the "answer" to this God-question, critical as it may be, becomes secondary to the "process" of one's speaking-about-God.

[73] As CLINES notes: "By contrast [to the set patterns of the friends] ... Job's mind is confused, flexible, experimental, and his argument constantly in course of development" ("The Arguments of Job's Three Friends," 213).

[74] COX, *Man's Anger and God's Silence*, 86: "But every thinking person, everyone who lives by the mind, must have a certain degree of scepticism regarding traditional ideas and beliefs that seem to contradict reality as it is actually experienced, and must on occasion renounce those received ideas if they make no sense. This denial of unsubstantiated 'theory about God and his control of creation' may eventually lead to a 'knowledge of God' that transcends 'received faith'."

Yet the brandishing of this rational scalpel brings no cure; actually, it aggravates his religious dilemma.[75] Caught between a tradition that could not respond to him, and a deity who would not, Job risks permanent metaphysical disillusionment,[76] for in a world without apparent meaning, even philosophic logic can founder in absurdity. His only "hope" seems to lie in his intellectual integrity,[77] although with no divine-human tribunal in which to be vindicated, this rational posture can only languish. But "futility" will not be the last word in the Joban tale[78] — the ultimate theological language is yet to come.

With the tempestuous advent of the voice of Yahweh, new intellectual vistas are opened for Job which make existential "belonging" possible again.[79] In the poetic panorama provided by the divine discourse, Job clearly learns something new.[80] He speaks now quite haltingly, for his words no longer stem from a-critical belief or reasoned deduction. Rather his responses in the Theologue bespeak the language of contemplation — a mode of discourse as mysterious as the reality to which it purportedly refers. Yet only *after* these last words of Job is the divine affirmation relative to the rightness of his speech issued publicly. And only then is the character of Job restored, and his theological characterization completed.

---

[75] Cox, "Structure and Function of the Final Challenge," 57-58: "But Job's poetic insight was that God had *destroyed* reason, because he had destroyed hope ...."

[76] Cox, *Man's Anger and God's Silence*, 84: "The only religion that is intellectually tenable is one that acknowledges absurdity. The alternative is a religion in which everything is rational (that of the friends), and this means a religion in which God is understandable."

[77] Contrary to Westermann, Cox holds that "the certainty of Job lies not in trust in God, but solely in the power of the human mind to query the 'god-idea'" (*Man's Anger and God's Silence*, 85).

[78] Contrary to the thesis of G. Larue, "The Book of Job on the Futility of Theological Discussion," *The Personalist* 45 (1964) 72-79.

[79] Cf. Cox, "Structure and Function of the Final Challenge," 67: "... when it finally comes in the theophany that follows, God's answer, such as it is, deals with man's *intelligence* and not with his moral faculties."

[80] Cox, *Man's Anger and God's Silence*, 136-137: "He returns to the world of everyday living — it is the same but he is not. He is a different person, capable of bringing a new maturity and a more open mind to the human situation of life in the world."

On Theo-Figuration

As with the creative schema of any narrative, so the tale of Job engenders the development of its theo-linguistic theme by way of the successive characterizations of the protagonist. Reflecting the productive imagination of the author, the "images of integrity" by which Job is presented help to locate this literary classic in the realm of religious fiction — a "theo-novella" that is more story than history, but no less true. In fact, by virtue of the phenomenon of "iconic augmentation," the fictional truth of the Book of Job — its teaching about wisdom — appears even more real.[81]

With regard to the forms of Old Testament literature, the Book of Job defies literary classification. The prose narrative reads like a legendary tale,[82] while the poetic speeches include lament,[83] disputation,[84] skepticism,[85] and lawsuit.[86] The dramatic action of the story as a whole resembles the movement of lyricism,[87] whether in

---

[81] RICOEUR, "The Function of Fiction in Shaping Reality," 126: "Because fictions do not refer in a 'reproductive' way to reality as already given, they may refer in a 'productive' way to reality as intimated by the fiction."

[82] On the formal characteristics of a "tale," see G.W. COATS (ed.), *Saga, Legend, Tale, Novella, Fable: Narrative Forms in Old Testament Literature* (JSOTSup, 35; Sheffield 1985) 63-70.

[83] C. WESTERMANN, *The Structure of the Book of Job: A Form-Critical Analysis* (Philadelphia 1981), considers the book a "dramatized lament" based on the poetic dispute's (chaps. 4-27) being framed by the soliloquies of Job's lament (chaps. 3 and 29-31). Similarly, H. GESE, *Lehre und Wirklichkeit in der alten Weisheit: Studien zu den Sprüchen Salomos und zu dem Buche Hiob* (Tübingen 1958), considers the book a "paradigm of an answered lament" (*Klageerhörungsparadigma*).

[84] R. MURPHY, *Wisdom Literature: Job, Proverbs, Ruth, Canticle, Ecclesiastes, and Esther* (FOTL, 18; Grand Rapids 1981) 18, classifies these chapters as "disputation speeches"; J. CRENSHAW, "Wisdom," in *Old Testament Form Criticism* (Trinity University Monograph Series in Religion, 2; [ed. J.H. HAYES] San Antonio 1974) 253-254, considers "controversy dialogue" to be the prevalent form in the book.

[85] See DELL, *The Book of Job as Sceptical Literature*, esp. 44-52, where she cites the proponents of a "protest" reading of Job.

[86] HABEL emphasizes the centrality of the legal metaphor (*The Book of Job*, 54-57, with references).

[87] TERRIEN describes the work as "a lyrical meditation with a dramatis personae" ("Job," 878). Similarly, R. GORDIS, *The Book of God and Man: A Study of Job* (Chicago 1965), claims it is both lyrical and didactic, where "logic and passion, emotion and theory, are fused in the crucible of genius" (p. 7).

tragedy[88] or even comedy,[89] and may even portend the advance of horror.[90] The protagonist appears as the hero of an epic account,[91] one dealing with religious conversion[92] or existential transformation.[93] Employing all these forms and more,[94] the book seems to be *sui generis* in its composition.[95]

To speak of the Book of Job as a "theo-novella," then, is not an attempt to impose the strictures of contemporary genre classification on a decidedly unique story. Rather, in terms of a phenomenological hermeneutics, this composite identification serves the dual purpose of recognition and facilitation. On the one hand, it focuses on the fictional characteristics of a narrative.[96] On the other hand, it also suggests the wisdom locus of its canonical interpretation.

To consider the Book of Job as a "novella" is to acknowledge as essential to its configuration the imaginative characterization which informs the plot. Not as fully developed as would obtain in a novel, but more complex than that in a short story,[97] the characterization of

---

[88] See the survey of opinions for and against Job as tragedy in FISCH, *Poetry with a Purpose*, 26-42.

[89] WHEDBEE, "The Comedy of Job," 3.

[90] R.C. SCHLOBIN, "Prototypic Horror: The Genre of the Book of Job," in *Fantasy and the Bible* (*Semeia*, 60; [eds. G. ACHELE and T. PIPPIN] Atlanta 1992) 23-38.

[91] F. ANDERSEN, *Job:* An Introduction and Commentary (TynOTC; Leicester 1976) 36-37.

[92] J. ALEXANDER, "Job Considered as a Conversion Account," *SpTod* 42 (1990) 126-139.

[93] R.A.F. MACKENZIE, "The Transformation of Job," *BTB* 9 (1979) 51-57.

[94] On the particular function of various forms in the "Sitz-im-Buch" of Job, see G. FOHRER, "Form und Funktion in der Hiobdichtung," *Studien zum Buche Hiob* (BZAW, 159; Berlin 2 1983) 60-77. In addition to those forms mentioned by Fohrer, see N. HABEL, "Appeal to Ancient Tradition as a Literary Form," *ZAW* 88 (1976) 253-272.

[95] POPE, *Job*, xxxi. The thesis that the Book of Job is "unique" is also sustained by ROWLEY ("The Book of Job and Its Meaning," 142) and R. AHRONI, "An Examination of the Literary Genre of the Book of Job," *Tarbiz* 49 (1979-80) 1-13.

[96] COATS introduces a study on narrative forms in Old Testament literature by distinguishing between the generic qualities uncoverable in the "narrative" tradition and those more difficult to read in the "poetic" sources (*Saga, Legend, Tale, Novella, Fable*, 14). While he includes Job in the latter, our contention is that Job exhibits the phenomena of a fictional *narrative*. Cf. N. HABEL, "The Narrative Art of Job: Applying the Principles of Robert Alter," *JSOT* 27 (1983) 101-111.

[97] W.L. HUMPHREYS, "Novella," in *Saga, Legend, Tale, Novella, Fable*, 92: "It is this development of characters that essentially sets the novel and the novella apart from the short story."

Job is both varied and exaggerated. This admittedly purposeful creation on the part of the author results in a four-fold figuration which both accompanies and furthers the sapiential emplotment of the story.

The inventiveness of the author strikes the reader in the opening verses. In an uncustomary introduction, the author presents the main character with deliberate forthrightness:

$$\text{אִישׁ הָיָה בְאֶרֶץ־עוּץ אִיּוֹב שְׁמוֹ}$$

(1:1a) *A man there was in the land of Uz; Job was his name.*[98]

From the modicum of biographical information provided here (1:1-5), Job appears initially as "Any Man," not restricted to the historico-religious tradition of the chosen People.[99] Yet he is much more. Described by the narrator as one who is תָּם וְיָשָׁר וִירֵא אֱלֹהִים וְסָר מֵרָע ("blameless and upright, one who feared God and turned away from evil" - 1:1; cf. 1:8; 2:3), Job exemplifies the apex of religious integrity; depicted as enjoying abundant material fortune (1:2-3), he also represents the zenith of socio-cultural status. Thus, right from the start the protagonist looms exceedingly large on the narrative horizon. This is not just any man — Job is *"The* Man," a clinically created prototype of universal and ideal proportions in relation to whom some comparison will, no doubt, be drawn.[100]

Following this brief introduction, the Prologue sets out the problematic tension which will give impetus to the entire narrative. Despite all satanic attempts to the contrary, Job maintains his divinely

---

[98] According to WEISS (whose translation is given), the inverted opening (אִישׁ הָיָה) serves a stylistic and thematic purpose: stylistically it opens the tale with a light and vivid tone; thematically, it serves to emphasize the person concerned. Similarly the second inversion (אִ יּוֹב שְׁמוֹ) is used to point to this "famous" Job among those of similar nomenclature (*The Story of Job's Beginning*, 17-21).

[99] Despite the references to Job in Ezekiel (14:14,20), his provenance in "the land of Uz" sets him apart geographically from the cities of the Israelite tradition. Based on a detailed analysis, WEISS concludes that this reference is figurative: "The aim is to establish that Job, the archetype of he who fears Heaven and dreads sin, lived in the world of Wisdom" (*The Story of Job's Beginning*, 21-24).

[100] LÉVÊQUE, *Job et son Dieu*, 138: "Rien ne lui manquait de ce qui fait la pleine santé physique et morale: il nous est présenté comme un modèle d'équilibre humain et surnaturel."

appreciated status as a paragon of piety.[101]   He who customarily
sacrificed burnt offerings on behalf of his children (1:6) falls to the
ground in worship of a providential deity even when they are taken
from him (1:20). With a "fear" redolent of covenantal piety,[102] Job
is thus characterized as a sanctimonious servant of God.[103]

Yet all is not so simple. In the poetic Dialogues that follow, the
theo-linguistic complication is furthered as the idyllic protagonist seems
to lose his legendary lustre. The non-sense of his deprivations has
subverted the a-critical piety of his theism,[104] and ritual silence
cannot contain his wonder. Hence, based on the concrete certainty of
his own experience, rather than on the supposed surety of his inherited
tradition, Job cries out as the victim of an inexplicably divine disaster.
Akin to a "character of the Absurd,"[105] Job seeks to comprehend the
cosmic quandary of the human being's finite condition.[106]   Yet he
cannot. With only his intellectual integrity to sustain him, Job here
shows little fear in revolting against the platitudes of his friends and

---

[101] With TSEVAT, HUMPHREYS considers "piety" not in terms of "the details of
worship or narrow religiosity" but a reflecting "a total pattern of character expressed
by full allegiance to a deity, allegiance that will brook no rival" (*The Tragic Vision*, p.
122, n. 3).

[102] As will be noted, various notions of "fear" correspond to the sapiential
characterization of Job and thus act as a structuring principle in the narrative; cf. J.
GAMMIE, *Holiness in Israel* (OBT, 13; Minneapolis 1989) 138: "That the majesty and
holiness of God call forth reverence and fear runs throughout the book as a minor
theme."

[103] For HABEL, Job's worship reflects his status as a patriarch and "devout head of
household" (*The Book of Job*, 87-88), but for BRENNER, "The religiosity of Job the
pious is almost a parody of faith rather than a climactic manifestation of it" ("Job the
Pious," 44).

[104] As PENCHANSKY argues, the tale of Job concerns a dissonance in the very notion
of piety, the traditional understanding of which comes to be bifurcated and reversed
(*The Betrayal of God*, 54).

[105] Rightly COX describes Job as a *persona*, a type-character, but he limits this to
"a character of the absurd" (*The Triumph of Impotence*, 51-52). In the perspective of
the narrative whole which we propose here, Job appears rather as "a character of
wisdom."

[106] COX, *Man's Anger and God's Silence*, 22: "Job has been cast in the role of
'Everyman', victim of the human condition of innate fragility and insecurity." In the
philosophy of RICOEUR, this would correspond well with his notion of human
"finitude"; see his *Fallible Man* (New York ²1986).

their concept of "god." Before one and all he has become a rational rebel.[107]

Only with the speeches from the whirlwind in the Theologue will the intellectual tension of this story be somehow resolved. Clearly on the receiving end of this didactic exchange, Job assumes in this section a new figurative stance. Moved by that fear which attends such theophanic events, for which silence and reverence seem to be appropriate reactions, Job appears more contemplative than confrontational, more a mystic than a metaphysician. In his final words he has become a respectful repenter.

In the Epilogue the resolution of the theo-linguistic tension is completed by the divine decree, and the complexity which initiated the narrative intrigue vanishes as Job's ideal status is restored.[108] The novella here ends with one final image of the protagonist — though this one without corresponding theological language. Portrayed as "tast(ing) the sweetness of life, undisturbed by the prospect of its end,"[109] Job leaves the narrative scene a sated sage.

With this final characterization, the mythic drama of theo-linguistics is complete.[110] More than that, it is rendered superabundant and makes of this tale a "prophecy of meaning."[111] By means of the

---

[107] COX, *Man's Anger and God's Silence*, 44: "Here man, faced with a cosmos he cannot rationally control, finds his true identity: in a consciousness of his capacity to rebel, what Camus calls a 'metaphysical' rebellion, by which he means a revolt, not so much against the human condition as it is experienced as against the facile acceptance of text-book answers that do not fit the case but which nonetheless claim to determine the reality. This is the artist's choice: creative anger. And it is Job's choice: not submission, not despair, but anger, and because of this the *Book of Job* deserves its classic status, for where there is anger there is humanity."

[108] According to KAUFMANN, in his essay entitled "Job the Righteous Man and Job the Sage," Job's restoration includes God's affirmation of his speech, God's reproach of the companions, and God's gift of material possessions (in GLATZER, *The Dimensions of Job*, 70). Similarly, the final response of Job pertains to the structural "resolution" of the tale in the thought of both HABEL (*The Book of Job*, 72) and D. BERGANT, *Job, Ecclesiastes* (OTM, 18; Wilmington 1982) 204-207.

[109] GLATZER, *The Dimensions of Job*, 10.

[110] PERDUE, *Wisdom in Revolt*, 238: "Redemption is the final and climactic end of the mythic pattern which internally organizes the stages of dramatic enactment."

[111] For RICOEUR, the notion of "superabundance" or "extravagance" is the trait which both transgresses the narrative structure and specifies its religious content (see "Biblical Hermeneutics," 99). It thus becomes critical to a Christian hermeneutics, as RICOEUR claims in "Tasks of the Ecclesial Community in the Modern World," in

exaggerated figuration of Job's integrity, the truth of this biblical tale thus appears "larger than life."[112]   The righteous Job who offers "just-in-case" sacrifices, the rational Job whose intellectual theorizing articulates a metaphysical rebellion against the non-sense of this divinely created world, the repentant Job who utters no more the perorations of a litigant but instead the adumbrations of a sage, the mythical Job who dies a hero, "old and full of days" (42:17) — each of these figures is an ideal, a paragon of respective theological epistemologies.

In this sense, the Book of Job is not only a work of narrative artistry but a *theo*-novella, a fictional story whose structure and content mutually develop the theme of speech about God.[113]   By means of its heuristic emplotment, this narrative draws its readers into an interpretive engagement with its theological themes.[114]   Supported by the "iconic augmentation" of the Joban characters, it presents various theological approaches for consideration and evaluation. The interpreter must ask which "Job" is wise enough to have spoken correctly about God: the pious Job of the Prologue, the disputational Job of the Dialogues, or the repentant Job of the Theologue? Perhaps none of these? Or, as we suggest, all of them — in the mutuality of believing affirmation, rational investigation, and spiritual apprehension.

Theology of Renewal, II: Renewal of Religious Structures (ed. L.K. SHOOK) (New York 1968) 245: "To be Christian is to decipher the signs of this superabundance in the very order where humanity expresses its purpose. The Christian stands *as the adversary of the absurd, the prophet of meaning*, not by desperate will, but by recognizing that this meaning has been attested in the events which the Scriptures proclaim" [*emphasis added*].

[112] HUMPHREYS, "Novella," 95: "In all this the novella seeks to reflect life, to present the truth in life, not what happened once in the past, but what happens. ... The events of the story are set on a scale larger than most of life; the stage is more vast than that on which most of us play out our roles."

[113] Contrary to ROWLEY, who claims that "It is in the sphere of religion rather than in theology that the meaning of the book is to be found" (*The Book of Job*, 18).

[114] Cf. D. PATRICK and A. SCULT, *Rhetoric and Biblical Interpretation* (JSOTSup, 82; Sheffield 1990) 101: "While one could construe the ambiguous ending as evidence that the author could not resolve the issue that he posed, or lacked the courage to present it to an unreceptive community, it should be appreciated — in light of the aesthetic hypothesis — as a sophisticated rhetorical move. Rather than allow the reader to stand back and pass judgment on the adequacy of the resolution, the author forces us to complete the meaning of the work. The resolution has the parabolic quality of involving the audience in the action."

That this sapiential focus concerns a fictional hero does not thereby denigrate its truthfulness. Though clearly not "historical," in the sense of being open to validation by empirical standards, the Joban novella, with its paradoxical conclusion and its creative variations, is nonetheless "real."[115] It offers an entertaining and insightful account into earthly and heavenly events which, by their nature, are not susceptible to scrutiny by a public audience.[116] Thus, from the perspective of a phenomenological hermeneutics, the "poetic" presentation in a fictional narrative portends truth of another, no less significant, kind. As Ricoeur concludes, "could we not say that by opening us to the different, history opens us to the possible, while fiction, by opening us to the unreal, brings us back to the essential?"[117]

Thus, we come back to the focal point of our study — the interpretation of Job's "repentance." Having considered the literary configuration and theological characterization of the Book of Job, we are now in a position to analyze Job's final words, which receive their fullest sense only in light of the paradoxical affirmation in the Epilogue and in comparison with the theo-linguistic figures that appear in the seemingly discordant scenes of this unique story. Taken together, these literary elements contribute to the narrative world of Job, which manifests itself not as the ironic failure of wisdom, but as its optimistic summit.[118] With a bolt of theophanic help Job becomes a sage — he succeeds in knowing what is, and the fictionalized process by which he comes to do so makes of him an exemplar of wisdom for all ages.

---

[115] Cf. FISCH, *Poetry with a Purpose*, 41: "The clear force of these verses [42:7-17] is that we are in the realm of historical writing. True, we are not talking about factual history but we are speaking of the kind of prose that claims a connection with history. These closing verses of the book, indeed, serve to anchor the high poetic invention of the earlier chapters in a world of men and women, marrying and giving in marriage, bearing children, establishing themselves economically, receiving and giving gifts, and finally, if they are lucky, dying 'old and full of days'."

[116] HUMPHREYS, "Novella," 86. Cf. RICOEUR, "History as Narrative and Practice," 215: "... in this sense you can say that a religious tradition is characterized first of all by the stories that it tells and quite evidently by the symbolic interpretations (or any other kind) that it grafts onto these stories. But the first center is a narrative center."

[117] RICOEUR, "Can Fictional Narratives Be True?" 16.

[118] I offer a more critical analysis of this structure in "The Book of Job as Optimistic Wisdom," forthcoming in the *Journal of Theta Alpha Kappa* 18,1 (1994).

Chapter Three

THEOPHANIC BLUSTER?

Job and the Wind of Change

Most interpretations of the final chapters of the Book of Job center on the depiction of God as either "windbag" or "wonder": do the divine words represent a tempestuous obliteration of the protagonist's problem in light of more grandiose cosmic concerns? Or do they portray a rhapsodic reiteration of the insuperable epistemological gulf which stands forever between finite human beings and the majestic Creator? In either case, it seems, Job is ultimately silenced.

What seems to regulate both positions is the impression made by the particular intervention of Yahweh. Highlighting the narrative action at this point, the "theophany" acts as a controlling image, providing by its symbolic import the narrative infrastructure that undergirds Job's epistemological transformation. Thus, a consideration of the opening verses of the Theologue (38:1-3) is necessary; by focusing attention on the revelational scope of the ensuing discourses, this narrative introduction elucidates the proximate context of Job's repentant utterance.

THE ADVENT OF THE DIVINE (Job 38:1)

In the course of the Dialogues, the narrative figure of Job has come to assume the properly Hebraic dignity of a tragic hero. Progressively ennobled by the blatant truth of his personal experience, the protagonist has engaged in a debate of cosmic proportions and has crowned his obstreperous outrage with a clamorous self-defense and divine stand-off.[1] Yet the main character will not be left to rest on his rationalistic laurels. After the narrative interlude supplied by Elihu, the words of God descend from on high, purportedly to offer some resolution. But, in the theo-linguistic setting of the tale, the inclusion of this episode remains somewhat disconcerting.[2] While some would reject the term "theophany" as inaccurate,[3] others tend to dismiss the notion as inappropriate.[4] What role does this specifically religious event play in a wisdom narrative?

A "Stormy" Event

By way of literary intrigue, the author has woven into the narrative an expectation of Yahweh's coming onto the scene. Generically, the cosmic considerations proffered by God in these chapters constitute a structural parallel to the theological perspective voiced by the human

---

[1] Cf. FISCH, *Poetry with a Purpose*, 30: "The combination of such utter helplessness and such extraordinary self-confidence is what constitutes the posture of Job. His rebellion is founded upon a confidence that God is bound to acknowledge the virtue of the righteous man. He calls God so to speak to testify against God, the God who has made a covenant with man founded on justice and law to testify against the God of the thunderstorm and the cataclysm. Here is the impudent claim of the Hebrew Bible; it would have been for the Greeks a matter of unimaginable presumption."

[2] J.L CRENSHAW, "When Form and Content Clash: The Theology of Job 38:1 - 40:5," in *Creation in the Biblical Traditions* (CBQMS, 24; [eds. R.J. CLIFFORD and J.J. COLLINS] Washington 1992) 70: "One can hardly say that in this instance the medium is the message, for the singular function of theophany, the bringing near of the one who until now has dwelt in concealment, clashes with the content of the speech, the shattering of every human illusion of occupying a special place in God's sight."

[3] Perhaps the most extensive study on the topic is that of J. JEREMIAS, *Theophanie: Die Geschichte einer alttestamentlichen Gattung* (WMANT, 10; Neukircher-Vluyn 1965). This author, however, dismisses the Joban account as "stunted" since it concerns more an "answer" of God than an appearance (p. 69).

[4] J. GIBSON, *Job* (Daily Study Bible; Edinburgh 1985) 222: "It is not the kind of setting that would normally have been chosen by a Wisdom teacher or, for that matter, by one of Israel's prophets." So, too, COX, "Structure and Function of the Final Challenge," 65: "... theophanies have no real function in wisdom literature, where reason and experience, not revelation, are normative."

characters in the previous dialogues.[5] Specifically, the divine discourses actuate a formal counter-statement to the protagonist's imprecations in his opening and closing soliloquies.[6] In this sense the speeches of Yahweh offer a literary balance to the words of Job and thereby seek to alleviate the growing perplexity of those involved in the debate — characters and readers alike.[7] In whose favor the scales are tipped, however, remains to be determined.

Beyond the exigencies of literary art, a divine response is also expected from a religious perspective. Given Job's seemingly blasphemous attack on God and the traditional systems of belief, some conclusive remedy is called for in order that the biblical book exceed the tacit promotion of philosophical skepticism. Given the theological scope of the Joban tale, some authoritative resolution is needed in order that the canonical work transcend the narrative cry of an embittered existentialism.[8]

That some patent resolution is provided in these final chapters can, for the most part, be assumed.[9] *How* this is so remains another matter

---

[5] COX, "The Book of Job as Bi-Polar *Mašal*," 21: "The reader ... is thus presented with a bi-polar *mašal*, in which man's rational view of God is countered by God's view of himself."

[6] TSEVAT, *The Meaning of the Book of Job*, 7: "The challenge to God [in chaps. 29-31] is overt and clear. God is bound to act. If Job has perjured himself, God is to punish him even more than he is already punished, if that is yet possible. If not, he is pure; the oath proves it. Then he should be restored *in integrum*, for so judicial procedure requires. If neither of these immediate and plain alternatives result, God is challenged personally to respond to the oath." Those who stress that this section represents the counterpoint to Job's discourse in chapter three include S. BACHAR, "God's Answer to Job," *BM* 25 (1979) 25-29 and V. KUBINA, *Die Gottesreden im Buche Hiob:* Ein Beitrag zur Diskussion um die Einheit von Hiob 38,1 - 42,6 (Freiburger theologischer studien; Freiburg 1979) 153-155.

[7] R.A.F. MACKENZIE, "The Purpose of the Yahweh Speeches in the Book of Job," *Bib* 40 (1959) 438: "Besides the dialogue of Job with the Friends, and that of Job with God, there is the dialogue of the author with his readers. And it is this ... which justified and indeed required the composition and inclusion of the Yahweh-speech."

[8] WILCOX, *The Bitterness of Job*, 101: "So not only tradition but also reason demanded that the drama not end with Job's silencing of the friends; a reconciliation with reality, an acceptance, needed to be achieved somehow. Bitterness should not have had the last word."

[9] A minority opinion considers these chapters as totally irrelevant or entirely impertinent (e.g., POPE, *Job*, lxxxi). Such displeasure is given graphic description by L. STEIGER, "Die Wirklichkeit Gottes in unserer Verkündigung," in *Festschrift H. Diem* (München 1965) 160: "dürftig und leer ... drei Stunden Naturkunde für Hiob."

altogether. Seeing that the divine words recounted here fail to address
directly the issues so hotly debated in the preceding Dialogues,[10]
several commentators have suggested that the conclusiveness of these
chapters lies not so much in the content of the speeches as in the event
of the theophany itself.[11] But what sort of event is recounted here?

Riding on the narrative crescendo of speakers,[12] the divine
discourses are introduced with a straightforward simplicity:

וַיַּעַן־יְהוָה אֶת־אִיּוֹב מִן הַסְּעָרָה וַיֹּאמַר׃

(38:1)   *Then Yahweh answered Job from the storm and said:*[13]

What distinguishes this response from that of the previous characters
is precisely the locus of the voice that now speaks, namely "the storm"
(הַסְּעָרָ ה).[14]

At first glance, this introduction brings to mind references to
meteorological phenomena given previously in the tale.   In the
Prologue, a mighty "wind" (רוּחַ) is the vehicle of domicile destruction
as it causes the four-cornered collapse which leads to the death of Job's
children (1:19). In the Dialogues, Job's incredulous hypothesis of a
face-to-face recrimination with God is thwarted by his fear of being

---

[10] See the catalogue of omissions given by D. O'CONNOR, "The Futility of Myth-Making in Theodicy: Job 38-41," *PIBA* 9 (1985) 84-85.

[11] E. RUPRECHT, "Das Nilpferd im Hiobbuch: Beobachtungen zu der soggennante zweiten Gottesrede," *VT* 21 (1971) 231: "Der Inhalt dieser Antwort ist nicht wichtig. Wesentlich ist nur, dass er Hiob in einer Theophanie begegnet und sich ihm zuwendet als einer, der auch den einzelnen Menschen hört und auf ihn eingeht."

[12] ALONSO SCHÖKEL notes "l'intensità con cui resuona qui il verbo 'rispondere', predicato di Dio" and suggests that it functions "come ripetizione di un leitmotiv in crescendo fino alla sua risoluzione" (*Giobbe*, 619).

[13] This translation follows the Qerê reading. In terms of the thesis to be proposed, the lack of a definite article in 40:6 (מִן סְעָרָה) does not appear to be significant. Moreover, the variant readings found in some ancient versions (e.g., Syriac and Targum) are disregarded here as not reflecting the poet's symbolic intention. On these textual problems, see DHORME, *Book of Job*, 574.

[14] The standard introduction of speakers is given as וַיַּעַן --- וַ יֹּאמַ ר (4:1; 6:1; 8:1; 9:1; 11:1; 12:1; 15:1; 16:1; 18:1; 19:1; 20:1; 21:1; 22:1; 23:1; 25:1; 26:1; 32:6; 34:1; 35:1). It differs only here and in a few other instances: by the added mention of a "curse" (3:1); by the prefaced rationale for speaking (32:1-5); and by replacement with the notion of "continuing the discourse" (27:1; 29:1; 36:1).

crushed "in a whirlwind" (בִּשְׂעָרָה - 9:17). There, too, Job depicts the fate of the wicked in blustery terms: similar to straw before the "wind" (רוּחַ) and to chaff in a "tempest" (סוּפָה), they are swept away (21:18); like those snatched up in the night by a "tempest" (סוּפָה) from the east, they are whirled away (וִישָׂעֲרֵהוּ) from their place (27:20,21). Finally, a lashing "tempest" (סוּפָה) pertains to Elihu's picturesque defense of the thunderous majesty of God (37:9).

As is readily apparent, none of these particular terms is adopted by the poet to introduce the divine speeches in 38:1 and 40:6; it is not out of a blowing gale or rotating whirl or tumultuous squall that Yahweh speaks but simply "from the storm." Given the author's penchant for poetic ploys, such a distinction is not simply to be overlooked or easily to be dismissed as mere lexical equivocation.[15] Rather, while the basic sense of windiness remains evident, the significance of "the storm" must involve something more than heavy atmospheric disturbance. In fact, as a semantic study will demonstrate, the poet's use of the term evokes, yet also betrays, the traditional imagery of biblical theophanies.

In the historical narratives of the Old Testament, the only instance of סערה occurs in the story of Elisha's succession of Elijah, where it concerns the latter's being borne up to the presence of God in the heavens (2 Kings 2:1-12); no doubt, this picture would call to mind the wind and other elements of nature which form the prelude to God's whispering appearance to Elijah earlier on Mt. Horeb (1 Kings 19:9b-18). In the prophetic oracles, סערה usually occurs in the imaginative descriptions of God's final judgment. Whether in the condemnation of false and lying prophets (cf. Ezek 13:11,13; Jer 23:19; 30:23) or in the destruction of national rulers (cf. Amos 1:14; Isa 40:24; Jer 25:32), "the storm" is often accompanied by tempestuous winds and other violent forces of nature; it thus becomes the futuristic vehicle of divine wrath and heavenly rebuke. Accordingly, in the cultic hymns, the God who has power over the storm, whether to stir or still it (Ps 107:25-29), is worthy of praise (Ps 148:8).

---

[15] For GOOD, the same referents in both 9:17 and 38:1 are merely spelled differently (*In Turns of Tempest*, p. 435, n. 8).

By introducing the divine voice as coming "from the storm," the author of the Book of Job does evoke the graphic imagery of the theophany.[16] Yet what is characteristic of such an event is not, primarily, its horrific proportions; rather, is emphasizes a meeting between the divine and the human.[17] In terms of Old Testament history, this theophanic encounter is associated in the first place with salvation and only later with the power of condemnation.[18] Evoking the foundational event at Sinai, the actualization of God's presence in a theophany serves as a demonstration of divine favor; it legitimizes those called to holy service (Exod 19:16-19; cf. Lev 9:23-24; Ezek 1:4) and establishes as distinctive the people whom this God would accompany and protect (Exod 33:12-23; cf. Exod 13:21-22;14:19-20).[19] To be noted is the extraordinariness of such an appearance — anyone who experienced immediate contact with the divine risked almost certain death (Exod 33:20; cf. Deut 4:33; 5:24).

Nevertheless, despite the abundant treasure of theophanic imagery in the literary tradition of the Old Testament, "the storm" mentioned in Job 38:1 and 40:6 is not depicted with all the splendor of a privileged penetration of the divine into human affairs. Instead, the poet proceeds immediately to the recitation of Yahweh's words (וַיֹּאמֶר). By such a collocation, it would seem, the meaning of the theophany resides not in the tempestuousness of the event but in the definitiveness of the ensuing speeches. Hence, any direct association with the historical traditions is at best implicit, while any symbolic reference to eschatological judgment may be disregarded.

Nonetheless, "the storm" does correspond to Old Testament theophanies in that it initiates for Job a very real encounter with the divine, one that will assure his integrity yet alter his ways. By specifically re-employing the divine tetragrammaton (יְהֹוָה), the poet

---

[16] Other allusions to a theophany in the Yahweh-speeches are catalogued in GOWAN, "God's Answer to Job," 94.

[17] G. FOHRER, "Theophanie," in the *Calwer Bibellexicon* (eds. K. GUTBROD und R. KÜKLICH) (Stuttgart 1959) col. 1310: "Stets handelt es sich um eine Begegnung, in der der Mensch sich der Gottesmacht zum Heil oder Unheil ausgeliefert sieht."

[18] J.L. MCKENZIE, "Aspects of Old Testament Thought," in *The New Jerome Biblical Commentary* (eds. R.E. BROWN, J.A. FITZMYER, and R.E. MURPHY) (Englewood Cliffs 1990) 1294.

[19] See J. JEREMIAS, "Theophany in the OT," *IDBS*, 896-898.

evokes the salvific foundations of Old Testament life and lore.[20] In fact, the definitive presence of God, manifest in the divine words to follow, ultimately provides the vindicating "answer" (רַעַנ) to Job's theo-linguistic angst.[21]

A "Symbolic" Manifestation

That "the storm" portends the immediacy of the Almighty is readily apparent from the poet's adoption of the familiar image of a theophany. Nevertheless, the narrative import of this event for the interpretation of Job's change of stance is open to varying interpretations.

For some, the event reckons the swift end to an otherwise obtrusive human debate. In this view, the stormy arrival of Yahweh would insinuate a destructive disposition,[22] the verbalization of which issues forth in a divine self-defense of such overwhelming proportions as to render insignificant Job's creaturely pleas.[23] With nothing less than blind force,[24] the reasoning of Job would herewith be concussed.[25]

For others, the advent of Yahweh is comparably powerful, but directed toward a more positive end. Manifesting a beneficent presence, the divine appearance would demonstrate the creator's care for his faithful servant.[26] In what would amount to a re-activation of

---

[20] On the distinction among the divine names used in the Book of Job, see LÉVÊQUE, *Job et son Dieu*, 146-179.

[21] Cf. J.A. WHARTON, "The Unanswerable Answer: An Interpretation of Job," in *Texts and Testaments:* Critical Essays in the Bible and Early Church Fathers (FS. S.D. Currie; [ed. W.E. MARCH] San Antonio 1980) 48: "Consistently in the Psalms, the innocent sufferer uses the word [רַעַנ] in what must be taken as a virtually absolute sense (i.e., not as a 'reply' in words, but as the appropriate vindicating response)...."

[22] A. VON ROHR SAUER, "Salvation by Grace: The Heart of Job's Theology," *ConTM* 37 (1966) 269: "From this figure [of the tornado or cyclone] Job was to conclude that the Lord could dispose of him as easily as a whirlwind whisks away a house, a tree, or an individual."

[23] Cf. R.B.Y. SCOTT, *The Way of Wisdom in the Old Testament* (New York 1971) 159-162; P. SNELL, "A Journey of Faith," *TBT* 20 (1982) 334-337.

[24] Cf. P. VOLZ, *Hiob und Weisheit* (Die Scriften des Alten Testaments in Auswahl, 3/2; [ed. H. GUNKEL] Göttingen 1921) 85; ROBERTSON, *The Old Testament and the Literary Critic*, 51.

[25] Cf. P.C. CRAIGIE, "Biblical Wisdom in the Modern World, III: Job," *Crux* 16 (1980) 9.

[26] Cf. FOHRER, *Das Buch Hiob*, 534; G. VON RAD, *Wisdom in Israel* (London 1972) 221-226.

the self-disclosure of the covenant-god,[27] the arrival of Yahweh occasions an existential transformation of him who suffered.[28] In this way, the fact that Yahweh actually comes to Job provides an "answer" more significant than any logical communication.

Whatever the estimations of the commentators, the theophanic appearance does fulfill the protagonist's oft-lamented desire to meet his God and engage in a discursive confrontation — though not exactly as he foresaw it (cf. 7:11-21; 13:20-27; 23:2-7; 31:35-37).[29] Unlike judicial disputations in the human arena, however, the speeches of Yahweh issue "from the storm" as from an entirely different level of discussion.[30] Hence, the few words of an otherwise simple introduction convey the poet's appeal to, and invocation of, a new narrative context. In the hermeneutic philosophy of Ricoeur, this advertence pertains to the domain of symbolism. What this climactic episode entails, therefore, is something more than the words of just another interlocutor; instead, we are confronted here with the experience of a divine manifestation.

That the narrative localization of the Yahweh-speeches in "the storm" ushers in a symbolic world can be adduced according to Ricoeur's four-fold criteriology. First, the symbolic import of "the storm" is structurally *bound* to its literary context, where prior references allude to a similar event. In light of what has occurred before and what is feared to happen again, mention of "the storm" creates an atmosphere of impending doom. Yet, as the semantic distinction among terms noted above suggests, this particular "storm" will differ somehow from the threatening whirlwind or destructive tempest referred to in the preceding chapters of the book.

Further, "the storm" introduced here conveys the *double-sense* proper to symbols. Whereas on a literal level it refers to a common meteorological event, on a non-literal level it also articulates an extraordinary religious reality, namely the theophany. Nonetheless, in

---

[27] D.L. BERRY, "Scripture and Imaginative Literature: Focus on Job," *JGenEd* 19 (1967) 127-128..

[28] Cf. H.-P. MÜLLER, *Hiob und seine Freunde* (Theologische Stüdien, 105; Zürich 1970) 42; MURPHY, *Wisdom Literature*, 44.

[29] Cf. M.G. SWANEPOEL, "Job 12 — An(other) Anticipation of the Voice from the Whirlwind?" *OTE* 4 (1991) 192-205.

[30] LARCHER, *Le livre de Job*, 152: "Yahvé ne répondra pas à Job sur le même plan, mais en Dieu."

contradistinction to the otherwise conventional pattern of reporting a theophany,[31] the streamlined announcement in this introduction hints at the uniqueness of the Joban event. Indissolubly connected with the forthcoming divine words, "the storm" will rain upon this scene its own logomachy.

Moreover, the image of "the storm" becomes theologically *evocative*. Bound traditionally to the presence of the divine, its mention here encodes the imminent arrival of Yahweh.[32] Like theophanies of old, it intimates a salvific presence; like images of the future, it implies a definitive judgment. But whether or not this tell-tale tempest will involve an ominous rebuke remains to be "seen" in the way Job hears the words to come.

Lastly, reference to "the storm" is *donative* in meaning, for the symbolic sense obtains in and through the literal reference. Like the vertical path of precipitation accompanying an actual storm, the words of Yahweh will descend from the heavenly heights to saturate the ground of the earthly discussion. Like the torrents of such precipitation, the heavenly revelation will arrive in a veritable onslaught of questions and descriptions. In this way, association of the Yahweh-speeches with the meteorological phenomenon prefigures the movement and intensity of divine self-disclosure which will burst forth precipitously in the ensuing discourses.

Thus, "the storm" furnishes the context in which the divine action of speaking to Job will take place. In so doing it acts as what Ricoeur calls a "rule of interpretation" which, by way of the religious imagination, "reanimates anterior experiences, reactivates dormant remembrances (and) irrigates the adjacent sensory fields."[33] As the controlling poetic image, "the storm" engenders a new context for the question

---

[31] According to G. Henton Davies, "Theophany," *IDB*, 4:620, the characteristic pattern includes: "the divine initiative; various revelatory formulas; the encounter and the relationship between God and the human party; the account of the purpose of the theophany and the reverential awe of the human party."

[32] McKenzie, "Aspects of Old Testament Thought," 1294: "The one natural phenomenon with which Yahweh is most frequently associated is *the storm*."

[33] Ricoeur, "Poétique et symbolique," 50: "C'est dans l'expérience de la lecture que ce phénomène s'observe le mieux: en schématisant l'attribution métaphorique nouvelle, l'imagination réanime des expériences antérieures, réactive des souvenirs dormants, irrigue les champs sensoriels adjacents: c'est ainsi qu'elle procure des images au concept."

under discussion. It thereby presages a level of discourse that is more divine than human, a mode of thinking that will be more wondrous than rational — all this as a manifestation of the sacred breaking forth into the world of theological proclamation.

The traits common to such a manifestation suggest that in Job 38:1 and 40:6 this same phenomenon obtains, though with a particular nuance.[34] Articulated in the concreteness of a known meteorological phenomenon, the numinous presence of the divinity is hereby anchored in the reality of space and time. Yet, because the poet does not recount the storied details of a theophany, this manifestation pertains to another, non-physical level of human experience — the aesthetic — where the power of the imaginal supersedes that of the rational. Its efficaciousness will derive not from the threatening power of eschatological destruction but from the inherent strength of the revelatory words of Yahweh. In the sacral immediacy designated by "the storm," the paradoxical dualities heretofore debated are now manifested: the apparently inaccessible God now draws near; the previously hidden divinity comes to be revealed; the inimical "seeing" of God will be replaced with "insight" into the divine.[35]

Consequently, the Joban theophany appears to be *unique*.[36] Bound as it is to the subsequent words of Yahweh (cf. Exod 20:18-19; Ps 50:3,7,21),[37] "the storm" here is a properly literary phenomenon, one whose provenance is not the atmosphere of the cult but the artistry of fiction. In this narrative modality, the imaginative event points to a new horizon of meaning. In other words, by invoking "the storm" as the locus of the divine words, the poet introduces a proto-revelatory

---

[34] Cf. "Manifestation et proclamation," *AF* 44, 2-3 (1974) 58-64, where RICOEUR borrows from the thought of Mircea Eliade to present a phenomenological analysis.

[35] Cf. BRENNER, "God's Answer to Job," 132-33.

[36] Cf. WESTERMANN, *The Structure of the Book of Job*, 108-109: "Within the whole of the Job-drama, this theophany *must* have the character of a unique event; there *can only* be one. This must be said irrespective of the 'content' of the divine speech. The decisive revelations of God in the Bible always have the character of being unique events."

[37] ALONSO SCHÖKEL, *Giobbe*, 620: "Dio viene nella tempesta per rispondere, non per asportare o per strappar via Giobbe, come fece con Elia. Se la tempesta lo mostra inaccessibile, la parola lo avvicina."

symbol,[38] one whose concreteness initiates the vibrancy and vitality of the experiential speech-event to follow.

A SAPIENTIAL DIALOGUE (Job 38:2-3)

In the narrative world introduced by the symbolic storm, the words of Yahweh shine with a linguistic brilliance befitting transcendent illumination. By means of a dialogic interrogation, the divine discourses take issue with the supposed wisdom of Job's words. Invested with a power proper to poetic language, the proclamation of Yahweh reveals a world of mysterious possibility. But how does Job's experience of this world effectuate the existential re-orientation to which his enigmatic responses give voice?

Divine Interrogation

In the tempestuous world of the Yahweh-speeches, a wide range of earthly and heavenly topics is covered. Coming as they do from a divine source, one expects these verses to exhibit a certain superiority, both from a narrative and a religious point of view.[39] Yet opinions vary as to the form and function of the words offered to Job "from the storm."

---

[38] L. ALONSO SCHÖKEL, *A Manual of Hebrew Poetics* (SubsBib, 11; Roma 1988) 111: "The symbol is the proto-language of transcendent experience, and thus also of religious experience."

[39] Cf. P. SKEHAN, "Job's Plea and the Lord's Reply," *Studies in Israelite Poetry and Wisdom* (CBQMS, 1; Washington 1971) 120: "Bearing in mind, however, the rules of debate ... we can expect that if the Lord condescends to answer at all the three-part speech of Job 29-31, he will be made by the human author to appear as the better debater not only qualitatively but, prosaic as this may seem, quantitatively as well. He will be given more to say, and if he does not answer Job point for point, which is not the accepted technique, at least he will answer Job's speech part for part, and thus 'excel' or overtop it in some measurable way." H.D. PREUß, "Jahwes Antwort an Hiob und die sogenannnte Hiob-literatur des alten Vorderen Orients," in *Beiträge zur alttestamentlichen Theologie* (FS. W. Zimmerli; [eds. H. DONNER, R. HANHART and R. SMEND] Göttingen 1977) 336: "Denn wenn nach dem bisher möglichen Befund allein das Hiobbuch es ist, das innerhalb der altorientalischen Hiobliteratur an seinem Schluss eine Theophanie mit Gottesrede(n) als Lösung des Problems bietet ...."

In terms of genre classification, the speeches of Yahweh could pertain to a number of different domains. The theophanic context would suggest a cultic environment,[40] one in which the divine answer to a human lament takes hymnic form.[41] Or, in a juridical perspective, the speeches would elaborate the disputation of the divine adversary; formally, they present Yahweh's challenge to the human rival.[42] Ultimately, given the wisdom milieu in which the tale unfolds, the divine discourses may best be considered as educative, though exactly what Job is taught is likewise open to debate.

For some, Job learns that he is incapable of any ultimate knowledge. By expanding the area of human ignorance,[43] the divine discourses deepen, rather than solve, the existential enigma and heighten, rather than dispel, the cosmic mystery.[44] In this respect, the Yahweh-speeches may reflect a greater difficulty more than a fitting resolution,[45] perhaps even giving evidence of the general failure of wisdom.[46]

For others, however, the words "from the storm" are positively instructive. Whether intended to correct Job's delusions, or to establish

---

[40] Cf. S. TERRIEN, "The Yahweh Speeches and Job's Responses," *RevExp* 68 (1971) 500; A. WEISER, *Das Buch Hiob* (ATD, 13; Göttingen 1968) 12, 241.

[41] Cf. G. FOHRER, "Gottes Antwort aus dem Sturmwind (Hi 38-41)," *Studien*, 116; H. GESE, *Lehre und Wirklichkeit*, 63-78.

[42] H. ROWOLD, "Yahweh's Challenge to Rival: The Form and Function of the Yahweh Speech in Job 38-39," *CBQ* 47 (1985) 199-211.

[43] H. GREENBERG, "In Dust and Ashes," in GLATZER, *The Dimensions of Job*, 223-224: "God's voice from the storm explained nothing to Job — it merely expanded the area of his not knowing and not understanding; it opened before him unlimited horizons of the inconceivable and impenetrable, and deepened the mystery of existence."

[44] PATRICK and SCULT, *Rhetorical and Biblical Interpretation*, 101: "The reader is forced to admit that the reality of God does not dispel the mystery of existence, but heightens it. ... One might say that we are forced to admit that God will be God, and not the predictable guarantor of anyone's scheme of coherence." Cf. W. LILLIE, "The Religious Significance of the Theophany in the Book of Job," *ExpTim* 68 (1957) 356.

[45] COX, "Structure and Function of the Final Challenge," 65.

[46] B. VAWTER, *Job and Jonah: Questioning the Hidden God* (New York 1983): "In the first place, that Yahweh says anything at all is proof of the failure of wisdom" (p. 83); "No further vision is given. Wisdom has failed. The God who spoke to Job out of the whirlwind has overwhelmed him with his all-presence and all-power, but he has offered no path by which man may seek the divine. The God of the theophany of Job is a *deus absconditus* even more remote than the God on whom Job refused to call" (p. 86).

anew the creator-creature distinction, or to redeem the human imagination,[47] the interrogative style of the Yahweh-speeches serves a
purposeful educational plan. Akin to the method employed in the
Socratic dialogues,[48] these discourses represent a divine self-revela-
tion that, in turn, engineers a "*conversio sapientis*" for Job.[49]

That here we are privy to a sapiential dialogue, however one-sided,
is indicated by the introductory words of Yahweh:

$$\text{מִי זֶה מַחְשִׁיךְ עֵצָה בְמִלִּין בְּלִי־דָעַ ת}$$
$$\text{אֱזָר־נָא כְגֶבֶר חֲלָצֶיךָ וְאֶשְׁאָלְךָ וְהוֹדִיעֵנִי}$$

(38:2-3) *Whosoever* [50] *[would] darken* [51] *[the] design* [52]
with sayings lacking insight?
Gird now your loins like a man,[53]
for I want to question you and you will inform me.[54]

---

[47] Respectively A. DILLMAN, *Das Buch Hiob* (cited in J. VAN OORSCHOT, *Gott als
Grenze: eine literar- und redaktions-geschichtliche Studie zu den Gottesreden des
Hiobbuches* [BZAW, 170; Berlin 1987] 232); KUBINA, *Die Gottesreden im Buche Hiob*,
143-159; D. PATRICK, *Arguing with God:* The Angry Prayers of Job (St. Louis 1977)
92-95.

[48] COX, *Man's Anger and God's Silence*, 96; cf. D. PELLAUER, "Reading Ricoeur
Reading Job," *Semeia* 19 (1981) 79.

[49] F. STIER, *Das Buch Ijjob* (cited in VAN OORSCHOT, *Gott als Grenze*, 240).

[50] The translation of מִי זֶ ה is de-personalized here (not "who is *this
one*") as possibly representing an instance of a demonstrative added to an interrogative "without
any notable change in meaning" (*GBH*, §143g); cf. the use of מִי הוּא in Job 4:7;
13:19; 17:3.

[51] As the primary performance-term in this verse, the participle מַחְשִׁיךְ here is
rendered as a verb; because its action stands in reference to a generic agent, it is here
given a suppositional sense ("would").

[52] The definite article is adjoined here in order to preclude the facile interpolation
of עֵצָה as Yahweh's possession ("*my* counsel").

[53] To read גִּבּוֹר here, as do DRIVER/GRAY, *Book of Job*, 326 ("mighty man") and
PERDUE, *Wisdom in Revolt*, 203 ("warrior") is unnecessary; while the terms may be
interchangeable (cf. GORDIS, *The Book of Job*, 442-443, and HABEL, *The Book of Job*,
520-521), the reference here concerns the distinct nature of the interlocutors not the
level of their physical strength, the divine superiority of which has never been in
question (cf. 9:4-10,19; 12:13-16; 23:13).

[54] The verbal modality translated here reflects the use of an indirect imperative after
a cohortative (*GBH*, §116f).

Comparable to patriarchs (Moses in Exod 19:16) and prophets (Ezek 1:4), Job receives a direct response from his God. But the question and directive which inaugurate the Yahweh-speeches here (cf. 40:7) serve to call attention to the particular features of this divine intervention.

Posed at the outset as a universal question rather than an individualized inquisition (38:2),[55] the basic focus of the divine interrogation centers on Job's grasp of the cosmic "design," a multidimensional project that pertains uniquely to the Creator. Such knowledge would involve a divining discernment of the primordial plan,[56] and by its very nature this would lead to a corresponding power in the regulation of the world order.[57] With the "darkening" of this design,[58] its eternal purposefulness is clouded, its infallible certainty doubted, its dynamic efficacy muddled, its intra-mundane execution hidden — in sum, its character as foundational to existence is made turbid.[59] But beyond the practical question of providential control over the world, there lies a deeper issue, that of bringing into play the very wisdom of

---

[55] According to PERDUE, "This rhetorical question does not merely seek the identity of the one who has dared to challenge divine rule, but more importantly expresses contempt for the opponent. מִי זֶה ('Who is this?') is often used by one who scoffs at the status and power of a challenger" (*Wisdom in Revolt*, 203). However, in view of the de-personalized syntax (see notes 50 and 52 above), the comment of RAVASI seems more appropriate: "Il contro-interrogatorio di Dio inizia con la domanda-base di cui la seguenza degli altri interrogativi non sarà che l'esplicitazione. È una domanda 'universale' pronunciata alla terza persona indefinita" (*Giobbe*, 741).

[56] This is confirmed in the idiomatic reference (אִם־יָדַעְתָּ בִינָ ה) which initiates the first part of the Yahweh-speeches in 38:4. In the sapiential tradition (cf. Prov 4:1,5), "to know discernment" is equivalent to having gained wisdom (HABEL, *The Book of Job*, 537).

[57] This is posed in the second part of the Yahweh-speeches (40:8ff) as pertaining to the question of divine "justice" (מִשְׁפָּטִי ... תַּצְדִּק). In the sapiential tradition this "justice" comes to be seen as the practical application of wisdom (COX, *The Triumph of Impotence*, 137).

[58] Reciprocally, the Hiphil participle מַחְשִׁי ךְ has a causative and declarative sense. A distinction between the two need not be stressed; however, given both the immutability which is characteristic of עֵצָה and the concluding affirmation of right speaking which is predicated of Job (42:7,8), the declarative sense may be preferable.

[59] These understandings of עֵצָה are given respectively by COX, *The Triumph of Impotence*, 121; LÉVÊQUE, *Job et son Dieu*, 511; RAVASI, *Giobbe*, 743; TERRIEN, *Job*, p. 247, n. 3; and FOHRER, "Gottes Antwort aus dem Sturmwind," 125-126.

God.[60] The implication, then, is plain and clear: heretofore, the manifold insightfulness requisite of such divine counsel has been lacking in the utterances of the protagonist.[61] As a result, the clarifying power of transcendent wisdom is needed to remedy the situation.[62] For this reason Yahweh will speak, he whom Job has already acknowledged as in fact possessing the "wisdom and power, counsel and understanding" here under discussion (12:13).

With regard to the mode in which this discursive interaction will take place (38:3), the poet portrays the encounter with an image of vigorous effort — "gird your loins." This image need not emphasize the conflictual relation of the interlocutors as verbal foes or even judicial combatants,[63] but may instead allude to the inherent distinction between them in terms of sapiential capabilities.[64] Yet, although he is bound to take up his epistemological stance only "like (the) man" he is, nevertheless Job is implored to enter into the full partnership of an "I-you" dialogue. By means of questioning and answering, this encounter purports to be more informative than fomenting. Neither an

---

[60] HABEL, *The Book of Job*, 536: "This design reflects the profound wisdom and knowledge of God; Job's obfuscation of that design must be exposed as ignorance. As part of his defense against Job's presumptuous claims, Yahweh challenges Job to demonstrate a level of knowledge and discernment equal to the wisdom of God. ... The challenge to this 'hero' is not one of strength (as in 40:7ff.) but of knowledge, wisdom, and discernment. The irony in the wording of Yahweh's challenge lies in the use of the verb 'know' (*yd'*) in place of "answer" in v. 3b."

[61] As RAVASI explains, the knowledge lacking in Job's words (בְמִלִּין בְּלִי ־ דָעַ ח) incorporates several epistemological aspects — "razionale-sperimentale ... estetico-volitiva ... etico-religiosa" — all of which contribute to "la vera conoscenza (come) un'attività dell'essere intero dell'uomo" (*Giobbe*, 743-744). ANDERSEN understands עֵצָ ה here as "the 'advice' dispensed by a wise man" and, hence, as "a good parallel to knowledge" (*Job*, 273).

[62] F.J. BOLTON, "The Sense of the Text and a New Vision," *Semeia* 19 (1981) 88: "The point of this text seems to be that wisdom, not merely theoretical explanations and information, is required to deal with Job's concern."

[63] An allusion to a "contest" is signaled by C. GORDON, "Belt Wrestling in the Bible World," *HUCA* 23 (1950-51) 131-136; cf. O. KEEL, *Jahwes Entgegnung an Hiob:* Eine Deutung von Ijob 38-41 vor dem Hintergrund der zeitgenössichen Bildkunst (FRLANT, 121; Göttingen 1978) 27, 54. That such a contest is intended here is convincingly disputed by H. GINSBERG, "Interpreting Ugaritic Texts," *JAOS* 70 (1950) 158.

[64] LÉVÊQUE, *Job et son Dieu*, 513: "Yahweh lui offre une joute sapientielle; et ce déplacement de l'axe du dialogue atteste à la fois l'intention éducative de Dieu et sa volonté de ne pas entrer dans le système d'images où Job s'est enfermé."

ironic upbraiding nor a condescending imposition,[65] the event thus
bodes well for Job. In this not-to-be-refused invitation to dialogue lies
the prospect of a thorough re-invigoration of his mode of life,[66] for
the theo-linguistic void of Job's rationalistic comportment is about to
be filled with the awe-inspiring poetry of divine wisdom.

Theo-Poetic Proclamation

In the poetic grandiosity of the divine discourses,[67] Job hears
much about the primordial design, as he is buffeted by a litany of
cosmic wonders, the recitation of which redounds to the marvelous
character of the one responsible for their creation. Though multidimensional in content,[68] these speeches focus on God and the world
as mutually related entities in the existential order. Yet the significance
of each is diversely understood.

In the theological dimension, what Job encounters in the stormy
speeches is tantamount to a demonstration of "holiness" understood as
that which sets the divinity apart from all else. The God with whom
Job had wished to dispute is re-presented as transcending human
concerns, one whose existential distance renders him ordinarily

---

[65] COX, *Man's Anger and God's Silence*, 96: "It is less than justice to the author
to take seriously the idea that the poetry of chapters 38-41 represents either verbal irony
or sarcasm on the part of God — it is too powerfully constructed for that, and such a
literary tactic would not have been convincing to a contemporary reader. Nor is it
simply a gracious condescension on God's part; the firmly logical sequence and the
tightly-knit structural pattern responds too closely to the tenor of the Dialogue."

[66] S. TERRIEN, *Job: Poet of Existence* (Indianapolis 1957) 21: "... he (the poet of
Job) knew and promoted in the immediacy of God's confrontation *a mode of life*."

[67] R. ALTER, *The Art of Biblical Poetry* (New York 1985) 87: "If the poetry of Job
... looms above all other biblical poetry in virtuosity and sheer expressive power, the
culminating poem that God speaks out of the storm soars beyond everything that has
preceded it in the book, the poet having wrought a poetic idiom even richer and more
awesome than the one he gave Job."

[68] KUBINA concludes her critical study of these speeches with an exposition of four
theological "aspects": the dialogical, which emphasizes God's speech "to" Job rather
than over or around him; the soteriological, which emphasizes the nearness of God as
motivating Job's repentance; the universal-cosmological, which emphasizes the divine
counterpoint to the ungodly *ursünde* of humans; and the theocentric, which emphasizes
the glorification of God's ways as the fullness of human understanding (*Die Gottesreden
im Buche Hiob*, 143-160).

inaccessible to earthly remonstrance.[69] This metaphysical separation is made evident by the power of a divinity whose freedom is limitless and whose sovereignty is immutable.[70] Given the supreme might of his God, Job's speech could be considered an affront, the response to which consists in upholding God's honor and integrity.[71] It would seem, then, that the God of these chapters re-emerges as a "sage" and exits from the narrative scene as a "victor,"[72] though the extent of such a victory may be impugned by the irony of its laughable demonstration.[73]

In the cosmic dimension, the speeches of Yahweh contrast Job's world of reason with a "vision of unreason," an alternative world-view in which mystery prevails over absurdity and un-order remains a divine fact, however incomprehensible. In this perspective, duality is

---

[69] Cf. J.B. CURTIS, "On Job's Response to Yahweh," *JBL* 98 (1979) 511: "A Yahweh, so conceived as loftier than all of man's thoughts and ways, simply cannot be bothered by so human a problem as the unmerited suffering of the innocent." VAN OORSCHOT, *Gott als Grenze*, 258-259: "Gott selbst verteidigt seine Freiheit und Unverfügbarkeit sowohl gegen eine Tendenz damaliger Weisheitstheologie, die undialektisch das Weltgeschehen und Gottes Willen gleichzusetzen begann, als auch gegen den Protest Hiobs, der sich auf eigene Erfahrungen beruft und diese zum Maßstab der Bewertung des Handelns Gottes in Schöpfung und Geschichte macht. Hier wird jeweils die Grenze menschlicher und d.h. geschöpflicher Möglichkeiten überschritten."

[70] PREUß, "Jahwes Antwort an Hiob," 343: "Gott ist keine Kategorie unserer Weltdeutung und will es nicht werden, auch wenn gläubiges Vertrauen auf einen unbegreiflichen Gott immer schwierig bleiben wird." Cf. GUTIÉRREZ, *On Job*, 72-75.

[71] ROWOLD, "Yahweh's Challenge to Rival": "In his challenging questions Yahweh not only implies but openly declares that the only one who exercises creative and redemptive power in the world is Yahweh himself" (p. 209). "At this [confrontational] level, then, the Yahweh-speech functions as Yahweh's self-asseveration of creative lordship and as a denial of Job's stance as princely rival who can stand before Yahweh on his own terms and righteousness" (p. 210).

[72] These depictions are proposed, respectively, by N. HABEL ("In Defense of God the Sage") and T. METTINGER ("The God of Job: Avenger, Tyrant, or Victor?") in *The Voice from the Whirlwind:* Interpreting the Book of Job (eds. L.G. PERDUE and W.C. GILPIN) (Nashville 1992) 21-49.

[73] B. SARRAZIN, "Du rire dans la Bible? La théophanie de *Job* comme parodie," *RevScRel* 76 (1988) 54: "L'ironie est évidente. A cette ironie quelle intention donner? La présente lecture 'dialogique' n'est pas un lieu pour trancher, la réponse est plurielle. Sa cruauté évoque l'exercice d'un surmoi dévorant, conduisant à une mystique terrifiante; à moins qu'il s'agisse du regard humoristique d'un sage dont la foi inentamable s'amuse, pour exorciser la peur." Cf. ROBERTSON, "The Book of Job," 48-53.

celebrated as part and parcel of the universe: on the one hand, it is
acknowledged that justice, as humans conceive of it, is *not* a constituent
feature of the world's configuration;[74] on the other hand, the evils to
which life is subject are nevertheless subjugated to the creator's
ultimate control.[75] What is more, the riddle of meaning in which the
universe is mired belies a mystery of beauty and vitality whose very
wonder points to an inexhaustible, though inexpressible, cosmic
order.[76]

As a result, the rhetoric of Yahweh's interrogation need not be
considered a sardonic suffocation of Job's lamentation.[77] Instead,
given the volitional aim of these discourses,[78] it appears to be the
sublime supplanting of it.[79] In this respect, the intervention of

---

[74] TSEVAT, *The Meaning of the Book of Job*, 31: "God says: 'No retribution is
provided for in the blueprint of the world, nor does it exist anywhere in it. None is
planned for the nonhuman world and none for the human world. Divine justice is not
an element of reality. It is a figment existing only in the misguided philosophy with
which you have been inculcated'."

[75] KEEL, *Jahwes Entgegnung an Ijob*, 156-157; KUBINA, *Die Gottesreden im Buch
Hiob*, 143-158.

[76] FISCH, *Poetry with a Purpose*, 39: "The speeches celebrate the *vitality* of the
universe: abundant life and creation are their theme. ... There is terror in the universe
here revealed — darkness, cloud, thunderbolts, unimaginable distances in which man is
lost, but it is all vibrating with life and power and purpose." Cf. R. GORDIS, "The
Lord Out of the Whirlwind: The Climax and Meaning of 'Job'," *Judaism* 13 (1964) 62-
63.

[77] Contrary to the viewpoint of PENCHANSKY, *The Betrayal of God*: "He blusters
and bullies Job, never effectively answering Job's questions" (p. 48); "Yahweh's
speeches therefore represent not Job's answer but the final desolation and abandonment
of Job, the failure of his last hope for redress" (p. 53).

[78] FOHRER, "Dialog und Kommunikation im Buche Hiob," *Studien*, 141: "Dahinter
steht die israelitische Auffassung vom Sinn und von der Absicht der Rede. Sie soll
letzlich nicht durch theoretische, logische Begründing überzeugen, sondern unmittelbar
den Willen der Zuhörer beeinflussen. ... Denn eine Behauptung ist wahr, wenn man fest
an sie glauben kann und glaubt, wenn man seine ganze Seelenkraft hineinlegt, nicht
aber, wenn sie nur bestimmten Normen oder Tatsachen entspricht."

[79] J. MUILENBURG, "The Speech of Theophany," *HDB* 28 (1963-64) 42: "There is
awfulness here and terror and great majesty. Israel's most elevated speech, most
spacious and imposing and august, is reserved for the epiphanies of God. Her speech
is commensurate with its transcendent perspectives. It is not so much with beauty as
we ordinarily speak of it that we have to do here, but something infinitely (and the word
is chosen deliberately!) infinitely more. It is no human dialect to which we listen, but
the kinds of words out of which myths are born."

Yahweh need not be evicted from the domain of the true as merely a "weird experience" that brings appeasement.[80] Rather, the divine words dwell safe and sound in the extraordinary realm of sapiential poetry, whose power of conviction lies more in reflection than in rhetoric,[81] whose strength of certitude derives more from contemplation than from investigation.[82] In terms of Ricoeur's philosophy, the revelation by Yahweh to which Job will respond can be interpreted as a "theo-poetic proclamation."

The poetic dimension of this revelatory proclamation resounds in the extensive "re-description" of the world order. Replete with images that transcend ordinary, descriptive, didactic and prosaic language,[83] the speeches of Yahweh paint a cosmic picture that is more visionary than scientific,[84] more mythical than objectifiable.[85] As such, the focus of

---

[80] R. OTTO, "The Element of the Mysterious," in GLATZER, *The Dimensions of Job*, 226.

[81] GREENBERG, "Job," 303: "Poetry was the form taken by sapiential observation and speculation throughout the ancient Near East. With its engagement of the emotions and the imagination, it was the usual mode of persuasive discourse. Through its compression, poetry allows stark, untempered expression that, while powerful in impact, awakens the kind of careful reflection that leads to the fuller apprehension of a subject."

[82] GORDIS, *The Book of Job*, 560: "The thinker calls upon Job to grasp the world and recognize man's limitations. The poet summons him to steep himself in the beauty of the world and to experience it existentially. By seizing the two staffs of understanding and emotion, man can live wisely, bravely, and joyfully in a world that is miracle as well as mystery."

[83] RICOEUR, "Manifestation et proclamation," 67: "Par redescription j'entends ceci: c'est le propre du langage poétique en général d'abolir la référence du langage ordinaire, descriptif au premier degré, didactique, prosaïque, et, à la faveur de cette *épochè* de la réalité naturelle, d'ouvrir une dimension nouvelle de réalité qui est signifiée par la fable."

[84] Contrary to the "technical" emphasis by M. SAWICKI, "Technological Imagery in the Yahweh Speeches: What Did Job See?" *TBT* 91 (1977) 1304-1310 and the "evolutionary" explanation of L.S. FORD, "The Whirlwind Addresses Job," *SLJT* 24 (1980-81) 217-221.

[85] Cf. LANG, "Ein Kranker sieht seinen Gott," 141-143 and H.-P. MÜLLER, "Gottes Antwort an Ijob und das Recht religiöser Wahrheit," *BZ* 32 (1988) 214-217. On the other hand, O'CONNOR advances the thesis that the Yahweh-speeches concern "The Futility of Myth-Making in Theodicy."

these discourses is not so much a problem to be resolved, as a mystery to be deciphered.[86]

Given the poetic status of these speeches as figurative language or "picture-thinking,"[87] Yahweh's proclamation to Job acts as a limiting medium, one that reinforces the distance between the divine counsel as unconditioned and human insight as derivative.[88] Nonetheless, it is the imagery and thought of this poetic language which engenders meaning for Job, there where the epistemological import of the divine discourses will eclipse the rationalistic world of his lamenting dispute in order to illumine the sapiential horizon of a new way of life being offered to him.[89]

Controlled by the theophanic image of "the storm,"[90] the Yahweh-speeches thus become a direct and definitive revelation. In such a divine proclamation, the unique power of poetic language comes to the fore as that which is purposefully ambiguous, interiorly directed, and cathartic in scope.[91] And these dimensions are most appropriate in the expression of a divine self-disclosure, the "truth" of which pertains specifically to the biblical realm of theophanic manifestation. Prescinding from any verifiable adequation, the divine words demonstrate to

---

[86] In "The Language of Faith," RICOEUR renders suspect the "extension of rationality" which "produces a reduction from the mysterious to the problematic" and whose corollary is "the *autonomy of man* as an agent of his own history" (in REAGAN and STEWART, *The Philosophy of Paul Ricoeur*, 225).

[87] Cf. RICOEUR, "The Status of *Vorstellung*," 70-88.

[88] RICOEUR, "Biblical Hermeneutics," 142: "The concept 'limit' implies not only and even not primarily that our knowledge *is* limited, has boundaries, but that the quest for the unconditioned *puts limits* on the claim of objective knowledge to become absolute. 'Limit' is not a fact, but an act." Cf. G.M. TORTOLONE, "L'enigma di Giobbe: destino dell'uomo e silenzio di Dio," *Asprenas* 36 (1989) 22-38.

[89] P. RICOEUR, "Biblical Hermeneutics," 87: "It is the eclipsing of the objective manipulable world, an illumining of the life-world, of non-manipulable being-in-the-world, which seems to me to be the fundamental ontological import of poetic language."

[90] Cf. L. DORNISCH, "The Book of Job and Ricoeur's Hermeneutics," *Semeia* 19 (1981) 12: "In the beginning of each movement, there is concrete imagery followed by a question. In the working through of that question, a transformation takes place. One has moved from a language too narrow, which denies the fullness of meaning, to a fullness of language which is symbolic. As the language is transformed, so is the subject of the narrative. As Job's language changes, so does Job."

[91] Thus does RICOEUR distinguish poetry from, respectively, scientific, ordinary, or rhetorical language.

Job "the proposition of a world, of a world such that (he) could project there (his) innermost possibilities."[92]

By means of this poetic revelation, the speeches "from the storm" open a treasure of truthfulness for Job. Awakening him to something "more" than he had heretofore known,[93] these imaginative discourses offer a new modality for his theological understanding.[94] But even more so, in the very event of speaking these words, Yahweh extends to Job the opportunity to take part in this novel reality — through his personal appropriation of the wisdom here effused.

The speeches of chapters 38-41 thus constitute a sacral proclamation, understood phenomenologically as a mode of expression addressed to the boundary-situations of human life. Whirled into the extraordinary domain of the divine discourses, Job undergoes what could be labelled a "limit-experience." But here, the event of a heavenly revelation becomes for the earthly protagonist a culminating experience.[95] Raising this wisdom narrative to its climax, the words "from the storm" bring Job to the point at which a new existential response on his part will be possible.

The manner by which these blustery words enable the re-orientation of Job's life involves a "logic" proper to the divine — the *logic of*

---

[92] RICOEUR, "Nommer Dieu," 351: "Révélation, en ce sens, désigne l'émergence d'un autre concept de vérité que la vérité adéquation, réglée par les critères de vérification et de falsification: un concept de vérité-manifestation, au sens de laisser être ce qui se montre. Ce qui se montre, c'est chaque fois la proposition d'un monde, d'un monde tel que je puisse y projeter mes possible les plus propres."

[93] While some commentators (e.g., STEIGER and WILLIAMS) claim that there is nothing new in the Yahweh speeches that was not already known or acknowledged by Job in the Dialogues, some novelty clearly affects Job and induces his repentant change of stance. In our analysis, what is "novel" is the poetic eventfulness which suffuses the language of divine disclosure; from this emerges a new possibility for Job's theo-linguistic life.

[94] RICOEUR, "Philosophy and Religious Language," 80: "Through fiction and poetry new possibilities of being-in-the-world are opened up within everyday reality. Fiction and poetry intend being, not through the modality of givenness, but rather through the modality of possibility. And in this way everyday reality is metamorphosed by means of what we would call the imaginative variations that literature works on the real."

[95] RICOEUR, "Manifestation et proclamation," 70: "Ces expériences-limites ne sont pas seulement des expériences de crise et de décision, comme dans maintes théologies de la crise, pas seulement de détresse comme chez K. Jaspers; ce sont aussi des expériences de culmination, comme dans la parabole de la perle de grand prix, où 'trouver l'inappréciable' constitue la suprême joie."

extravagance. Contrasted mytho-poetically with the rationalistic tenets of traditional human realism,[96] this divine logic proclaims "the excess of sense over non-sense which gives rise to thought."[97] And it is this thought, occasioned by the theophanic discourse as superabundant hope,[98] which will be voiced by Job ultimately as "repentance." The question of how this final utterance expresses the theological re-orientation of Job's life brings us now to crux of our study.

---

[96] With reference to the paradoxical and hyperbolic qualities found similarly in the parables, RICOEUR claims: "C'est alors le contraste entre le réalisme de l'histoire et l'extravagance du dénouement qui suscite l'espèce de dérive par laquelle l'intrigue et sa pointe sont soudain déportés vers le Tout-Autre" ("Nommer Dieu," 359).

[97] P. RICOEUR, "Hope and the Structure of Philosophical Systems," in *Philosophy and Christian Theology* (PACPA; [eds. G.F. MCLEAN and F. DOUGHERTY] Washington 1970) 59. In a note the author expresses his desire "under the expression 'sense' and 'non-sense' ... to unite the logical, the ethical, the existential and the religious aspects of meaning and meaninglessness in life."

[98] Cf. RICOEUR, "Hope and the Structure of Philosophical Systems," 58: "Hope means the 'superabundance' of meaning as opposed to the abundance of senselessness, of failure and of destruction."

Chapter Four

VISIONARY SAGACIOUSNESS:

Job and the Language of Avowal

It has been said that interpretations of Job's responses to the speeches of Yahweh are as numerous and varied as are the interpreters! Given the "classic" nature of this biblical tale, such a multiplicity of viewpoints is almost inevitable. What, then, can our study hope to accomplish by offering yet another interpretation of these conclusive, albeit paradoxical, verses (Job 40:4-5; 42:2-6)?

The hermeneutical lens provided by Ricoeur's philosophy of interpretation focuses our consideration of the compelling truth of this religious work on the poetic character of Job's final words. As such, we will suggest, first, that Job's initial response can be explained as a symbol of reticence; read in this manner, his silence can be understood as a sophisticated shift toward interiority in the face of futile contentiousness. Job's "repentance" can then be explained in terms of a metaphorical twist in meaning; understood in tensionsal contrast to a knowledge that had heretofore been "wondrously far from" him, Job's concluding statement bespeaks an "originary affirmation," one that attests to the inner eye of a newfound wisdom which now informs his theological language. In order to substantiate this aesthetic interpretation, our study will proceed from a new translation of these critical verses.

THE WISDOM OF DIVINE DISPUTATION? (Job 40:2-5)

The reading of Job's first response (40:4-5) seems less problematic
than that of his abrupt and unforeseen "repentance" (Job 42:2-6).
Differences in translation are slight, and, notwithstanding variations in
nuance, nearly all interpretations are similar in rendering these verses
as the initial concession of the earthly protagonist: overwhelmed by the
existential enormity of Yahweh, Job apparently suppresses the linguistic
license with which he has reproved his God.

Yet one wonders how to reconcile such a concession with the
rightful rebellion of the main character.   Can a muted Job be an
exemplary prototype of the sage's struggle with the enigmatic issues of
human existence?   Were the controversy to conclude with the his
resigned capitulation, would not the intrigue of the book also collapse?
But Job's reply need not necessarily be read as forced submission.
Instead, based on a novel translation and read in the context of theo-
linguistic discourse, the question of divine disputation begins to be
resolved through a sophisticated silence which allows for the attainment
of biblical wisdom.

The Futility of Contentious Speech

The common assumption that Job's reply expresses a concession to
the divinity is founded on a particular translation of the verses in
question. In the conclusion to the first segment of the divine speeches
(40:1-2), Yahweh poses to Job a question that, for all intents and
purposes, compresses the divine-human debate into a single issue of
theological prominence.

$$\text{הֲרֹב עִם־שַׁדַּי יִסּוֹר   מוֹכִיחַ אֱלוֹהַּ יַעֲנֶנָּה׃}$$

While reference seems to be made here to a divine imperviousness to
human criticism, the phrasing of this verse varies in translation:

(40:2*a*)

    (#1)   *Shall a fault-finder contend with the Almighty?*

[or]

    (#2)   *Can he who contends with* (or *presents a case against*) [1] *the Almighty instruct [him]* [2] (or *yield*)?*[3]

(40:2*b*)   *Let him who argues with God answer it* (or *him*)![4]

The philological difficulties which occasion the difference in translations include the syntactical enigma of 40:2*a* and the pronoun references (or lack thereof) in both stichs of the verse.

Any rendering of the divine question must grapple first with a problematic construction and rare terminology. Should the infinitive absolute הרב be made equivalent to a finite verb and the form יסור be rendered as a noun?[5] Or should רב be re-vocalized to the participle, with יסור understood as a Qal imperfect verb?[6] Either translation can be problematic: the former appears to furnish the poetic figure of a chiasm in relation to 40:2*b*, but it depends on a questionable convergence of rare linguistic phenomena;[7] the latter would offer a

---

[1] So HABEL, *The Book of Job*, 520 and PERDUE, *Wisdom in Revolt*, 216.

[2] Both KJV and NIV introduce this pronoun. In another variant, HABEL reads "me" in both stichs (*The Book of Job*, 520).

[3] The JB translates "Is Shaddai's opponent willing to give in?". Those who translate "to yield" or "to cede" include DHORME, *Book of Job*, 614; POPE, *Job*, 316; and GOOD, *In Turns of Tempest*, 163.

[4] The NIV translates "him." Similarly, a demonstrative pronoun is supplied by both DHORME, *Book of Job*, 614, and GORDIS, *The Book of Job*, 440.

[5] This translation (#1) is favored by RSV, NAB, and DRIVER/GRAY, *Book of Job*, 2:325. However, יסור as a noun would constitute a *hapax*.

[6] This translation (#2) is given by the KJV and NIV; similar in subject is NEB ("Is it for a man who disputes with the Almighty to be stubborn?"). GORDIS also reads the participle but claims that a re-vocalization is unnecessary "since רוב with a Holem is the older form of the participle Qal of *mediae Vav* verbs, a form which has survived in several passages in the Bible" (*The Book of Job*, 464).

[7] These questions are discussed in the only study specifically dedicated to the peculiarities of this verse, namely, K. FULLERTON, "On the Text and Significance of Job 40:2," *AJSL* 49 (1932-33) 197-211; they include "(a) the use of the infinitive absolute in a question, (b) the apparently rather awkward separation of יסור as subject from the verb רב, and (c) the fact that יסור, interpreted as a noun, is found only here in the Old Testament" (pp. 197-198).

synonymous parallel with the exhortation that follows, but it submits
the text to the dubious practice of providing a supposedly corrective
emendation.

If one accepts the syntactical sequence of the Masoretic text, further
difficulties in parallelism arise with regard to the antecedent reference
of the supposed contestation. To resolve this poetic difficulty, several
translations introduce a personal pronoun ("him"/"me") as the explicit
object of the human's purported instruction. Others simply re-vocalize
יסור in order to read there a verb of concession ("yield").

Because of such philological peculiarities, the translator must work
with uneasy critical hypotheses, and these assumptions, in turn, tend to
influence or re-inforce a given understanding of this verse. Here, it
seems, the confrontational stance with which the Yahweh-speeches
were introduced in 38:1-3 is continued. Whether by reading יסור in
the nominative or by re-vocalizing רב to the participle, the translations given above focus attention on the subject of these actions — by
obvious implication, Job. As a result, the divine question gives the
appearance of being a personalized opposition. This implication of
divine-human confrontation is augmented by the interpolation of
personal pronouns not attested in the text and/or by the unwarranted
emendation of an admittedly rare verb.

From this oppositional perspective derives the verbal modality latent
in the text: In comparison with the divinity, "will" a human dare to
criticize God? Being so puny, "can" he argue with the Almighty?
"Let" him so answer, if he can. And so, it seems, the narrative cards
are sturdily stacked against the earthly protagonist — any potential for
rebuttal seems merely an ironic possibility. The choice to re-vocalize
יסור is but a logical extension of this position. Intimating the quasi-
juridical decisiveness of a formal verdict, Yahweh thus indirectly
incites the submission of Job. Faced with what appears to be obvious,
the earthly disputant does not seem to have too many choices.

But the interpolation of personalized opposition appears to be more
an exegetical assumption than a textual truism. Is the issue at hand
really a personal affront to God? Were the expectation fulfilled that
here a divine-human opposition comes to poetic blows, it seems to
contradict the prose perspective to the tale. Is it not narratively inconsistent that God would be so opposed to the one whom he repeatedly
praises as his uniquely blameless and upright servant (cf. 1:8; 2:3;
42:7,8)? Would he who holds such beneficent power act as an

antagonistic adversary to him whom he so lavishly blesses (cf. 1:2-3; 42:12-15)?

Moreover, were this divine intervention given as an ironic rebuke intent on quelling the dispute once for all, it does not seem to have achieved the desired outcome! Job does, in fact, provide a rejoinder — immediately, with a symbolic silence and later, with a paradoxical repentance. Yet, in neither of these responses does Job yield his position, for that would subvert his intellectual and existential integrity. To the contrary, his words come to be affirmed by divine decree (42:8) as pertaining to that right-speaking which contrasts with the "folly" of the other interlocutors.

The answer of Job to the divine question is given in these words:

הֵן קַלֹּתִי מָה אֲשִׁיבֶךָ   יָדִי שַׂמְתִּי לְמוֹ־פִי :
אַחַת דִּבַּרְתִּי וְלֹא אֶעֱנֶה   וּשְׁתַּיִם וְלֹא אוֹסִיף:

Here, too, the translations are essentially the same in rendering Job's reply:

(40:4)	*Behold, I am small, what/how can I answer you?*
	I put my hand over/to my mouth.
(40:5)	*I spoke once, but I will not answer again (or insist);*[8]
	twice, but I will proceed no further.

The basic interpretation of this reply is constructed on a consideration of Job's existential identification and the temporal sequence relative to his protestations.

For the most part, הֵן is rendered as a conclusive exclamation ("Lo" and "Behold").[9] Taken together with the basic sense of smallness in קַלֹּתִי,[10] this opening statement draws attention to the

---

[8] This emendation to אָשֵׁן ה is suggested by DHORME (*Book of Job*, 615), DRIVER/GRAY (*Book of Job*, 348) and several other older studies.

[9] Variations include: "Oh" — as a somewhat ironic interjection (GOOD, *In Turns of Tempest*, 162-163); "Although" — as a conjunction of concession (CURTIS, "On Job's Response," 506-507); and "Since" — as that which introduces a fact upon which a conclusion or action is based (PERDUE, *Wisdom in Revolt*, 216-217).

[10] The "root" sense of קלל is that of being light, small, or of little account (BDB, 886); variations in translation include: "unworthy" (NIV), "vile" (KJV), and "mean" (DRIVER/GRAY).

protagonist as he voices an existential self-admission, namely, that of
having been made strikingly aware of his relative insignificance in the
grand cosmic scheme.[11]   In turn, this stance before the divine provides the experiential rationale for the gesture and decision that follow.

From the recognition of the swiftness of his fleeting disuptations,
Job concludes that to "turn back" (אֲשִׁיבֶךָ) in defensive reply would
be utterly futile.   And so he chooses to say nothing.   Implicitly
understood as pertaining to the domain of the future, or re-vocalized as
a lack of insistence, the translation of Job's decision to speak no more
denotes an impeding of any other fastidious fulminations so as to stave
off any further reprisals.

It would seem, then, that Job has gotten the message!   Having
experienced first-hand the vengeful force of the divine challenge, Job
is so humiliated as to be reduced to a totally uncharacteristic silence.
Humbly admitting his comparative existential weakness, Job gives in to
the divine discourse and agrees to dispute no more.

Accompanying his statement is a juridical and sapiential gesture
which accents the self-imposed obligation to keep silent.[12]   That the
act of putting hand to mouth is rich in symbolism appears obvious, but
the explanations of its significance vary.   Powerful in emotion, this
gesture could signal respectful fear (as in Job 21:5; 29:9), dumbfounded astonishment (cf. 9:2-13), or shameful defeat.[13]

Thus, what seems to be acknowledged here is a vanquished
deference to the aweful power and authority of Yahweh.   In recognition
of all human inadequacy before the mystery of the divine,[14] Job
chooses that very silence which would be expected as fitting reticence
before the overwhelming presence of the infinite God.[15]

---

[11] A few authors note the absence of any reference to human beings in the Yahweh-
speeches and conclude thereby that at least part of the divine message is meant to
highlight the non-anthropocentrism of the universe; see, in particular, WILLIAMS,
"Deciphering the Unspoken," 70-72.

[12] B. Couroyer, "'Mettre sa main sur sa bouche' en Égypte et dans la Bible," *RB* 67
(1960) 198-199.

[13] Respectively, KUBINA, *Die Gottesreden im Buche Hiob*, 79; HARTLEY, *The Book
of Job*, 517-518; and C. MUENCHOW, "Dust and Dirt in Job 42:6," *JBL* 108 (1989)
608.

[14] PERDUE, *Wisdom in Revolt*, p. 218, n. 2; cf. RAVASI, *Giobbe*, 780.

[15] TERRIEN, "The Yahweh Speeches and Job's Responses," 505.

Yet, as with the divine question in 40:2, Job's reponse here need not necessarily be interpreted as portraying one hopelessly silenced by a divinely instigated humiliation. Were this the case, need anything more be said by Yahweh? Yet the divinity continues to engage this human in an I-you dialogue relative to a discernment of the cosmic design and Designer.[16] In such a sapiential context, does the divine discourse really reduce Job to the existential rubble of "worthlessness" or "nothingness"?[17]

From the human perspective, Job's self-imposed silence need not represent only a prudent prevention of further disputation. Does not his subsequent speech mitigate against such a "silenced" reading? In fact, the ambiguity of his gesture and the fact of his later response support the notion that Job's silence here can be construed otherwise. Besides, would it not be incongruous, in light of Job's previously prolix positions and the subsequent affirmation of the rightfulness of his speech, that here he should concede verbal defeat?

Given the development of the narrative as a whole, these interpretive issues call into question the traditional understanding of these verses. In fact, the "oppositional" or "submissive" interpretations of 40:2-5 seem doubly derogatory, neither becoming of the creative genius of the author nor satisfactory for the genuine interest of a reader.[18] But if these verses are re-read in light of their discursive context, Job's silence may appear as a deliberate response, one which purposefully contributes to the resolution of the thematic question of the tale. In this sense, his laconic stance represents less a resigned capitulation to the tempestuous bluster of the divine discourse than a heedful consciousness of the revelatory words of a mysterious encounter.

---

[16] That these chapters constitute such a dialogue is suggested by the repeated introduction to the speeches (38:1-3 and 40:6-7) and by the leading question in each section (38:4; 40:8).

[17] Respectively, L.B. NEWELL, "Job: Repentant or Rebellious?" *WTJ* 46 (1984) 306, and FOHRER, "Der innere Aufbau des Buches Hiob," *Studien*, 16.

[18] D. PATRICK, *The Rendering of God in the Old Testament* (OBT, 10; Philadelphia 1981) 77: "The dialogue elicits our sympathy for and identification with Job, and the resolution should confirm his integrity."

A Matter of Interiority

As the narrative highpoint in this biblical tale, the Yahweh-speeches seem designed to resolve the tension created by the bitter blasphemy of the otherwise pious hero. And, despite their apparent irrelevance,[19] the divine discourses do cut to the very core of the book's theme. In this sense, a revised translation of the question posed to Job recognizes 40:2 as a summary of the issue under discussion:

$$\text{הָרֹב עִם־שַׁדַּי יִסּוֹר מוֹכִיחַ אֱלוֹהַּ יַעֲנֶנָּה׃}$$

(40:2)   *To contend[20] with the Almighty, can [that] be corrective?[21]
Engaging[22] the Most High in dispute, can [that] give it
answer?*

In a verse laden with four verbal elements, the train of thought is here centered on the question of speech, particularly speech of a disputational nature. In the second, and clearer, of the two stichs, a contentious pleading or reasoning (יכח - cf. Job 13:3; 16:21; 22:4) is placed in relation to a quasi-juridical answering (ענה). Read as a synonymous parallel, the first stich considers a contentious quarreling (עם + רב) in relation to an instructive chastening (יסור - cf. Job 4:3). In both cases, the object of the contentious speech is the divinity, understood in terms of total sovereignty.[23] As a result, this question resituates the matter fully in the realm of theo-linguistics.

In this context, the contrasting juxtaposition of the verbs appears to generate a repetitive question: "can" such speech be of any possible sapiential benefit? While the allusion to Job's earlier diatribes is clear,

---

[19] A list of topics raised in the Dialogues but ignored in chapters 38-41 is given by O'CONNOR, "The Futility of Myth-Making," 84-85.

[20] Here רב is read with the Masoretic text as an infinitive (absolute).

[21] Here יסור is read as a Qal imperfect verb, parallel to יַעֲנֶנָּה ; having no distinct object, it is rendered in a quasi-stative manner. [For a possible explanation of the *dageš forte* in the Qal, see *GBH* §77, a, (2).]

[22] The translation seeks to maintain the Hiphil sense of the participle מוֹכִיחַ.

[23] Hence, the specific mention of "Shaddai" and "Eloah" need not be translated as if there were two distinct referents in the dispute; cf. LÉVÊQUE, *Job et son Dieu*, 146-179.

this question is generic;[24] understood in a wisdom perspective, it encapsulates the theme being considered in the book. Resumptive of the basic issue in the Yahweh-speeches ("it"),[25] the question here is both theoretical and factual: both in the general approach taken by the biblical sages and in the specific comportment adopted by the narrative's protagonist, do reproachful rebukes provide an adequate response to the existential problematic of life?[26]

The divine question need not, then, be read as the chastening challenge of one insulted by a personal affront, nor as the backhanded inducement of one looking for human submission.[27] Rather, it resumes the leading question with which the Yahweh-speeches were introduced in 38:2-3 and in so doing focuses particular attention on this sapiential issue.[28] With the pointed thrust of these disputational verbs, the theo-linguistic question is summarily posed, and its directedness makes a reply from Job necessary.

His response to the divine question follows immediately:

הֵן קַלֹּתִי מָה אֲשִׁיבֶךָ   יָדִי שַׂמְתִּי לְמוֹ־פִי :
אַחַת דִּבַּרְתִּי וְלֹא אֶעֱנֶה   וּשְׁתַּיִם וְלֹא אוֹסִיף:

---

[24] Cf. Job 11:2, where רב refers to the totality of such speech.

[25] FULLERTON, "On Job 40:2," 197: "This represents the feminine suffix in יעננה in its frequent neuter significance and probably refers to all the questions which Jahweh has put to Job in chapters 38 and 39 rather than to the question in the first clause of verse 2." He prefers this reading to the "smoother reading of the third masculine singular ... or the omission of the suffix altogether ..." (p. 204).

[26] Cf. WILCOX, *The Bitterness of Job*, 100: "Whatever the honesty and grandeur of Job's complaint, what satisfaction can be found in the morally bitter life? Given Job's theology, it leads to blasphemy; but theology aside, I believe that Job's bitterness represents a kind of psychological or spiritual illness, a lack of psychic health; and I suspect that underneath it are philosophical presuppositions that are untenable."

[27] Cf. JANZEN, *Job*, 242: "The point of this divine response [in Jer 12:5] is not to put the prophet down with an impossible question, but to express surprise over the quickness with which the prophet succumbs to discouragement and disillusionment and to challenge the prophet to a deeper loyalty and vocational endurance. ... It is the same with Job."

[28] FULLERTON, "On Job 40:2," 207: "By thus returning to the introductory questions at 38:2-3 after all the intervening questions in chapters 38-39, the author would seem to intend to point the meaning of these questions more sharply; and by providing a special introduction [in 40:1] for this final summarizing question he gives to it a peculiar force."

(40:4)   *If I am [a] lightweight, how could I retort?* [29]
           my hand, I place [it] over my mouth.

(40:5)   *Once I spoke, but gave no answer;*
           twice [indeed], but caused no augment. [30]

Given the renewed understanding of the divine question in 40:2, this response can be re-interpreted as something more significant than tacit submission on Job's part.

Clearly, the opening clause of Job's reply grounds his subsequent affirmation. The emotion-charged response is founded on Job's relative status in this linguistic joust: in comparison with the blusterous power behind the words from the storm, Job is but a "lightweight," one whose very smallness would make a swift demise easily possible in a raging tempest. "If" this diminutive stature be the basis on which Job's rejoinder will stand,[31] there seems little chance of his verbal survival: "how" could any response on his part effect a change in the divine stance?[32] Having readily acknowledged that God is invested with unsurpassable authority and power (cf. 9:4-10; 12:13-16; 23:13), Job could not possibly turn back his dialogue-partner with any verbal "retort" of his own.[33] Re-admitting as much, he takes an unexpectedly tacit turn.

With the gesture of putting hand over mouth, Job symbolically invokes the power of silence and thereby initiates a new stance before the divine. Literally, such a move on his part would prevent any reactionary utterances from passing his lips; in a linguistic struggle for

---

[29] Literally, שׁוּב with the pronominal suffix means "to turn you back"; given the discursive context and the known partner in dialogue, "you" is here assumed in the turning back of a reply or "retort."

[30] The poetic translation here seeks to convey the causative sense of the Hiphil אוֹסִיף within a synonymous parallel of negation; here the negating adverb (לֹא) concerns directly the action of the verbs more so than their temporal extension.

[31] By reading the particle הֵן with the value of "if" (*GBH*, §167-l; cf. Job 9:11,12; 12:14,15; 19:7; 23:8), an ambiguity remains which neither canonizes ("behold") nor concedes ("although"/"since") Job's small status.

[32] Given the context, our translation of מָה with a verb reads the generalizing, adverbial meaning of "how" (*GBH*, §144e) rather than the interrogative pronoun "what."

[33] Cf. GOOD, *In Turns of Tempest*, 352: "Job may add to the resignation of one who thinks that no reply can be made to this power the resignation of one who thinks that the power would pay not attention to a reply in any case."

truth and right and good, such verbal emissions would probably admit of more vehemence than wisdom! More important, however, is the non-literal significance given in and through this gesture. As ensured by his own hand, Job's decision not to speak reveals a conscious choice, destined in this case to some ulterior end. This silence does not evoke the fateful fright championed by his Friends in the previous dialogues but instead initiates a deliberate and purposeful plan of action by the protagonist.

In this respect, Job's silence is neither absolute nor defiant.[34] Its sphere of concern is not a potentially fastidious future,[35] but the pretentious past wherein Job "spoke" intensively and repeatedly concerning what he judged to be true on the basis of his personal experience.[36] Yet, neither the religious protestations of the Prologue nor the reasoned disputation of the Dialogues have given any relief to Job's existential angst.[37] Indeed, despite the multiplication of his previous words, no increase in theological understanding had come his way.

Now, perhaps, it would. With a turn to interiority, Job's not-speaking will become listening, as the words from the storm continue. There within, the transcendent wisdom of Yahweh will be appropriated by Job in such was as to elicit the definitive response with which the Theologue will be brought to its paradoxical conclusion.

---

[34] Cf. CURTIS, "On Job's Response," 507: "With biting sarcasm and hostility Job declares it useless to try to talk to a god who is so concerned with great matters (like cosmology) that he does not even recognize that the small problems (like the suffering of the innocent) exist."

[35] As ANDERSEN notes, the translation "to proceed no further" suggests "giving up" and the translation "to do so no more" suggests "the renunciation of an admitted fault," neither of which is applicable to the main character (*Job*, p. 285, n. 2).

[36] These verbal aspects, which can be ascertained from the interplay of the Dialogues, may also be suggested by the Piel form (דִּבַּרְתִּי), though this is not certain [cf. *GBH* §52d and notes (1) and (2)].

[37] In general, instances of "ascending numeration" concern not the exact number of instances but their plurality; however, were אַחַת ... וּשְׁתַּיִם read in a more literal fashion, this could possibly refer to the two preceding sections of the tale understood in their linguistic totality.

THE INNER EYE OF WISDOM !

In his patently small share of the sapiential dialogue with Yahweh, Job has shifted from contentious disputation to sudden silence. Situated before the divine with an attitude of purposeful listening, Job stands to benefit from a newfound acquisition of wisdom.[38] Through the door opened by his turn toward interiority, the divine voice whirls with a flurry of mytho-poetic imagery,[39] and to this revelatory discourse Job replies, in the end, with the avowal of his "repentance."

How this ultimate stance on the part of Job can be interpreted depends to a significant degree on the translation of this thoroughly enigmatic text. What follows is a comparative analysis, the results of which lead to a novel reading of these ambiguous verses. In light of the translation which we present below, we will suggest an interpretation of Job's responses as an "originary affirmation" attesting to his newfound poetic wisdom.

'Wondrously far from me' (Job 42:2-3)

Compelled to respond to the renewed speech from the storm,[40] Job precedes his utterance of repentance in 42:6 with the ambiguous affirmation of 42:2-3. Although this two-sided statement has not received as much critical attention, its translation nevertheless contributes directly to the interpretation of Job's final stance before Yahweh.

Suffering the burden of a "semantic overflow,"[41] the consonantal text appears thus:

---

[38] LÉVÊQUE, *Job et son Dieu*, 531: "La puissance de Dieu a pris le relais de l'impuissance de Job, pour l'introduire dans les profondeurs de la Sagesse."

[39] Cf. J.G. GAMMIE, "Behemoth and Leviathan: On the Didactic and Theological Significance of Job 40:15-41:26," in *Israelite Wisdom:* Theological and Literary Essays in Honor of Samuel Terrien (eds. J.G. GAMMIE, W.A. BRUEGGEMANN, W.L. HUMPHREYS, and J.M. WARD) (New York 1978) 217-231.

[40] ALONSO SCHÖKEL, "Toward a Dramatic Reading," 59: "Above our criticism of the God whom we imagine, there sounds the voice of God each time more real. Job could not be silent." It should be noted that, unlike his words in 40:4-5, this second "reponse" of Job does not arise as an answer to a specific question.

[41] KUBINA, *Die Gottesreden im Buche Hiob*, 109: "Die überwältigende Fülle der Eindrücke, die Hiob in seiner 'Schau' Gottes gewinnt, wird durch syntaktische Überfülle (5 Sätze in einem Vers!) demonstriert."

יָדַעְתָּ כִּי־כֹל תּוּכָל   וְלֹא־יִבָּצֵר מִמְּךָ מְזִמָּה:
מִי זֶה מַעְלִים עֵצָה בְּלִי דָעַת
לָכֵן הִגַּדְתִּי וְלֹא אָבִין נִפְלָאוֹת מִמֶּנִּי וְלֹא אֵדָע:

For the most part, however, translations are similar in their rendering
of the text:

(42:2)   *I know that you can do all things,*
                 and that no purpose of yours can be thwarted.

(42:3)   *"Who is this that hides counsel without knowledge?"*
              Therefore, I have uttered,
                 what (or but) I did not understand,
              things too wonderful for me,
                 which (or but) I did not know.

Whether one translates וְלֹא אָבִין and וְלֹא אֵדָע as relative clauses
referring to the "things" of which Job spoke or as independent clauses
of negation, nearly all translations render נִפְלָאוֹת מִמֶּנִּי substantively
and understand it to be the object of הִגַּדְתִּי , in apposition to the
negating clauses.[42]

Based on this translation, the primary interpretations of Job's
position view it as a sapiential skepticism. The language in 42:2 is
explained as expressing the supplicant's submission to the divine oracle
given in response to his lament (cf. Pss. 20:6; 41:11; 56:9).[43] The
claim that follows in 42:3, then, is understood to be an admission of
insurmountable ignorance, a seemingly appropriate concession given the
grandiose perspective of mysteriously divine wonders (cf. Job 5:9;
9:10; 36:26).[44] Read in a liturgical light (cf. Ps 119:75), Job's
statement becomes a quasi-penitential confession; his having previously
spoken without understanding would constitute the fault for which he

---

[42] Cf. the conjecture of F. STIER, who in verse 3 reads הֻגַּדְתָּנִי ("you have made
known to me") and inserts גְדוֹלוֹת ("great things") as in the LXX (*Das Buch Ijjob*,
351-352).

[43] Cf. FOHRER, *Das Buch Hiob*, 532, and LÉVÊQUE, *Job et son Dieu*, 523.

[44] DHORME, *Book of Job*, 646.

will ultimately repent.[45]   Or, read in a sapiential context (cf. Prov 30:2; Sir 42:17-21), Job's affirmation echoes the epistemological tenet that comprehension of divine marvels is beyond human grasp; his knowing now that he does not know would disengage the confrontational stance from which he will ultimately retract.[46]

Two less prevalent interpretations have also been suggested, each of which emphasizes a slightly different translation concerning the "things too wonderful" being declared. For some, the marvels spoken of God, or known by him,[47] depict a deity far removed from petty human concerns; such an ironic caricature of blind force tantamount to continuing chaos yields bitterness in Job, who would only feign submission to this sort of God. For others, instead, the wonders here being declared would evoke religious amazement;[48] the interjection of such incomprehensible graciousness changes Job's lament into praise and would allow him to abandon for good his mournful stance.

Each of these interpretations, however, can be problematic; though based on acceptable translations, they tend to run aground of the narrative context.   A "submissive" explanation, which reads Job's statement as an open confession of faulty utterances now to be rejected, would deny validity to the subsequent affirmation of Yahweh that Job has spoken "rightly" (42:7,8). Likewise, a "skeptical" understanding, which reads these verses as an admission of inherent ignorance now to

---

[45] D.J. O'CONNOR, "Job's Final Word — 'I Am Consoled' (42:6b)," *ITQ* 51 (1985) 187. Cf. the translation of B. LANG, "Ein Kranker sieht seinen Gott," 144: "... so habe ich ohne Verstand geredet — gar Lästerliches — ohne Wissen."

[46] L.J. KUYPER, "The Repentance of Job," *VT* 9 (1959) 94: "The context ... suggests that Job now, after his encounter with the Lord from the whirlwind, is painfully aware of the inadequacy of his arguments and demands before God." Cf. LÉVÊQUE, *Job et son Dieu*, 525; ALONSO SCHÖKEL, *Giobbe*, 672; and HARTLEY, *The Book of Job*, 536.

[47] According to GOOD, reading the Ketib of 42:2a ("you know") allows for several possible tones of voice: submissive, sarcastic, indignant, obsequious (*In Turns of Tempest*, 370-371). Cf. JANZEN, who favors the Ketib reading "as a human affirmation of the inexhaustible resourcefulness of the covenant God" (*Job*, 251-252).

[48] D. PATRICK, "The Translation of Job XLII 6," *VT* 26 (1976) 371: "If we construe the perfect [הִגַּדְתִּי] as indicating a present action here (or perhaps as a 'prophetic perfect'), the basic sentence would be a declaration of praise." Cf. M. FISHBANE, "The Book of Job and Inner-biblical Discourse," in PERDUE and GILPIN, *The Voice from the Whirlwind*, 90-91; he suggests that in the rhetorical structure of 42:2 (using the masculine verb יִבָּצֵר in conjunction with the feminine noun מְזִמָּה), Job praises the omnipotence of God, thereby inverting the hubris of the Tower of Babel generation.

be accepted, tends to canonize the failure of the quest for wisdom. As to the variant interpretations, could the resolute bitterness of "ironic insolence" really provide a satisfactory conclusion to the tale, either for the protagonist or the reader? Then again, to what wonders would Job's "laudable lyricism" refer in a discourse which culminates with emotive despising and existential repentance?

At this point another translation of Job's second response may be considered:

יָדַעְתָּ כִּי־כֹל תּוּכָל   וְלֹא־יִבָּצֵר מִמְּךָ מְזִמָּה ה:
מִי זֶה מַעְלִים עֵצָה בְּלִי דָעַת
לָכֵן הִגַּדְתִּי וְלֹא אָבִין נִפְלָאוֹת מִמֶּנִּי וְלֹא אֵדָע:

(42:2)   I realize that you are capable of all,
            and no project is restrained from you.
(42:3)   "Whosoever would obscure the design without knowledge?"
            Admittedly I made pronouncements, but I had not understood,
                wondrously far from me, but I had not realized.

This rendering, in accord with the sapiential context of the divine-human dialogue that takes place in these final chapters, will call attention to the distinctiveness of the theophany experience as it contributes to the wisdom of Job.

Both formally and stylistically these verses deal with the acquisition of wisdom, understood here as the virtuous interplay of knowledge and speech.[49] In terms of literary convention, the inclusive repetition of ידע ("to know") signals the specific issue of these verses, namely, the depth of understanding of the protagonist. Moreover, in the rhetorical style common to the dialogues,[50] the words of Job's interlocutor are cited; although not repeated with precision (cf. 38:2), the third-person indefinite style of this quotation re-directs attention to the general question of illuminating knowledge and, by implication, to the words which express such insight. Finally, the verb הִגַּדְתִּי governs Job's admission as the declared acknowledgment of what one has come to know (cf. 26:4; 31:37).

---

[49] J.L. CRENSHAW, "The Acquisition of Knowledge in Israelite Wisdom Literature," *WW* 3 (1987) 247.

[50] GORDIS, *The Book of God and Man*, 185-189.

Thus, by his statement in 42:2, Job admits to having realized the potency of Yahweh.   Specifically, this realization concerns the activation of Yahweh's discretionary "project" or perspicacious plan for creation and human life.[51] But this knowledge, understood in its fully biblical sense,[52] is broader than mere perception, deeper than simple cognition.[53] It is, rather, an experiential discernment that grasps the significance of what is conceived or imagined.

In turn, Job comments in 42:3 on the extent to which his knowledge had informed his speech. Yet his admission is not focused primarily on the content of his discourses; explicit reference to the "things" which Job has said is actually an interpolation on the part of the translator, one which supplies for the otherwise characteristic absence of objective complements in the responses of Job (cf. 40:5; 42:6). Rather, in keeping with the question of Job's own capability to explicate the divine design (38:2,4; cf. 40:8), the statement here becomes a two-fold assertion concerning the *manner* of his speech.

First and foremost, he avows that his speech lacked knowledge,[54] and the parallel negation in וְלֹא אָבִין and וְלֹא אֵדַע , when read with the force of independent clauses, repetitiously strengthens this admission. It should be noted, however, that this declaration concerns not his present linguistic state but his *previous* utterances: as the alternation of verbal forms suggests, when Job spoke earlier his words had *not yet* been informed by his sapiential realization.[55]

But more significant than this epistemological fact is the existential claim that the making of knowledgeable pronouncements had surpassed his own capacity for wisdom. This second aspect of Job's declaration is highlighted by the unusual use of the participle נִפְלָאוֹת. Parallel to the act of declaring (Hiphil הִגַּדְתִּי), the participle could be a *qualifier*

---

[51] Cf. Lévêque, *Job et son Dieu*, 524.

[52] According to Ravasi, the knowledge of recognition is "intellettuale, volitivo, affettivo ed effettivo" and here contributes to a "confessione sperimentale ed esistenziale" (*Giobbe*, 814).

[53] In this respect, as Wilcox rightly argues, Job's statement would intend more than a simple acknowledgment of divine omnipotence (*The Bitterness of Job*, 191-193).

[54] Cf. A. Blommerde, *Northwest Semitic Grammar and Job* (BibOr, 22; Roma 1969) 140, who argues for the emphatic ל with כֵּן.

[55] Here the perfect הִגַּדְתִּי , translated in the domain of the past by virtue of allusion to the Dialogues, places as prior to itself the imperfects וְלֹא אָבִין and וְלֹא אֵדַע (see *GBH*, §113o).

of Job's speech rather than its object.[56]   The feminine plural form would then have either of two possible referents: the "sayings" alluded to in the quotation (cf. בְמִלִּין in 38:2) or the previous discourses of Job understood generically (cf. the similar use of the feminine in 40:4 and 42:7,8 with a neuter significance in reference to speech taken as a whole). Not representing a semantic construct (cf. 37:14), a substantive translation of נִפְלָאוֹת can, therefore, give way to an adverbial rendering (cf. 37:5), justifiable here as conforming to and furthering the sapiential focus on the manner of Job's speech. In this way, a parallel reading emerges: compared to the all-powerful capability of Yahweh for disclosing the mysteries of life (cf. 11:6 where the verb נגד has the divinity as its proper subject), proficiency at so expounding upon wisdom had been "wondrously far from" Job.

Thus understood, the affirmation of 42:2-3 need not convey skepticism. On the one hand, the un-informed quality of his previous speech is not so much the matter of uncharacteristic blasphemy as it is the inevitable outcome of a not-yet fully sapiential aptitude. On the other hand, such an epistemological lacuna is here realized not in virtue of its timeless insurmountability but as characteristic of the protagonist's past. Further, Job's assertion in these verses seems to convey more than merely ironic insolence before, or even pronounced praise of, the divinity with whom he speaks. Rather, befitting the integrity which substantiates his boldness, Job forthrightly announces that his own level of theo-linguistic wisdom had not been sufficient.

Yet the protagonist proceeds to an even more significant declaration. Reading his response in its sapiential context, it would seem that the theophanic encounter with Yahweh has, indeed, generated some new knowledge for Job, a novel realization by which he distinguishes present from past. No longer founded on the pious presuppositions of the Prologue or the rational deductions of the Dialogues, Job's knowledge now bears the mark of a veritable conviction, one whose sapiential surety and transformative tendency result from a truly religious experience. It is the depth of knowledge gleaned from this experience that comes to be affirmed in 42:2-3 as present now but lacking in his past utterances. In turn, this intensified understanding invigorates the subsequent words with which Job concludes his speech.

---

[56] As a verbal adjective, a participle concerns more the agent of an action than its object (*GBH*, §40).

Seeing He Repents (Job 42:2-6)

Despite numerous philological perplexities, the words of 42:4-6 form the grand finale to the Theologue. Following upon the words of 42:2-3, these verses continue to deal with the same sapiential issue (יָדַע) though now in a changed perspective. Whereas verses 2-3 represent an affirmation about Job's past speech, verses 4-6 offer the full-powered statement of his present knowledge.[57] Moving from knowledgeable speech to existential decision,[58] Job will give voice here to the definitive expression of his wisdom.[59]

A Question of Translation

This conclusive response is introduced by somewhat confounding words:

שְׁמַע־נָא וְאָנֹכִי אֲדַבֵּר אֶשְׁאָלְךָ וְהוֹדִיעֵנִי:

(42:4)   *Listen here, that I, I may speak;*
           "I want to question you and you will inform me."

The critical question in the rendering of this verse concerns the determination of whose words are being spoken, for the linguistic allusions read here will affect the tonal impact of Job's final statement.[60]

In the clearer of the two strophes, the words of 42:4b repeat exactly those of 38:3b (cf. 40:7a). Seeing that no questions on Job's part are

---

[57] JANZEN, *Job*, 253: "One may hazard the suggestion that the frequency of occurrence of this verb 'to know' fittingly characterizes the climactic speech of Job, following so many chapters of confused questions and conflicting opinions." However, whereas this same author argues that יָדַע governs an *inclusio* between verses 2 and 4, we suggest that the *inclusio* is formed between verses 2 and 3, and that verse 4 initiates a new affirmation relative to the "present" state of Job's knowledge.

[58] Cf. HABEL, *The Book of Job*, 578-580.

[59] KUBINA, *Die Gottesreden im Buche Hiob*, p. 109, n. 243: "Beachtenswert ist auch das 'Spiel' mit den Vokabeln יָדַע (und Deriv.) in 42,2f und שָׁמַע in 42,4f; beide Begriffe sowie ihre Verwendung bezeugen den 'weisheitlichen' Standort des Verfassers gleicherweise wie seine Sonderstellung innerhalb dieser Geistesrichtung."

[60] The various possibilities are discussed in GOOD, *In Turns of Tempest*, 371-373.

actually put forth, the words spoken here can hardly be the protagon-ist's own humble plea for further instruction. Rather, they should be read as a quotation of Yahweh's introduction, cited by Job here as a means of maintaining narrative focus on the issue of knowledgeable speech.[61] In this respect verse 4 provides both a transition from verses 2-3 and a motive for the new response in verses 5-6.

The words of 42:4a, on the other hand, are better attributed to Job himself. They do not, in fact, complete the quotation of Yahweh's words in 38:3 (cf. 40:7a).[62] Moreover, the tone of admonition evident in the imperative is hardly necessary in the midst of the already authoritative divine speech. Rather, akin to the prayerful entreaty of a supplicant (cf. Pss 27:7; 54:2; 64:1; 84:8; 143:1), these words reflect the resumption of Job's protestation, as before he had characteristically seized the linguistic initiative (cf. 13:13; 21:2-3).[63]

In this perspective, the words of 42:4 represent the decisiveness of Job as he initiates the conclusive response with which the dialogic scope of the Yahweh-speeches as a whole will be fulfilled. With daring boldness Job implores Yahweh in a colloquial admonition. Bespeaking the emotion underlying his urge to respond ("Listen here"),[64] Job draws the divine attention to his impending statement. The defini-tiveness of his forthcoming speech follows from a purposeful intent ("that I, I may speak"), one which accentuates the words of Job himself as an intensive rejoinder to the words of Yahweh.[65]

Thus, in response to the divine request to be informed which occasioned Yahweh's intervention in the narrative debate (cf. 42:4b and

---

[61] Cf. HABEL, *The Book of Job*, 581: "By citing these quotations from Yahweh's speeches, Job is making it quite explicit that he is responding formally to the challenge of Yahweh as his adversary"; MUENCHOW, "Dust and Dirt," p. 608, n. 47: "Doing so keeps the underlying issue of the challenge to rival fresh in the reader's mind."

[62] GORDIS, *The Book of Job*, 492: "Job does not cite 40:7a because these words of challenge by God, 'Gird up your loins like a man,' could not be appropriately cited by Job in his response. This is particularly true, since Job wishes to emphasize the difference between merely 'hearing' about God and 'seeing' Him."

[63] GOOD, *In Turns of Tempest*, 372.

[64] On נָא as a particle/interjection of entreaty or admonition in a colloquial style, see BDB, 609 and *GBH*, §105c.

[65] In our translation, the repetition of the pronoun seeks to convey an emphatic character, which may be intended here in the combined use of a separate personal pronoun (וְאָנֹכִי) and the Piel verb (אֲדַבֵּר). On the nuance of "purpose-consecution" suggested by the Waw (וְהוֹדִיעֵנִי), see *GBH*, §115c and §634b.

38:3*b*), Job will indeed speak. Beyond the apologetic soliloquy with which his words ended in chapter 31, the statement of Job here purports to be truly definitive. Issuing from the sophisticated silence with which he has attended to the divine discourse (40:4-5), his final affirmation will surpass the un-informed speech of his former diatribes (42:2-3). To his God, Job will now respond with the fullness of human wisdom.

Following upon this rhetorical introduction,[66] Job takes up his own words to make an assertion concerning the ways in which he has come to know of God:

$$ \text{לְשֵׁמַע־אֹזֶן שְׁמַעְתִּיךָ וְעַתָּה עֵינִי רָאָתְךָ:} $$

(42:5)   *By sound of ear, I have heard (of) you,*
             but now my eye, (she) sees you.

The critical question in this verse concerns the sense of, and relation between, Job's "hearing" and "seeing," for the epistemological distinction read therein will ground the transformation expressed in his final stance.

Adapting an otherwise rare idiomatic expression (cf. Ps 18:45; Sir 43:24), Job first speaks of a "hearing" mode, one which concerns more the substance of the message heard than the physical act of hearing (cf. Num 14:15; Deut 2:25; Isa 23:5; Jer 37:5).[67] Assumed by most commentators to refer to the dialogic interaction with his Friends, Job's hearing "of" God would be a second-hand learning about the divinity, one mediated by, and corresponding to, the tenets of long-standing tradition (cf. Job 8:8,10).[68] Yet this eventful hearing also takes place in and through the Yahweh-speeches, in that transcendent discourse

---

[66] JANZEN, *Job*, 254: "The same rhetorical connection is thus seen to exist between verses 4 and 5 as was seen to exist between verses 3*ab* and 3*cd*. In the earlier instance, words first spoken by God, and then quoted by Job as God spoke them, are finally re-phrased in Job's own terms."

[67] W. MORROW, "Consolation, Rejection, and Repentance in Job 42:6," *JBL* 105 (1986) 220.

[68] Cf. DHORME, *Book of Job*, 646 and TSEVAT, *The Meaning of Job*, p. 22, n. 57. For MORROW, this may be "an elliptical reference to the wisdom theology of retribution heard from the lips of Job's comforters and which he himself shared" ("Consolation, Rejection, and Repentance," 221).

which acts as the "cultic space" of a divine-human encounter.[69]
Hence, the "hearing" of Job takes into account the entirety of his
learning — both then and now, through the arguments of the stalwarts
of tradition and the imagery of the voice from the storm, Job can claim
"I have heard (of) you."[70]

Beyond the auditory mode, however, Job also claims to "see"
Yahweh, a stupefying statement in both its poetic sense and existential
import.[71] Translated in the generic present, with emphasis more on
the perceptive fact than the physical act,[72] the affirmation is clear and
direct — by virtue of his own faculties ("my eye"), Job "sees" Yahweh
("you"). Yet, owing to the semantic particularity of the Joban
theophany, reference here to an actual gazing upon the divine seems
unwarranted. Nevertheless, the question remains as to what this vision
entails, for it situates Job in the rare company of privileged patriarchs
and prophets. In turn, it will serve as a hermeneutical key to the
interpretation of his subsequent "repentance."[73]

The wisdom of Job's response is grounded in the spiritual awareness to which the poetic vision of Yahweh makes recourse. In terms
of an epistemological phenomenon, this unique "seeing" comprises
three mutually related aspects. In the first place, Job's seeing entails
something *experiential*; radically real, it yields an unmistakable

---

[69] LÉVÊQUE, *Job et son Dieu*, 526: "Et l'espace cultuel de cette rencontre ne saurait
être matérialisé: c'est le champ même du dialogue, où Job accomplit son sacrifice
spirituel."

[70] Our translation of שְׁמַעְתִּיךָ seeks to include both possible referents, where the
present perfect rendering presents the action as having begun in the past (the hearsay
of the Dialogues) *and* as continuing in the present (the divine speeches of the
Theologue).

[71] HUMPHREYS, *The Tragic Vision*, 116: "Attempt as one might to tone down the
force of this, the uniqueness of the claim made in Job's submission cannot be denied.
Only here — in a work that too often, for all its recognized power, is consigned to the
periphery of the Hebraic tradition — is the claim to see god made simply, without a
qualifier. Only here, as the Hebraic tradition comes closest to a full confrontation with
the vision of tragedy and the development of a tragic hero, does a man see god."

[72] Cf. Job 13:1-2, where the connection between sensation (seeing and hearing) and
understanding is made explicit.

[73] Cf. R. LAURIN, "The Theological Structure of Job," *ZAW* 84 (1972) 86-89, who
holds that 42:5 provides the key to the overall structure of the book.

certainty that surpasses the standard logic of knowing.[74] Moreover,
this seeing is uniquely *personal*; with an intimacy born of devoted
familiarity, it takes place within, and gives witness to, an interactive
communion.[75] Finally, the vision of which Job speaks is vividly
immediate; sudden and unexpected, it occasions a direct perception,[76]
one whose insightfulness would not otherwise be possible.

Thus, the distinction between seeing and hearing affirmed here
appears to be decisive for Job. Whereas elsewhere in the narrative
hearing and seeing are parallel in time (cf. 13:11; 29:11), the emphasis
on the present moment in 42:5 ("now") suggests a differentiation
between Job's experience in the Theologue and in the Dialogues.[77]
However, the distinction between hearing and seeing need not be
construed in terms of a fundamental opposition;[78] neither the reasoned
speech of the Dialogues nor the figurative poetry of the Theologue are
here dismissed as qualitatively inferior modes of knowing. Rather, the
vision which Job attributes to the immediacy of a personal experience
of the divine serves as a defining moment, "as the final verifying
experience of communication and communion with God."[79] In other
words, the self-disclosure of Yahweh revealed in the divine discourses
of chapters 38-41 complements and completes Job's customary mode
of knowing. As a result, in his mystical encounter with the God of the

---

[74] RAVASI, *Giobbe*, 816: "Ora Giobbe ha intuito il senso di se stesso perché ha
intuito quello di Dio. Più che un'analisi dei concetti e dei termini del problema
teologico, l'uomo ha bisogno innanzitutto di un'esperienza personale dell'azione divina
nella sua vita." Cf. LILLIE, "The Religious Significance of the Theophany," 356-357.

[75] FOHRER, "Dialog und Kommunikation," 145: "'Gott schauen' meint ja nicht die
bloße Sinneswahrnehmung, sondern die Begegnung im personalen Sinn, die eine
vertraute Gemeinschaft bewirkt. 'Gott schauen' meint: dem Vertrautenkreis Gottes
angehören und mit ihm reden." Cf. LÉVÊQUE, *Job et son Dieu*, 526: "Job a vu
Yahweh, dans une *koinônia* tout intime qui réalise et surpasse ce qu'il espérait en
xix,26s ...."

[76] TERRIEN, *Job*, p. 269, n. 2: "Le sens visuel s'applique dans la mentalité
hébraïque à la perception sans intermédiaire. Il n'existe pas de contradiction entre cette
métaphore sensorielle et les nombreux exemples d'une polémique dirigée contre une
expérience sensuelle de la divinité ...."

[77] Cf. Job 30:1, where וְעַתָּה ("but now") introduces the discussion of Job's
present travails in contrast with his past felicity.

[78] GOOD translates "With ears' hearing I hear you, / and now my eye sees you" (*In
Turns of Tempest*, 171) and proposes a non-disjunctive interpretation (pp. 373-375).

[79] G.G. HARROP, "But Now Mine Eye Seeth Thee," *CJT* 12 (1966) 83.

storm, understood as including both the experience of the theophany and the content of the Yahweh-speeches,[80] Job has finally acquired wisdom.

The result of this visionary sagaciousness Job voices in his concluding utterance:

עַל־כֵּן אֶמְאַס וְנִחַמְתִּי עַל־עָפָר וָאֵפֶר:

(42:6)   *Therefore I despise yet repent*
           of dust and ash.

In this verse, questions abound concerning the form of the text, especially the sense of the two verbs and the reference of the idiomatic expression to which they are somehow connected. In fact, the philological difficulties here are so gregarious as to subvert any clear rendering of the text.[81] Nevertheless, by way of a hermeneutical "feedback loop," critical choices can be made which will justify our translation of this verse and inform our interpretation of Job's paradoxical position.[82]

Concerning אֶמְאַס, from what verbal root is it formed: מאס ("to reject, despise"), whose meaning will be debated below, or מסס ("to melt, be poured out"), which can express either humiliation[83] or dissipation?[84] Given the former (מאס), should it be read as a

---

[80] PERDUE, *Wisdom in Revolt*, 199: "It is the evocative imagery and experience of theophanic event, coupled with the metaphorical content of the speeches, that present a new linguistic vision of creation, divine rule, and human existence."

[81] In the case of 42:6, the presupposition of T. TILLEY, "God and the Silencing of Job," *ModT* 5 (1989) 258, is most appropriate: "... at crucial points, the text of the book is so indeterminate that the 'text' of Job is, to a significant extent, made, not found."

[82] PATRICK/SCULT, *Rhetoric and Biblical Interpretation*, 89: "Though one obviously has to be able to read the text before deciding what it is about, there is a 'feedback loop' in which the judgment as to what the book is about requires revision of the translation."

[83] So DHORME, *Book of Job*, 646 ("I sink down"); TERRIEN, "The Yahweh Speeches and Job's Responses," 505 ("I lose myself into nothing"); GORDIS, *The Book of Job*, 491 and HARTLEY, *The Book of Job*, 535 ("I abase myself").

[84] So WESTERMANN, *The Structure of the Book of Job*, 126 ("I dissolve in tears"); CLINES, *Job 1-20*, xlvi ("I melt in reverence before you"); J.H. EATON, *Job* (OT Guides, 5; Sheffield 1985) 29 and O'CONNOR, "Job's Final Word," 181 ("I melt away").

reflexive verb[85] or a transitive one? If the latter (מסס), is its object
to be drawn from the context — in Job's speech or attitude or ignorance
— or should it be read in the remainder of the verse? And with what
degree of intensity should this verb be rendered: is it to "disown,"[86]
"repudiate,"[87] "recant,"[88] "retract,"[89] "renounce,"[90] "reject,"[91] or "despise"?[92]

Concerning the verb נִחַמְתִּי , is it to be read in the Piel or Niphal
form?[93]   If the Piel, is it also a partitive form, meaning "to
accept,"[94] or simply an emotive term, meaning "to be consoled,
comforted"? If the Niphal, does it convey the sense of sorrowful
contrition ("to be penitent")[95] or decisional reversal ("to change one's
mind")?[96]

Concerning עָפָר וָאֵפֶר , what is its reference? If עַל is locative
("in, on, upon"),[97] a literal meaning would be suggested; but is this

---

[85] As in the KJV, RSV and NIV. The reflexive reading finds an ancient precedent
in the LXX (*ephaulisa emauton*) and in the Vulgate (*ipse me reprehendo*).

[86] NAB.

[87] DRIVER/GRAY, *Book of Job*, 373 and A. GUILLAUME, *Studies in the Book of Job*,
with a New Translation (ALUOS supplement, 2; Leiden 1968) 75.

[88] POPE, *Job*, 347.

[89] HABEL, *The Book of Job*, 575. Cf. FOHRER, *Das Buch Hiob*, 532 ("widerrufe
ich"); ALONSO SCHÖKEL/SICRE DIAZ, *Giobbe*, 669 and RAVASI, *Giobbe*, 811 ("mi
ritratto"); and J. LÉVÊQUE, *Job, le livre et le message* (CahEv, 53; Paris 1985) 51 ("je
me rétracte").

[90] Cf. A. LACOQUE, ""Est-ce gratuitement que Job craint Dieu?" *Mélanges André
Neher* (Paris 1975) 178: "Dans le mouvement le plus émouvant du libre, Job *renonce*
("*ma'as*") à toute confirmation de son bon droit et de sa respectabilité." (*emphasis
added*)

[91] PERDUE, *Wisdom in Revolt*, 232; cf. KUYPER, "The Repentance of Job," 94.

[92] GOOD, *In Turns of Tempest*, 171.

[93] Cf. H. van Dyke PARUNAK, "A Semantic Survey of נחם ," *Bib* 56 (1975) 512-
532.

[94] So A. CERESKO, *Job 29-31 in the Light of Northwest Semitic: A Translation and
Philological Commentary* (BibOr, 36; Roma 1980) 206.

[95] GINSBERG translates "Therefore am I contrite and penitent, humble in the dust"
("Job the Patient," 90), while EATON translates "Therefore I melt away, sorrowing on
the dust and ashes" (*Job*, 29).

[96] PATRICK, "The Translation of Job XLII 6," 370; JANZEN, *Job*, 254.

[97] DRIVER/GRAY, *Book of Job*, 373; GORDIS, *The Book of Job*, 492; HARTLEY, *The
Book of Job*, 537. Cf. the objection by PATRICK that a locative translation "is without
parallel in Biblical usage" ("The Translation of Job XLII 6," 369).

specific (the dunghill)[98] or generic (the ground)?[99] If, instead, עַל is referential ("about, concerning"),[100] a symbolic figure would be evoked; but does it concern the ritual postures associated with suffering,[101] penitence,[102] and mourning,[103] or is it a reference to the transitory nature of life itself?[104] In either case, how is this phrase related to the verbs which precede it?[105]

Depending on how one responds to these questions, the rendering of this verse, and by extension the interpretation of Job's characterization, will vary. A brief survey, which groups various opinions under four typical headings, will highlight the hermeneutical ambiguity that characterizes Job's final statement.[106]

---

[98] DHORME, *Book of Job*, 647; POPE, *Job*, 349 (cf. p. 21); FOHRER, *Das Buch Hiob*, 536.

[99] A. VAN SELMS, *Job: A Practical Commentary* (Texts and Interpretation; Grand Rapids 1985) 156, suggests that Job casts himself "on the ground" in deep respect for God; MUENCHOW argues that Job's "falling down upon the ground" expresses his shameful status ("Dust and Dirt," 610).

[100] Citing numerous parallels, PATRICK concludes that נחם followed by על (or occasionally אל) means "to change one's mind *about* something one had planned to do" ("The Translation of Job XLII 6," 370). Cf. the objections by MUENCHOW, based on the sense of the idiom and the placement of the *athnach* ("Dust and Dirt," pp. 609-610, n. 53).

[101] HABEL, *The Book of Job*, 583: "'Dust and ashes' therefore seem to represent the status and role of Job as isolated sufferer and humiliated litigant."

[102] ALONSO SCHÖKEL, *Giobbe*, 673: "Ciò che in 2,8.12 era espressione di lutto, qui è gesto di penitenza."

[103] PATRICK, "The Translation of Job XLII 6," 370-371.

[104] TERRIEN, "The Yahweh Speeches and Job's Responses," 505: "The contextual mention of dust and ashes indicates the mortal extremity in which he finds himself, for it refers to a rite suggestive of the ceremony of burial." Other translations suggest this understanding by personalizing it: NJV, 1980 ("Wherefore I abhor my words and repent, being but dust and ashes"); S. MITCHELL, *Into the Whirlwind: A Translation of the Book of Job* (Garden City 1979) 92 ("Therefore I will be quiet, comforted that I am dust"); A. WOLTERS, "A Child of Dust and Ashes? (Job 42:6b)," *ZAW* 102 (1990) 116-119 ("Therefore I recant and repent, a child of dust and ashes").

[105] A strophic division between וְנִחַמְתִּי and עַל־עָפָר וָאֵפֶר is suggested in the Masoretic text by the placement of the *athnach*.

[106] MORROW concludes his own survey by suggesting that the various translations complement different emphases of the divine address and that the "vague and ambiguous language of 42:6" indicates the author's purposeful creation of "a situation that can be interpreted in several ways according to the theological inclinations of the reader" ("Consolation, Rejection, and Repentance," 225).

A Survey of Interpretations

The first type of reading highlights the *confessional* nature of Job's repentance, the substance of which would concern his "return to the religious temper of mind."[107] In this perspective, his final statement could be "a metonymy for the entire process of repentance,"[108] understood as a "change in his mind so radical that it could be called a conversion."[109] His repentance could also be the expression of penitential contrition,[110] either for his ignorance[111] or his erring words — be they hasty or foolish or critical or sinful.[112] It could reflect a change of heart from his previously righteous pride,[113] which would have implicated him in evil by thrusting God to the periphery;[114] now he would be confessing his humiliating "fall from the

---

[107] A.S. PEAKE, "Job: The Problem of the Book," in *Theodicy in the Old Testament* (Issues in Religion and Theology, 4; [ed. J. CRENSHAW] Philadelphia 1983) 107; this author fully exemplifies this type of interpretation when he concludes that Job "has become a man of broken and contrite heart, penitent and self-loathing, who, because he knows himself to have nothing and deserve nothing, can most readily cast himself upon God, whose wisdom and omnipotence no longer crush but uphold and uplift him" (p. 108).

[108] MORROW, "Consolation, Rejection, Repentance," 119; cf. SNAITH, *The Book of Job*, 38-43.

[109] ANDERSEN, *Job*, 269; cf. ALEXANDER, "Job Considered as a Conversion Account."

[110] RAVASI, *Giobbe*, 816: "Giobbe è un convertito che si è pentito e ha lasciato dietro le spalle gli errori e la povertà della sua precedente religione (v. 6)."

[111] O'CONNOR, "Job's Final Word," 187: "Job acknowledges his fault when he admits finally that he uttered what he did not understand."

[112] Respectively, VAN SELMS, *Job*, 156; BERGANT, *Job*, 206; DRIVER/GRAY, *Book of Job*, 348; and NEWELL, "Job: Repentant or Rebellious," 315.

[113] See O'CONNOR, "The Hybris of Job," *ITQ* 55 (1989) 125-141. Cf. K. NAKAZAWA, "On the Dénouement of the Joban Poem," *Kirisutokyo Gaku* 19 (1977) 1-17, who translates 42:6*a* as "I reject my righteousness," and N. ARARAT, "Concerning Job's 'Fear of God'," *BM* 29 (1983-84) 263-278, who argues that only after Job ceases to be self-centered does God restore him.

[114] S. POLLOCK, "God and a Heretic," in GLATZER, *The Dimensions of Job*, 271: "He has seen something of the mystery of evil and has realized his own implication in it, discovering a root of pride in his heart which has hitherto been hidden from his consciousness, but in which he now dimly recognizes the ancient and deadly plague of the soul." J. CRENSHAW, *A Whirlpool of Torment: Israelite Traditions of God as an Oppressive Presence* (OBT, 12; Philadelphia 1984) p. 74, n. 39: "... I see Job's remarks as an expression of repentance for allowing his own ego to thrust God to the

heights of bold and fearless self-affirmation."[115] With a gesture that demonstrates "the essence of the shame response,"[116] Job would thereby acknowledge the "nothingness"[117] which, at base, founds his existence.

Differing from this penitential tone, a second type of reading suggests that Job's repentance is *lyrical*, one that would reflect the intense emotion that corresponds to a "psychology of theological awe."[118] The recognition afforded by his theophanic experience could, in this case, provide for Job's comfort; with "an inward relaxing of his soul's anguish and an appeasement,"[119] he would enjoy both spiritual consolation[120] and psychological integration[121] in the realm of faith. As a result, Job could renounce the dejected outlook of his previous protests.[122] Ultimately, he would be "yield(ing) himself in active reverence to find peace in the living presence of the God he thought he had lost,"[123] the same God who now enables him to abandon his mourning in favor of confident joy and praise.[124]

---

periphery. His sin was the salvaging of personal purity at God's expense." Cf. RAVASI, *Giobbe*, 819: "Giobbe nel dolore si pente della sua particolare *hybris* che gli aveva fatto ridurre Dio a oggetto discutibile e che lo aveva tentato di sostituirsi a lui nel giudicare cosmo e storia."

[115] HUMPHREYS, *The Tragic Vision*, 113.

[116] MORROW, "Consolation, Rejection, Repentance," 610.

[117] A. DE WILDE, *Das Buch Hiob:* eingeleitet, übersetzt und erlautert (OTS, 22; Leiden 1981) 396, translates "Deswegen erkenne ich meine Nichtigkeit an / und halte mich für Erde und Staub."

[118] TERRIEN, "Job," 1194; cf. his *Job*, 271: "Job ne reçoit ni rétribution de sa moralité ni punition pour l'amour de soi, mais Dieu s'offre à lui 'en personne transpersonnelle', et pour Job, cet instant de communion suffit."

[119] OTTO, "The Element of the Mysterious," 226.

[120] D. O'CONNOR, "The Comforting of Job," *ITQ* 53 (1987) 256: "Job at last finds consolation ... the consolation of wisdom, the consolation of knowing the truth (21:2)."

[121] BRENNER, "God's Answer to Job," 136: "Job has achieved an integration of all the elements— emotional, spiritual, and intellectual— that make up his faith." Cf. M.L. GRAMLICH, "Job — Before and After," *TBT* 94 (1978) 1494-1502.

[122] GUTIÉRREZ, *On Job*, 87.

[123] ROWLEY, *The Book of Job*, 266.

[124] PATRICK, *Arguing with God*, 119. Cf. PERDUE, *Wisdom in Revolt*, 232: "Since God delivered a disputation in the two speeches, and not a legal decision, a doxology from Job would be not a confession, but rather a statement of confidence in impending divine judgment."

In an entirely opposite vein, a third type of reading regards Job's repentance as *skeptical*. Corresponding to several possible tones of voice, Job's final words would convey "tongue-in-cheek" irony,[125] "clever" pragmatism,[126] insolent rejection,[127] or even revulsive denunciation before "the god who responds to the anguished plea of his most devoted worshipper with contemptuous and arrogant boasting."[128] At the very least, his repentance could signal that futile resignation by which he puts up with,[129] or even leaves behind,[130] the vicissitudes of life. In so doing, Job would be giving voice to a thoroughly realistic human experience, namely, "that often one does not receive a satisfactory answer but all one can do before such a God is to bow down and repent."[131]

A fourth type of reading concerns the *evidential* character of Job's response as it would indicate the manifold actuality of his theophanic experience. In this regard, his repentance could reflect the juridical decision by which he "withdraws his case against Shaddai now that Yahweh has spoken with Job face to face."[132] Admitting the need for

---

[125] ROBERTSON, "The Book of Job," 52.

[126] J. WILLIAMS, "'You have not spoken truth of me' — Mystery and Irony in the Book of Job," *ZAW* 83 (1971) 247: "Job 'repents', of course, but this is clever of him in the circumstances; it is the only way to deal with one who is rather easily threatened and who does not observe covenants."

[127] In his *Studies in Job* (Leiden 1939) 25-26, B.D. EERDMANS suggests that Job does not actually "repent" because he is proud of his vision and such an act would be unworthy of himself.

[128] CURTIS, "On Job's Response," 505.

[129] E. WÜRTHWEIN, "Gott und Mensch in Dialog und Gottesreden des Buches Hiob," *Wort und Existenz:* Studien zum AT (Göttingen 1970) 283: "Hiob findet zu einem Verhalten zu Gott in Demütigung und schweigender Hinnahme des über ihn von Gott Verhängten." Cf. W. URBROCK, "Job as Drama: Tragedy or Comedy?" *CurTM* 8 (1981) 37: "They [the words of 42:6] express Job's reconciliation to the indifference of providence."

[130] P. DE BOER, "Does Job Retract? Job xlii,6," *Selected Studies in Old Testament Exegesis* (OTS, 27; [ed. C. VAN DUIN] Leiden 1991) 194, translates "Therefore I have had enough of it all and leave dust and ashes behind" ("daarom heb ik er genoeg van en laat stof en as voor wat ze zijn"). Cf. VAWTER, *Job and Jonah*, 85: "... he wishes to cut the losses of his former speculation and move on to other considerations."

[131] DELL, *The Book of Job as Sceptical Literature*, 207-208.

[132] HABEL, *The Book of Job*, 582.

something more than the juridical in his situation,[133] Job recants the grievous charges he has brought against the divinity[134] and "surrenders to God the last vestige of his self-righteousness, i.e., he withdraws his avowal of innocence."[135] Or Job's repentance could constitute an existential conclusion relative to the place of his own concerns in light of the cosmic amplitude of creation.[136] Whether negatively, "by the realization that his suffering was a drop in the endless mystery of being and living,"[137] or positively, by affirmation of the royal status of humanity as it is "challenged to take up the divine *image* through engagement with the partly determinate, partly indeterminate character of the world"[138] — in either case Job is ultimately reconciled with, and vindicated before, his all-powerful God.[139] Or, finally, Job's repentance could express the epistemological impasse engendered by the incongruity and paradox of the divine discourse.[140] Accepting the unfathomable design of life, Job "succumbs ... not to authority or power, but to mystery."[141]

---

[133] Cf. G. ERIKSON and K. JONASSON, "Jobsbokensjuridiska grundmönster," *STK* 65 (1989) 64-69.

[134] Cf. D.N. FREEDMAN, "Is It Possible to Understand the Book of Job?" *BRev* 4,3 (1988) 26-33.

[135] HARTLEY, *The Book of Job*, 537.

[136] P.E. BONNARD, "Job où l'homme enfin extasié," *LumVie* 13 (1964) 30.

[137] GREENBERG, "In Dust and Ashes," 224; cf. LILLIE, "The Religious Significance of the Theophany," 358: "What he realized was the divine greatness, which threw himself and his troubles into complete insignificance."

[138] JANZEN, *Job*, 257.

[139] GORDIS, *The Book of Job*, 491; cf. the conclusion of S. HUBERMAN-SCHOLNICK, "The Meaning of *mišpat* in the Book of Job, " *JBL* 101 (1982) 529: "Job speaks at the end of the drama not as an innocent hero who rejects the divine Judge for improperly accusing him of wrongdoing, but as an enlightened and humbled man who accepts an all-powerful King. His acceptance is based on a full understanding that *mišpat* integrates the ideas of human jurisprudence and divine sovereignty."

[140] WHEDBEE, "The Comedy of Job": "The mystery and incongruity remain -- they are now accepted but not resolved (p. 26); "His confession is authentic but paradoxical: his new wisdom is that he does not know all, his new perception is that he does not see all; but he knows enough and sees enough" (p. 29).

[141] COX, *Man's Anger and God's Silence*, 106. Cf. MACKENZIE, "The Transformation of Job," 56-57: "Job's final retraction ... is not to be understood merely as resignation and submission to a higher power. It is full acceptance of the mystery, confirmed by this personal contact with the Almighty."

Given the ambiguity of the text, each of these four readings enjoys a certain measure of acceptance. The *confessional* interpretations of humble conversion seem to correspond to the sort of religious fear expected of a true believer like Job. The *lyrical* interpretations of reverential praise highlight the linguistic dimension of the question at hand and account well for the experiential transformation that has come about through Job's theophanic encounter. Then again, the *skeptical* interpretations of frustrated understanding highlight the intellectual concern of Job and justly emphasize the lack of clear resolution in this domain. Finally, the *evidential* interpretations of newfound belonging are in full accord with the decisive, yet mysterious, character of Job's response.

Given the interactional phenomenon at work in this narrative, each of these four readings tends to bespeak the subjectivity of the interpreters, whose respective expectations necessarily affect their understanding of the text. Nevertheless, each of these readings owes its plausibility to a particular combination of textual choices made by the interpreter, which, in turn, governs a respective line of thought.[142] In terms of the development of the narrative, however, the determinations surveyed here may be subject to some critique.

Most evident is the lack of a sound basis for the facile readings of Job's repentance as *confessional*. In general, this approach fails to correspond both to the tenor of the narrative and to the formal pattern of repenting in the Old Testament.[143] More specifically, several objections can be raised against such a reading. Is the main character,

---

[142] TILLEY, "God and the Silencing of Job," 260: "... no version of 42:6 has been established as the right rendering. Yet the meaning of this climactic verse determines Job's final stance. This leads to a crucial problem. As this verse is critical for understanding Job, the meaning of the whole book of Job becomes fluid. In short, the multiple possibilities for rendering 42:6 mean that the interpreters make, rather than find, the text which they interpret."

[143] First, the poet does not employ the technical term for such repentance (שׁוּב), a root which "combines in itself both requisites of repentance: to turn from evil and to turn to good" (J. MILGROM, "Repentance in the OT," *IDBS*, 737); given the presentation of Job in the Prologue as a man of integrity, these attributes would not be something new. Second, the standard form is inverted, for "(a) doxology of confession normally would follow judgment, not precede it" (PERDUE, *Wisdom in Revolt*, 223). Cf. R.O. COLEMAN, "Repentance in the Old Testament," *BibIll* 12 (1986) 30-31.

heretofore a paradigm of virtuous integrity, actually in need of conversion?[144] Is Job's search for meaning in life so contradictory to the notion of informed faith that it would require his contrition?[145] Given his personal uprightness, affirmed in the Prologue and sustained in the Dialogues, is abject humiliation an appropriate conclusion to the characterization of Job? Most importantly, how can contrition or humiliation on Job's part coincide with the explicit affirmation by Yahweh that Job has spoken correctly in the divine regard (42:7,8)?[146]

The *lyrical* readings also lack full support in the text, for any quick shift to adoration threatens to ignore the issue of Job's plight as significantly as does the divine discourse itself. In particular, emphasis on the fact that Job abandons his lament tends to obscure the emotive tenacity of his concluding remarks.[147] Moreover, the notion that Yahweh's tempestuous tirade provides Job with consolation could border on the hypocritical.[148] Ultimately, the claim that Job's final words give voice to praise may stretch beyond the matter of the text.[149]

The *skeptical* readings, for their part, seem to disregard the hermeneutical clues provided by the narrative context. On the one hand, a cunning Job who rejects the divinity would make a mockery of the characterization of Yahweh's "faithful servant" in the Prologue and

---

[144] LÉVÊQUE, *Job et son Dieu*, 447: "une conversion n'aurait pas de sens puisqu'il ne s'est jamais détourné de Dieu, et que de toute façon Dieu prend soin de lui barrer le chemin du retour."

[145] GORDIS, *The Book of God and Man*, 126: "... it was no act of *hybris*, of insolence or arrogance, for a Hebrew to demand justice of his God."

[146] Cf. J.C.L. GIBSON, "The Book of Job and the Care of Souls," *SJT* 42 (1989) 303-317, who rightly argues against the notion of an abject collapse because it is not in keeping with Job's character, because it would exonerate the friends position, and because it would make useless the affirmation of 42:7.

[147] This is the major contestation of CURTIS, "On Job's Response," 504-505.

[148] VOLZ, *Hiob und Weisheit*, 1: "Die in den Wolken erscheinende Gottheit bringt der gequälten Seele keine Antwort, und das objectiv gehaltene schöne Naturgedicht kann ein verwundetes Herz nicht heilen." Cf. ALONSO SCHÖKEL, *Giobbe*, 671: "Una soluzione emotiva non soddisferebbe Giobbe e non sarebbe coerente con il dramma. L'autore ha fatto bene a non permettere al suo Dio facili sentimenti."

[149] GOOD, *In Turns of Tempest*, 377: "nothing in the text hints at any such thing."

Epilogue.[150] On the other hand, continuing revolt on the part of Job suggests that the Theologue makes no significant difference in the development of the plot, except, perhaps, to reinforce the portrayal of Yahweh as cosmic buffoon, in which case Job's change of stance makes little sense.[151] In the end, the futility of this reading seems unworthy of the genius of the narrative, and what fails to satisfy the protagonist of the narrative[152] could hardly be of benefit to the reader in terms of ongoing meaningfulness.[153]

Lastly, the *evidential* readings risk hermeneutical heresy if they portray the final stance of the main character as one of absolute surrender. Were Job's last words the decree of a judicial retraction, his response would become anti-climactic. Were this verse the acceptance of an existential re-alignment in virtue of his relative insignificance in the cosmic scheme, Job's affirmation would run counter to the heroic contestation by which he is characterized in the progression of the narrative and to the imaginal dominion with which humans are distinguished in the tradition of the Old Testament (cf. Gen 1:26-28; Ps 8). Finally, were his conclusive statement merely a human concession to the impenetrability of life's mystery, it could instigate the narrative's self-collapse in the ruins of an epistemological defeatism.

---

[150] CRENSHAW, "When Form and Content Clash," 82: "The difficulty with the detection of irony in Job's response is that it ignores the sages' belief that God saw into the depths of human hearts. Such duplicity on Job's part would not have escaped Yahweh's sight, in the sages' view."

[151] As MOORE notes, the "ironic" interpretations, in particular, mistakenly assume that "the poet's theological position is to be identified with his portrayal of Job's attitude" as it is pitted against the prose narrative, but they do not then take into account the change suggested by Job's repentance ("The Integrity of Job," pp. 20-21, n. 12).

[152] C.R. SEITZ, "Job: Full Structure, Movement, and Interpretation," *Int* 43 (1989) 15: "It will not do — with Jung and a score of modern critics — to bend the text and see Job's response as tongue-in-cheek, as though he is bluffing to get God off his back. Here the reader confuses his or her point of standing with that of Job, who is satisfied with the divine response."

[153] WILCOX, *The Bitterness of Job*: "It [the implication of Job's principled integrity] says that this moral sense is a threat to life itself: it makes us less happy and less likely to live. It is hostile to life; it is no-saying; it condemns the real world" (p. 110); "... a moral sense makes us suffer sometimes; but it does not necessarily lead — one would think — to a suffering, painful, view of reality itself. But *Job's* moral sense does just that. That makes one suspect that something is wrong with it, and not just with his cultivation of the bitterness it evokes" (p. 116).

The Phenomenon of Repentance

At this point, another reading of Job's last words may be suggested, one based on the translations given above:

$$\text{שְׁמַע־נָא וְאָנֹכִי אֲדַבֵּר   אֶשְׁאָלְךָ וְהוֹדִיעֵנִי׃}$$
$$\text{לְשֵׁמַע־אֹזֶן שְׁמַעְתִּיךָ   וְעַתָּה עֵינִי רָאָתְךָ׃}$$
$$\text{עַל־כֵּן אֶמְאַס וְנִחַמְתִּי   עַל־עָפָר וָאֵפֶר׃}$$

(42:4)   *Listen here, that I, I may speak;*
         "I want to question you and you will inform me."
(42:5)   *By sound of ear, I have heard (of) you,*
         but now my eye, (she) sees you;
(42:6)   *therefore I despise yet repent*
         of dust and ash.

Here, Job gives voice to the wisdom he has gained.

In these climactic verses, Job's sapiential acquisition leads to a two-fold affirmation concerning the subject *of* human life.[154] The rare idiomatic pair "dust and ash" provides the rhetorical referent for Job's claim.[155] Serving as "the ultimate symbol of humanness" by evoking both mortality and the potential for creation,[156] *dust and ash* here refers to the existential make-up of human life in its earthly status. Poetically posed as a universal descriptor,[157] this phrase sharpens the

---

[154] Those who read "dust and ash" as the accusative of *both* verbs in 42:6a include PATRICK ("The Translation of Job XLII 6," 369); GOOD (*In Turns of Tempest*, 376); and PERDUE (*Wisdom in Revolt*, p. 237, n. 1).

[155] The phrase עָפָר וָאֵפֶ ר occurs elsewhere only in Gen 18:27 and Job 30:19, where it connotes the lowliness of human life. Elsewhere in Job, "dust" tends to symbolize mortality (4:19; 10:9; 17:16), and for the Friends it suggests the corrupt nature of life. Here in 42:6, our literal rendering of the Hebrew singular (rather than "dust and ash*es*") seeks to convey the substantial rather than material aspect of the phrase.

[156] N. HABEL, "'Naked I came …': Humanness in the Book of Job," in *Die Botschaft und die Boten* (FS. H.W. Wolff; [eds. J. JEREMIAS und L. PERLITT] Neukirchen-Vluyn 1981) 390.

[157] Consistent with the narrative ploy of universalizing the personal implications of Job's tragedy (cf. COX, *Man's Anger and God's Silence*, 36), one could possibly read עָפָר וָאֵפֶר as an extension of קַלֹּתִי in Job's first response (40:4).

sapiential focus of Job's response: the fundamental issue in this theo-linguistic debate concerns the stuff of *this* life, the one created by God, the world of here and now, with its pervasive paradoxes and perennial problems, about or concerning which the questions of undeserved suffering, divine justice, and the like have been raised.[158]

That Job *despises* this *Lebenswelt* reflects the emotive response of one whose own experience of injustice is tragically real.[159] Employing a term that "is a much more visceral notion of detesting than the rather intellectual abandonment of a prior opinion,"[160] Job here unleashes before Yahweh an existential rage akin to that which had inspired his inter-human diatribes (cf. 7:16; 34:33). Thus, more than the resigned conclusion of pragmatic logic, by which Job would cease to press his previously confrontational position, this expression actualizes a positive and enduring affirmation.[161] It highlights his continuing and contemning reaction to the problematic senselessness of life (cf. 7:16; 9:21).[162] For Job the world is (still) not just — and that is cause for revulsion.

Nevertheless, the second verb in 42:6a expresses a sapiential transmutation— Job *repents* of this very problem. Here Job suddenly and unexpectedly changes his perspective, without however recanting

---

[158] MOORE argues that the thematic of the book concerns a preoccupation "with the issue of the value of life" ("The Integrity of Job," 24). Cf. POLZIN, *Biblical Structuralism*, 104.

[159] The same strength of emotion, though with a different reference, is found in HABEL's earlier translation of 42:6a as "Therefore I despair" ("Naked I Came," 388). On the debate concerning the emotive rendering of אמאס, KUYPER concludes that "The usage hardly allows the extreme emphasis of 'to despise, to abhor'" ("The Repentance of Job," 94), while CURTIS posits "a fundamental meaning like 'to feel loathing contempt and revulsion'" ("On Job's Response," 503).

[160] GOOD, *In Turns of Tempest*, 26.

[161] S. WAGNER, "מאס *ma'as*," *TWAT*, vol. IV, p. 627: "*m's* ist hier (ganz singulär) Terminus des positiv zu bewertenden Bußgeschehens."

[162] POLZIN, *Biblical Structuralism*, 104-105: "In short, Job is portrayed throughout the book as a man who always recognizes the power of God and his own subordination to Him, and for this very reason rejects life as God has constituted it. Nowhere in the book is Job the unbeliever; rather he is the supreme realist who rejects not God but life as God has shaped it for man."

the rhetoric of his former position.[163] Instead, his assertion devolves from the new and positive frame of being occasioned by the divine discourse and expresses that which is now significant for his own existential belonging. For Job, now, the world does not have to be just.

What is novel in this reading, and what will be significant for the interpretation of Job's final stance, is not simply the unusual terminology which is employed but the manner with which these two aspects of Job's affirmation are inter-related. In the first place, his rebellion against the non-sense of human life *and* his reversal with regard to the needed resolution of this enigma are *both* the result of his life-long experience: for the former, his own experience of divine injustice which contrasts with the platitudes voiced by his friends, and for the latter, his immediate experience of God in the voice from the whirlwind. Due, *therefore*, to both the realism of his travails and the surety of his vision,[164] Job's dual affirmation differs radically from the submissive turning back to God previously counselled by his Friends (cf. 11:14-15; 22:21-30). For them, penitence would lead to approbation by God, whereas for Job repentance proceeds from apprehension of the divine.

It follows, then, that in the interpretation of this verse *both* aspects of Job's statement are to be retained as justifiable. In this case, the bi-dimensionality of Job's final stance parallels the duality of his mode of knowing (42:5,6):

> *hearing (about)*   *but*   *now seeing God*
> **THEREFORE**
> *I (still) despise*   *YET*   *repent*
> *concerning the (in)justice of this life.*

---

[163] Contrary to JANZEN, who highlights the translation "(I) change my mind" but explains this as occurring "in such a transformation as both requires and enables him to give up what he formerly thought" (*Job*, 255). So, too, K.M. O'CONNOR, *The Wisdom Literature* (Message of Biblical Spirituality, 5; Wilmington 1988) 101: "He sees God face to face and he relinquishes his claim to be right."

[164] DEBOER, "Does Job Retract?" 193: "The only thing that happens to Job is this vision. However one sees this, it explains *how* he gets the spiritual force needed to overcome the numbing power of his incomprehensible suffering." Cf. RAVASI, *Giobbe*, 819.

In this reading, the two verbal elements need not be read as a poetic hendiadys;[165] instead, the continuing, repetitive sense of "despises" is supervened by the novelty and uniqueness of "repents."[166]

Devolving from this structure, and consistent with the narrative progression from the Dialogues to the Theologue, the novel rendering of the conjunctive *waw* best maintains the semantic contiguity, *yet* difference suggested by the juxtaposition of the two verbs. Nevertheless, this distinction, like that in 42:5, need not be construed as an exclusive opposition.[167] The concluding verse maintains the denunciation of cosmic mismanagement which would be consistent with Job's sapiential integrity; yet it precludes a rebellious rejection of God,[168] for Job's poetic repentance attests to the epistemological transformation effected in him as a result of his encounter with the God of the storm.

Nonetheless, the vocabulary of repentance in 42:6 engenders a certain perplexity when attempting to interpret Job's ultimate stance. On the one hand, "to repent" tends to imply a complicity in sinfulness, which forms the basis for the confessional interpretations. On the other hand, to repent while continuing "to despise" may suggest the futility of resignation, whereby Job would be giving in either to the apparent insignificance of his questions or to the unfathomable nature of their answer. To lend credence to our translation and to the interpretation of Job's final words as the affirmation of a newfound wisdom, we turn

---

[165] JANZEN admits the possibility of such a hendiadys, meaning "Job utterly changes his mind," (*Job*, 255); WOLTERS cites Van Selms as having recognized this construct ("A Child of Dust and Ashes," p. 118, n. 13).

[166] DE BOER argues that the construction here is an example of the *waw*-perfect consecutive, in which case "(t)he second verb is often a continuation of what is indicated by the first" ("Does Job Retract?" 192). However, the position of the *athnach* stress suggests that this may *not* be an instance of the inverted perfect construct; in this case, the *waw* is simple, not energic, and merely indicates juxtaposition (see *GBH*, §115c). As a result, the perfect נִחַמְתִּי retains the aspect of a singularly unique and instantaneous action (*GBH*, §119x), translated here in the "present" domain because it is an action "being performed at the very moment of the utterance" (*GBH*, §112f).

[167] Cf. BDB, 252 (e): "it (ו) connects *contrasted* ideas, where in our idiom the contrast would be expressed explicitly by *but*; in such cases prominence is usu. given to the contrasted idea by its being placed immed. after the conj." Such usage is especially evident in Proverbs.

[168] Contrary to CURTIS, "On Job's Response," 505.

now to a consideration of the phenomenon of repentance and the particular configuration it takes in this theo-linguistic narrative.

In what is acknowledged to be one of the few studies of its kind, T.E. Fretheim has investigated the biblical notion of repentance in terms of a divine activity. As a basis for his study, he describes five elements which comprise this phenomenon:

> Repentance is a metaphor whose roots are to be found in the dynamics of *interpersonal relationships.* Generally, the use of the word "repentance" presupposes that one has *said or done something* to another and, finding that to be hurtful or inadequate or dissatisfactory in some way, *seeks to reverse* the effects through contrition, sorrow, regret, or some form of "turning." It is a word which assumes *real change* on the part of the one who repents; something formerly said or done is no longer held to be right or appropriate. It is also a word for which *temporal sequence* is integral; it is a change with respect to some past statement or action.[169]

While these elements are fundamental to the common understanding of the phenomenon, a consideration of Job's use of the term will highlight the divergences which characterize his as a "repentance" proper to the wisdom of this biblical narrative.

In the first place, the narrative dynamic does concern the *relationship* between humanity and divinity — from the Prologue, where Job receives heavenly praise for his comportment, through the Dialogues, where the good favor of this relation is put into question by the otherwise inexplicable state of affairs, to the Theologue, where the two parties come to interact in a relatively direct communication. As this relation has developed, one fact emerges with clarity: Job does not abandon his God. Committing neither physical nor psychological suicide,[170] Job does not, in fact, curse Yahweh "to his face" (cf.

---

[169] T.E. FRETHEIM, "The Repentance of God: A Key to Evaluating Old Testament God-Talk," *Hor* 10,1 (1988) 50. [*emphasis added*]

[170] Cf. COX, *Man's Anger and God's Silence*, 43-45 and WILCOX, *The Bitterness of Job*, 107-110. For POLZIN this narrative fact reflects the "code" of the book: "Through all the meandering of the story it [being sent down to *Sheol*, the land of the dead] was never given to Job at his request, its affirmation longed for but never attained. It is the one state avoided by all the transformations of the story and it is hard to avoid the conclusion that this also is in some sense the point of the story. ... The message of the book centers around the courageous affirmation of apparently irreconcilable spheres

1:11; 2:5), despite whatever restive, accusatory and even condemning tones his diatribes assume.

Nevertheless, in this relationship something is clearly askew. And at this point, as Ricoeur explains it, there begins what we could call Job's quest for wisdom:

> It (wisdom) is addressed directly to the sense and the non-sense of existence. It is a struggle for sense in spite of non-sense. Unjust suffering holds a central place there, to the extent that suffering itself poses its enigma at the juncture of the order of things and the ethical order. ... At its limit wisdom discourse encounters a hidden God who takes for a mask the anonymous and inhuman course of things.[171]

Upon the axis of this established lack of equilibrium, the enigma of Job's repentance turns, for despite his Friends insinuations and recriminations, the narrative fact remains that Job has neither *said nor done* anything "wrong" (cf. 27:5) and therefore has no reason to feel "guilty."[172] In fact, one apparent aim of the narrative is to sound the death knell for any theory of retribution in which all deeds and consequences are inextricably linked. This being the case, Job's repentance must have for its object some inadequacy which obstructs the relationship but for which he is not to blame as the ignoble cause. In light of his solidly apologetic peroration in chapters 29-31, and by virtue of the explicit statement in 42:3, that inadequacy can only be his human finitude in the realm of knowledgeable speech: prior to his encounter with the voice from the storm, Job had lacked wisdom.

---

instead of the insane negation of those spheres to avoid conflict and contradiction" (*Biblical Structuralism*, 100-101).

[171] RICOEUR, "Nommer Dieu," 356. Cf. RICOEUR, "Sur l'exégèse de Genèse 1,1–2,4a," 82: "C'est-ce pas alors la fonction de la sagesse d'assurer la jonction entre les valeurs de salut et les valeurs cosmiques?"

[172] Cf. RICOEUR, *The Symbolism of Evil*: "Whereas sin is a qualitative situation — it is or it is not, — guilt designates an intensive quantity, capable of more and less" (p. 107); "Job is the zero degree of guilt joined to the extreme of suffering (and) from this conjunction is born the scandal which also is extreme" (p. 315, n. 1).

The implication of this insufficiency Job does *seek to reverse*, though not through the ethos of penitential return found in the customary parlance of repentance. Instead, the change effected in and by Job's repentance devolves from his immediate encounter with Yahweh, an experience which, in Ricoeur's description, combines the fact of divine manifestation and the consequent potential for human consolation:

> No teleology issues from the whirlwind, no intelligible connection between a physical and an ethical order. There is only the display of the whole of Being in the fullness of the Word. There remains only the possibility of acceptance, of resignation, which is the first stage of a consolation beyond the desire for protection.[173]

Job's repentance is thus something more than a change "back" to his prologue piety or a change "from" his dialogue disputation. Owing to the particular circumstances of the Theologue,[174] it may be construed as a turn "toward" the divine that goes beyond, without negating, the preceding developments in the Dialogues.

For Job, this *change* is certainly *real*. Yet it differs substantially from the reversal described by Fretheim. With no hint of regret, nor outpouring of admiration, Job affirms the duality of his existential conviction and then takes up life anew. In terms of the thematic discussion, he will be forevermore silent; his only subsequent speech, unreported in the narrative, will be that on behalf of the very interlocutors whom he had previously dismissed as "worthless physicians" (13:4) and "miserable comforters" (16:2). Thus, the Epilogue makes evident that the Job who speaks in chapter 42 is not the same character as before.

As a result of this real change, the meaningfulness of the Theologue comes to be highlighted, for Job can and does repent only *after* his experience of Yahweh in the voice from the storm. In terms of the

---

[173] RICOEUR, "Religion, Atheism, Faith," 89. Cf. his *Freud and Philosophy:* An Essay on Interpretation (New Haven 1970) 548: "Job receives no explanation of his suffering; he is merely shown something of the grandeur and order of the whole, without any meaning being directly given to the finite point of view of his desire."

[174] Dealing specifically with the verb םחנ , FRETHEIM clarifies that this term "appears to include not only the sense of reversal, but a reversal prompted by one's being moved by the situation in view" ("The Repentance of God," 51).

temporal sequence integral to the phenomenon of repentance, the tempestuous event of the theophany and the divine "rhetoric of interrogation" have somehow disclosed to Job the inexplicable design of Yahweh, in a way unlike what was possible in the deductive reasoning of the Dialogues.[175] For Job, in the dynamic intimacy of this communication with Yahweh, "(w)hat is revealed is the possibility of hope in spite of ...."[176] As a result, his final affirmation includes, yet surpasses, his previous discursive interventions. It draws together both the results of experiential reasoning *and* the fruits of theophanic revelation in order to encapsulate the wisdom of his narrative life.[177] In sum, whereas the triumph of experiential reasoning over impersonal tradition may lead to cognitive dissonance (in which the Job of the Dialogues has come to "despise" life), *yet* the experience of encounter with God provides existential consonance (through which the Job of the Theologue comes to "repent").

Hence, by saying that Job "repents," the author has given to his character a uniquely suitable locution with which to conclude his speech. In terms of the phenomenon indicated by this verb, "to repent" gives depth to the narrative's sapiential focus on how to speak about God given the human situation. It is an existential term, rather than a purely academic one, and for this reason pertinent to the realm of wisdom; it is a religious term, rather than a specifically juridic one, and for this reason appropriate to a properly biblical narrative. Yet, when placed on the lips of the man from Uz, this same term comes to mean something more than what is understood in the commonly accepted religious language. Transgressing the standard categories of

---

[175] COX, *Man's Anger and God's Silence*, 116: "By this rhetoric of interrogation, the use of questions that are also statements in question form, a dynamic of communication is set up: each of them, interrogator and interrogated, knows what the only answer can be, and is aware of the other's knowledge. A relationship of shared cognition is established. Yahweh is drawing Job into the dialectic of thesis-antithesis, making him see the same familiar world in different colours."

[176] RICOEUR, "Toward a Hermeneutic of the Idea of Revelation," 87.

[177] A. LACOQUE, "Job or the Impotence of Religion and Philosophy," *Semeia* 19 (1981) 39: "Job's *nehama* (repentance) is yielded by his wisdom, not by any feeling of culpability .... Rather than having discovered something about himself (a hidden iniquity perhaps), Job has discovered something about God: that He did not remain untouched during Job's torture."

sin and sorrow, it assumes not a logical signification but a symbolic one, the potential force of which is explained by Ricoeur:

> With symbolic language, we are in turn faced with a language which says more than what it says, which says something other than what it says and which, consequently, grasps me because it has in its meaning created a new meaning.[178]

It is this new meaning which expresses the wisdom proper to Job.[179]

The symbolic novelty of Job's repentance, in turn, governs our nuanced interpretation of his ultimate stance. In opposition to the culpability presupposed in the confessional interpretations, Job's repentance implies, at most, the finitude of human knowing.[180] In contrast with the laudatory leap suggested by the lyrical interpretations, Job's repentance remains consistent with his having despised the senselessness of the cosmos.[181] Likewise in contrast with the deconstructive denigration implicit in the skeptical interpretations,[182] Job's repentance actually results from, and contributes to, a real transformation on his part.[183] Finally, in distinction to the "giving in" resigna-

---

[178] RICOEUR, "The Language of Faith," 233.

[179] An appreciation of this symbolic potential in Job's final statement could assuage the conclusion of TILLEY, "God and the Silencing of Job," 268: "Readers may fear Job for good reason. The Book of Job makes no coherent claims. ... As part of the Jewish and Christian religious canons, it reveals that no way of speaking of God and suffering will do. ... The comfortable alternative to listening to Job is usually preferred by literary-critical, theological, and liturgical comforters: to play God and silence the voices of Job."

[180] GLATZER, *The Dimensions of Job*, 8: "Man's (reconstructed) knowledge is both: awareness of his limitation *and* of his capacity to live with this limitation in the context of the universe."

[181] FOHRER, "Der innere Aufbau," 17: "Es bleibt notvoll und rätselhaft, aber es quält ihn nicht mehr, weil die Gemeinschaft mit Gott alles andere überwiegt (vgl. Jes 51,7-8; Ps 73,25-28)."

[182] Cf. D. CLINES, "Deconstructing the Book of Job," *What Does Eve Do to Help? and Other Readerly Questions to the Old Testament* (JSOTSup, 94; Sheffield 1990) 123: "But when we believe its hero, we will believe him because we want to, because it suits our sense of the fitness of things, and not because he has divulged a truth about a transcendental signified that is one and incontrovertible."

[183] Cf. the conclusion to S.E. SCHREINER, "'Where Shall Wisdom Be Found?': Gregory's Interpretation of Job," *ABR* 39 (1988) 321-342: "Gregory assumed that buried within the words of the text, within the 'chaff' of history, within the events of Job's life, and within nature, lies a 'wisdom' which is perceptible only through the

tion of the evidential interpretations,[184] Job's repentance points rather to a giving up of rational requirements and existential exigencies herewith transvalued in virtue of his encounter with his God.[185]

Hence, in the statement "*I despise yet repents of dust and ash,*" Job expresses what is conclusive in terms of both his personal characterization in the narrative and its thematic progression: for the thinker, the inability to resolve the enigma of life remains; yet, for the sage, the ability to supersede this rational demand is offered by and in God.[186] And therein lies the inner eye of wisdom!

THE AESTHETICS OF REPENTANCE

Having explained the lexical aspects of the text in this new translation of Job's responses to the speeches of Yahweh, we can now expound upon our understanding of these verses according to the phenomenological hermeneutics of Ricoeur. In this perspective, our understanding of Job's ultimate stance will be built on the explanation of how his unexpected change of position is configured within the dramatic movement of the narrative. Here the "poetic" dimensions of the text play a significant role in as much as Job's responses to the voice from the storm contribute to the production of a distinct sapiential discourse.[187] Put simply, Job's final words constitute the language

---

double movement of turning inward and ascending to a higher level of reality. That higher perspective both transcends change and gives meaning to the changeable temporal realm."

[184] Cf. W. VISCHER, "God's Truth and Man's Lie — A Study in the Message of the Book of Job," *Int* 15 (1961) 136: "The small consolation of the incomprehensible wisdom of God is precisely that no one except God understands it ...."

[185] MACKENZIE, "Job," 486: "It (the divine speech) puts Job's problem in a new perspective and opens up a vista in which, although still without an answer, it ceases to require one."

[186] Cf. PERDUE, *Wisdom in Revolt*, 236: "For a sage, speech informed by knowledge and understanding shapes and creates a beneficent reality, whereas uninformed language distorts and destroys. Job's knowledgeless rhetoric, charged with accusations, is now replaced with at least the renewal of will to praise God's life-giving actions."

[187] RICOEUR, "Poétique et symbolique," 39: "Comme le suggère la racine grecque du terme (*poièsis* = fabrication d'une chose distincte de son auteur), la poétique s'attache au caractère *productif* de certains modes de discours, sans égard pour la

of avowal, wherein his ultimate "repentance" expresses what could be called an "originary affirmation" by means of which he renders testimony to the acquisition of wisdom.

Contributing to this phenomenological interpretation is an understanding of the setting in which Job's words are spoken. Read in the remote context of a quest for theo-linguistic wisdom,[188] Job's final words exhibit a *metaphorical sense*: with the final twist of despising yet repenting, the protagonist provides a conclusive, albeit confounding, answer to the narrative question.[189] Read in the proximate context as a direct reply to the proclamation by Yahweh, Job's words point to an *existential reference*: with an imaginative and emotive depth consistent with his integrity, Job boldly attests to his spiritual experience as that which infuses his existence with meaningfulness.[190] Given the conclusive judgment by Yahweh that follows, in which Job is confirmed as having spoken rightly (42:7,8), his language in these few verses reflects the veritable voice of wisdom.

Job's Poetic Wisdom

Understood in their theo-linguistic context, the responses of Job to the speeches of Yahweh can be further explained in virtue of their

---

difference entre la prose et la poésie (versifiée, rimée ou rythmée). ... Mais il importe de préciser dès le début que cette *production* est d'emblée double: c'est, à la fois, une production de *sens*, c'est-à-dire une expansion du langage 'interne' à lui-même, *et* un accroissement de sa puissance de découverte eu égard à des traits proprement 'inédits' de la réalité, à des aspects 'inouïs' du monde."

[188] Our thesis relative to the primary "theme" of the narrative — namely, that it concerns speech about God — constitutes a departure from Ricoeur's own comments on the Book of Job, which he tends to read in terms of a "tragic" understanding of the process which pits humans against God when evil is suffered.

[189] Ricoeur, "Biblical Hermeneutics," 97: "The signs of metaphoricity given by a single narrative, if there are any, have not to be found elsewhere than in the *plot* (in Via's sense), in the challenge which this plot displays for the main characters, and in the answer of these characters to the *crisis* situation."

[190] Cf. Ricoeur, "Tasks of the Ecclesial Community," 248: "It seems to me that the interpretation of the faith is today bound to the reconstitution and assumption of a critique of religion which is not confined to intellectual objectivization, but which takes place on the anthropological level, I mean on the level of the genesis of man — not, of course, of his biological genesis, but of the genesis of the meaning of man as man."

properly "poetic" power, where purposeful ambiguity precludes systematic precision, where artful wonder surpasses ordinary description, and where cathartic transformation prevails over rhetorical argumentation. In this hermeneutical realm, Job's "symbolic" silence implies a new sophistication, while his "metaphorical" repentance suggests an imaginative innovation.

Given the mysterious ambiance generated by both the tempestuous advent of the divinity and the "challenge" of Yahweh's mytho-poetic speeches,[191] the first response of Job (40:4-5) admits of a certain ambiguity. His gestured silence could, as traditionally rendered, be considered a conclusion or result. In that case, it would represent the outcome of his having been subjected to the tempestuous power of a divine discourse, one which has reduced Job to a humiliated position consonant with his status as human creature before the all-powerful Creator. It would be a silence of submission.

Or, owing to the multiplicity of sense inherent in such a symbolic gesture, Job's response could be the verbal signal of something more, namely, his own re-positioning in a more receptive epistemological mode.[192] Read in this way, Job's silence is an introduction or initiation. In marked contrast with his previous protestation, wherein a prolix power characterized his dispute with the tradition of his Friends and his lament over the God of his religion, Job's silence activates a new stance. Faced with the stormy words of the divine interlocutor whom he had so ardently sought (cf. 13:22-23), Job

---

[191] RICOEUR, *The Symbolism of Evil*, 321: "Through these symbols (God) gives him to understand that all is order, measure, and beauty — inscrutable order, measure beyond measure, terrible beauty. ... There is nothing in that revelation that concerns him personally; but precisely because it is not a question of himself, Job is challenged."

[192] Cf. RICOEUR, *Le conflit des interprétations*, 68: "s'il y a quelque sens à parler d'une herméneutique du sacré, c'est dans la mesure où le double-sens d'un texte, qui me parle par exemple de l'Exode, débouche sur une certaine condition itinérante qui est vécue existentiellement comme mouvement d'une captivité à une délivrance; sous l'interpellation d'une parole qui donne ce qu'elle ordonne, le double-sens vise ici à déchiffrer un mouvement existentiel, une certaine condition ontologique de l'homme, par le moyen du surcroît de sens attaché à l'événement qui, dans sa littéralité, se place dans le monde historique observable; le double-sens est ici le détecteur d'une position dans l'être."

becomes passive, his speech laconic.[193]   Now, in stark contrast to the Dialogues, he will be quiet.

But this silence need not be construed as cowering capitulation. Rather, in terms of the narrative development, it can symbolize Job's renewed resolve.   In the previous discourses among the human interlocutors, each had managed to present his own perspective, whether that of religious tradition or personal experience, without actually engaging the other in a true dialogue; effectively talking past each other, no significant communication had occurred.[194]   In his reply to Yahweh, though, Job relinquishes this ineffectual approach. Foregoing any boisterous debate, he chooses instead the way of quiet consideration.   From the former exteriority of public controversy about divine justice in the world, he moves now toward the interiority of personal contemplation of the divinity and the cosmos as they are made present to him.

This religious silence can be explained, in Ricoeur's terms, as a "pre-ethical" listening: "It is a mode of being which is not yet a mode of doing, and for this reason it escapes the alternatives of submission and revolt."[195]   Understood thus, Job's reaction need not be considered a "giving in" to the superior strength of divine pressure.   Rather, it can be interpreted as a "receiving from" the theophanic revelation of divine wisdom.   In this sense it represents the phenomenological equivalent of a "hearing which understands":

> Not only is hearing existentially prior to obeying, but keeping silent precedes speaking.   To keep silent is not the same as to be dumb, however.   To keep silent is to let things be said by others.   Silence opens a space for hearing.[196]

And what Job hears is the hearkening of divine wisdom.

Consequently, Job's silence can be read as symbolizing a certain sapiential sophistication.   By placing his hand over his mouth, he clamps shut the medium of critical complaint which was operative in

---

[193] PATRICK/SCULT, *Rhetoric and Biblical Interpretation*, 101:   "Job's compact, cryptic utterances hint at a profound change in his soul, a 'shaking of the foundations' of mystic proportions."

[194] FOHRER, "Dialog und Kommunikation," 135-146 (esp. 138-141).

[195] RICOEUR, "Religion, Atheism, Faith," 71.

[196] RICOEUR, "Religion, Atheism, Faith," 73-74.

the immediacy of a contemplative experience.[197] On the basis of such an experience, Job will be impelled to speak anew.[198]

Emboldened by his silent insightfulness,[199] Job utters his conclusive response. Not having been asked a direct question, his words ring with the decisiveness of an outright affirmation: "Therefore, I despise yet repent of dust and ash" (42:6). Both paradoxical and ambiguous, these words can nevertheless make sense in light of Ricoeur's phenomenology of "metaphorical" language. Reflecting the process of cognition, imagination and feeling proper to such language, this climactic verse can be interpreted as a "meaningful self-contradictory attribution."[200] Specifically, its metaphorical significance becomes clear in light of the figurative functioning of the narrative as a whole.[201]

As Ricoeur has theorized, metaphoricity represents that strategy by which poetic discourse "grasps together" what, taken literally, would be at best impertinent and at worst absurd. Proceeding from the

---

[197] Cf. A. VERGOTE, "Experience of the Divine, Experience of God," *God: Experience or Origin?* (eds. A. DE NICHOLAS and E. MOUTSOPOULOS) (New York 1985) 77-90 and CRENSHAW, "The Acquisition of Knowledge," 245-252.

[198] WESTERMANN, *The Structure of the Book of Job*, 125: "Job 40:4-5 is not, strictly speaking, an answer; it is an act of silencing which precedes the answer itself. It is against the background of this act of silencing that the answer itself in 42:2-6 stands." Cf. RICOEUR, "The Language of Faith," 231: "We are in quest of a language which would be appropriate to the kind of *imagination* which expresses most characteristic existential possibilities. Yes, it is necessary *to say*; it is this opening of human possibility, this *attempt* of my projects by which I advance toward my being."

[199] Cf. A.M. OLSON, "The *Silence* of Job as the Key to the Text," *Semeia* 19 (1981) 113-119.

[200] RICOEUR, "Parole et symbole," 146: "Ainsi la métaphore n'existe pas en elle-même, mais dans une interprétation. L'interprétation métaphorique présuppose une interprétation littérale qui se détruit. L'interprétation métaphorique consiste à transformer une contradiction, qui se détruit elle-même, dans une contradiction signifiante. C'est cette transformation qui impose au mot une sorte de 'torsion': nous sommes contraints de donner une signification nouvelle au mot, une extension de sens, grâce à quoi nous pouvons 'faire sense', là où l'interprétation littérale est proprement in-sensée. Ainsi la métaphore apparaît comme la riposte à une certaine inconsistance de l'énoncé interprété littéralement."

[201] RICOEUR, "Biblical Hermeneutics," 94: "Fictional narratives seem to constitute a distinctive class of metaphorical processes. The bearers of the metaphor are not the individual sentences of the narratives, but the whole structure, the narratives as a whole, what Aristotle had called the *mythos* in the poem."

As Ricoeur has theorized, metaphoricity represents that strategy by which poetic discourse "grasps together" what, taken literally, would be at best impertinent and at worst absurd. Proceeding from the tension maintained between two otherwise incompatible terms,[202] such "figurative" statements consist of an imaginative *rapprochement* between logically distant or even contradictory semantic fields.[203] On a narrative level, this rapprochement appears in the creative emplotment by which the author synthesizes what would otherwise be heterogeneous aspects of the tale. As Ricoeur explains,

> To tell a story is to emplot events in such a way that we grasp as a whole the series of episodes which has led the characters of the story from this initial situation to that terminal situation through a certain number of turns of fortune, of peripeties, and recognitions .... That some new insight is conveyed by the art of storytelling cannot be doubted.[204]

In the imaginative schema proper to the Joban narrative, the new insight appears in the protagonist's radical change of stance, one that clashes abruptly with his previous characterization. Given the embittered figure of chapters 3-31, recognized as justifiable in all but his Friends' eyes, to "despise" would be quite appropriate, but to "repent" is patently absurd — taken literally, it constitutes an overt contradiction to Job's otherwise established integrity.

Yet "repent" he does, and with this poetic twist the figurative force of the narrative comes to light. More than a pious ornamentation or skeptical degradation, the repentant mode in which Job concludes his discourse reflects a *cognitive* innovation. Corresponding to the poetic

---

[202] This emphasis on predicative "tension" distinguishes Ricoeur's theory of metaphoricity from the "substitutive" approaches of classical rhetoric. Applied to the Book of Job, the maintenance of tension in Job's response obviates any "ironic" interpretation inasmuch as irony intends a "sacrifice" of meaning in the recognition "that ... 'some statements cannot be understood without rejecting what they seem to say,' that is, without taking their words to mean something else than what they seem to say, a something which undercuts their apparent meaning" (JANZEN, citing Wayne Booth, in *Job*, 17).

[203] RICOEUR, "The Function of Fiction in Shaping Reality," 130-131.

[204] P. RICOEUR, "The Biblical Worldview and Philosophy," *NICM Journal* 6,3 (1981) 96.

power of over-signification,[205] the image of a repentant Job contributes to the narrative's "invention" of meaning, for

> The metaphorical process and the narrative composition are similar ways of imitating reality by narrating it at a mythical level of discourse. In both cases, fiction and redescription go hand in hand. In both cases it is the heuristic fiction that bears the function of discovery.[206]

What is discovered by Job is a new pertinence in spite of impertinence, and with this narrative innovation a new congruence is conferred upon the various theo-linguistic episodes of this story. Given the disparate modes of speech about God heretofore narrated, the rightfulness of which is affirmed only in the case of Job, the final statement of the main character can be "read as" the invention of meaning proper to this wisdom tale.[207] Taken metaphorically, his last words exhibit the definitive outcome of his now fulfilled integrity.

This cognitive claim brings with it an *affective* transformation, one that corresponds to the strategy by which metaphorical statements and fictional narratives innovate meaning.[208] Understood here in terms

---

[205] RICOEUR, "The Biblical Worldview and Philosophy," 96: "The clash of meanings, which should normally shatter the assertion which contains such incompatible terms, generates, within the specific context of a poem, a new insight instead of sheer absurdity. Poetic usage of language makes absurdity signify, or rather *oversignify*. ... Metaphor is one of the strategies thanks to which language is compelled to transgress its previous limits and becomes able to bring to language the not yet said, the still unsaid."

[206] RICOEUR, "The Biblical Worldview and Philosophy," 99; cf. "The Function of Fiction in Shaping Reality," 129.

[207] RICOEUR often refers to the "as if" character of metaphor: "Dans la *Métaphore vive*, je me suis risqué à parler non seulement de sens métaphorique, mais de référence métaphorique, pour dire ce pouvoir de l'énoncé métaphorique de re-configurer une réalité inaccessible à la description directe. J'ai même suggéré de fair du 'voir comme'..., à quoi se résume le pouvoir de la métaphore, le révélateur d'un 'être-comme'..., au niveau ontologique le plus radical" ("Poétique et symbolique," 61). In our extension of this analysis to a narrative, the "reading as" which founds interpretation can stand in an intermediary position between this "seeing as" and "being as."

[208] Cf. RICOEUR, *The Rule of Metaphor*, 41: "Considered from a functional point of view, imitation constitutes a unitary whole in which mythic elevation, displacement of language by metaphor, and the purging of feelings of fear and pity work side by side."

of thought assimilated, the "feeling" dimension in poetic language encompasses more than simple sensation or pure subjectivity:

> It is a process of interiorization succeeding a movement of intentional transcendence directed toward some objective state of affairs. To *feel*, in the emotional sense of the word, is to make *ours* what has been put at a distance by thought in its objectifying phase. Feelings, therefore, have a very complex kind of intentionality. They are not merely inner states but interiorized thoughts. ... Feeling is not contrary to thought. It is thought made ours.[209]

The thought which Job makes his own derives specifically from his visionary experience of Yahweh in the voice from the storm. Moved no longer by the sacrificial fear with which he was invested in the Prologue, nor by the intellectual rage with which he was consumed in the Dialogues, the Job of the Theologue has experienced the nearness of the divinity, and this spiritual encounter engenders a new way of being attuned to the state of affairs in this human life.[210] Given the silence with which Job exits from the discursive scene and returns to the pursuit of religious supplication, his repentance ultimately suggests the self-assimilation of meaningfulness — taken poetically, it enacts his newfound sense of "belonging" in the world.

Job's Originary Affirmation

Job's second response brings the divine-human encounter in the Theologue to its conclusion, and with it the movement of the book reaches a critical juncture. As poetic ploys by means of which the author conveys his message, Job's symbolic silence and metaphorical repentance contribute to the "positive insight" of the narrative.[211] That

---

[209] RICOEUR, "The Metaphorical Process," 154.

[210] RICOEUR, "The Metaphorical Process," 156: "... feelings have *ontological* bearing, (for) they are ways of 'being-there,' of 'finding' ourselves within the world, ... Because of feelings we are 'attuned to' aspects of reality which cannot be expressed in terms of the objects referred to in ordinary language."

[211] RICOEUR, "The Metaphorical Process," 152-153: "It is in fiction that the 'absence' proper to the power of suspending what we call 'reality' in ordinary language concretely coalesces and fuses with the *positive insight* into the potentialities of our being in the world which our everyday transactions with manipulatable objects tend to conceal."

message, as we interpret it in the terminology of Ricoeur's phenomen-ological hermeneutics, involves an "originary affirmation" in the domain of wisdom's quest for meaning. In this understanding, Job's concluding words can be read as proceeding from the "second naïveté" of silent "reflection" and as giving expression to a "passion for the possible" by way of repentant "divestment."

Though he says little in the Theologue, Job's interventions nevertheless suggest the response of one who has undertaken to *reflect* upon and interpret the divine discourses spoken in his regard. What is clearly at stake in the divine-human dialogue is the existential position of this (and every) human as a thinking being. Faced with the tempestuous grandeur of cosmic creation, Job acknowledges his comparative smallness in the theo-linguistic arena and assumes the child-like stance of one who knows to keep quiet (40:4-5).[212] In this first response he admits to no immediate intuition which could be exchanged summarily for his previous questioning. Yet he does seem to recognize that in this discursive engagement with Yahweh lies the potential for the sapiential resolution of his existential concerns. His reticence, then, is not so much the result of being dumbfounded as that of being held spellbound in the power of the divine words, the "appropriation" of which will henceforth direct his "effort to exist and desire to be."

In effect, Job's uncharacteristic reserve can be likened to what Ricoeur calls a *second naïveté*,[213] the choice in favor of which distinguishes his comportment in the Theologue. Read not in terms of skeptical frustration but as "a critically mediated attitude of expectation toward the reality-claims of religious faith,"[214] Job's deliberate deci-

---

[212] Cf. P. RICOEUR, "Le conflit des herméneutiques: épistémologie des interpréta-tions," *CISymb* 1,1 (1963) 184: "Comme des enfants, non point retour à l'infantilisme, mais nous entrons, je dirai presque, nous entrons dans la symbolique lorsque nous avons notre mort derrière nous et notre enfance devant nous. C'est dans cet échange de la naissance et de la mort que la symbolique s'accomplit. ... L'herméneutique s'arrête; nous laissons parler les symboles. C'est sur ce retour au silence que je voudrais terminer, mais un silence, si vous voulez, qui ne soit plus absence de parole mais véritablement parole de la parole elle-même."

[213] On the Ricoeurian notion of a "second naïveté," cf. *The Symbolism of Evil*, 347-357, and "Manifestation et proclamation," 70-76.

[214] This definition is proffered by M. WALLACE *The Second Naiveté: Barth, Ricoeur, and the New Yale Theology* (Studies in American Biblical Hermeneutics, 6; Macon, GA 1990) xiii.

sion to be silent makes allowance for an epistemological enrichment whose immediacy is characteristic of wisdom in its religious tenor.[215] And thus does he begin to close his own, personal circle of interpretation.[216] Gyrating through the primitive immediacy of belief in the Prologue and the experiential reality of doubt in the Dialogues, Job's quest for comprehension turns now on the revelation of the divine discourses, where "listening to the word is not possible without a conversion of the values of the *tremendum* and the *fascinosum* into obedience and fervor."[217] In this way the reticence of Job's first reply actually opens the way for his forthcoming affirmation.

In his second intervention, Job's words give testimony to the religious event which undergirds his sapiential position; in phenomenological terms, his statement in the last chapter expresses an intellectual *divestment* in response to his discursive engagement with Yahweh in the speeches from the storm.[218] Commencing in 42:2-3, where Job acknowledges the finitude of his own consciousness by admitting that prior to his encounter with Yahweh wisdom had been "wondrously far from me," this divestment culminates in the affirmation of 42:4-6.[219] Announced with a decisive boldness which flies in the face of otherwise

---

[215] L. DORNISCH, "Symbolic Systems and the Interpretation of Scripture," *Semeia* 4 (1975) 16: "... this enriched experiencing may not be called knowledge by the philosopher or the scientist, but it belongs to the long-standing traditions of wisdom and intuitive thought elaborated by the Wisdom tradition of the Jewish scriptures, ..."

[216] On the relation between "second naïveté" and "the hermeneutical circle," see RICOEUR, "The Symbol ... Food for Thought," 203-205.

[217] RICOEUR, "Manifestation et proclamation, 74: "Une parole qui nous est adressée plutôt que nous ne la parlons, une parole qui nous constitue plutôt que nous ne l'articulons — une 'parole qui parle' — ne réaffirme-t-elle pas le sacré autant qu'elle l'abolit? Cela est si vrai que l'écoute de la parole n'est pas possible sans une conversion des valeurs du *tremendum* et du *fascinosum* en obéissance et en ferveur. Je ne conçois pas, pour ma part, d'attitude religieuse qui ne procède pas d'abord du 'sentiment de dépendance absolue'."

[218] Ricoeur adopts the term "divestment" (*dépouillement*) from J. NABERT, *Le désir de Dieu* (Paris 1966), book III: "Métaphysique du témoignage et herméneutique de l'absolu."

[219] RICOEUR, "The Hermeneutics of Testimony," 149: "The hermeneutical structure of original affirmation is a corollary of the finitude of human consciousness in which and by means of which the original affirmation is produced."

expected dread (42:4; cf. 9:17-19),[220] and based on the surety of his contemplative insight (42:5),[221] Job performs here the speech-act by which he "accomplishes the negation of the limitations which affect individual destiny ... when it has renounced all the objectifications that understanding imposes."[222] He "*despise(s) yet repent(s) of dust and ash*" (42:6).

The tensional duality proclaimed in this verse encapsulates the development of the narrative as Job moves from cognitive dissonance to existential consonance.[223] What occasions the attestation of the latter is not, however, any inference or deduction in the rational order.[224] Instead, it proceeds from an absurd logic — that of hope — which, in contrast to retributive thinking, "means the 'super-abundance' of meaning as opposed to the abundance of senselessness, of failure and of destruction."[225] On the basis of this more poetic logic, Job's final statement eclipses the realm of everyday reality and projects a new mode of being-in-the-world. It attests to a new level of meaningfulness that originates in, and is sustained by, spiritual experience. Because of his encounter with Yahweh, Job can "*despise yet repent of dust and ash,*" thereby affirming that "hope makes of

---

[220] Cf. P. RICOEUR, *Freedom and Nature:* The Voluntary and the Involuntary (Evanston 1966) 279: "The dread of a terrifying encounter is covertly reinforced by the fear which feeds on fabulous expectations. ... In this sense it is the inverse of boldness whose object is difficulty. Now if boldness lives on hope, that is, on acute expectation of the end which it proposes to attain in spite of difficulties which would evoke nothing but fear and hopelessness if considered in themselves, fear would outweigh it in case of the man who, being too preoccupied with himself, marks his place in life and its good with an avarice which makes him incapable of great tasks."

[221] RICOEUR, *The Symbolism of Evil*, 321: "... the contemplation of the whole initiates a movement which must be completed practically by the surrender of a claim, by the sacrifice of the demand that was at the beginning of the recrimination, namely, the claim to form by oneself a little island of meaning in the universe, an empire within an empire."

[222] RICOEUR, "The Hermeneutics of Testimony," 120.

[223] Cf. J. SOUTHWICK, "Job: An Exemplar for All Ages," *Encounter* 45 (1984) 390: "Cognitive dissonance is not only possible, but can be creatively profitable. The capability of holding together two contrary things enables us to understand our integrity, to allow this understanding to mingle with the truths and knowledge inherent in our inner being ..., and to bring forth new modes of creativity."

[224] RICOEUR, "The Hermeneutics of Testimony," 150: "To attest is of a different order than to verify in the sense of logical empiricism."

[225] RICOEUR, "Hope and the Structure of Philosophical Systems," 58.

freedom the *passion for the possible* against the sad meditation on the irrevocable."[226]

Thus, with his expression of hope-filled divestment, Job has traversed the path of wisdom: through an asceticism more intellectual than moral,[227] he has passed from self-conscious reflection to originary affirmation.[228] In the dialogic event of the Theologue, his existential "wandering" has reached its sapiential destination,[229] for in and through the Yahweh-speeches, Job has been able to experience something of the absolute,[230] to apprehend something of the divine,[231] to actualize something of freedom.[232] With his final words, then, the hermeneutical circle of his narrative life takes on a new and lasting dimension: having professed faith in a providential God, he seeks to understand the reasons for adversity; having understood the travesty of retributive thinking, he hopes in something more; having hoped, he understands anew the majesty of the created design.

---

[226] RICOEUR, "Hope and the Structure of Philosophical Systems," 58 [*emphasis added*]. Concerning the notion of "a passion for the possible" as the telltale mark of Ricoeur's theological hermeneutics, see K. VANHOOZER, *Biblical Narrative in the Philosophy of Paul Ricoeur: A Study in Hermeneutics and Theology* (Cambridge 1990) 3-16.

[227] Cf. COX, "Structure and Function of the Final Challenge," 67.

[228] For RICOEUR it is this movement which makes sense of the problem of testimony ("The Hermeneutics of Testimony," 119-120).

[229] Cf. RICOEUR, *History and Truth*, 324-328.

[230] RICOEUR, "The Hermeneutics of Testimony," 120: "It is by this 'divestment' that reflection is brought to the encounter with contingent signs that the absolute, in its generosity, allows to appear of itself."

[231] NABERT, *Le désir de Dieu*, 267: "For the apprehension of the divine, the divestment (*dépouillement*) essential for mystical experience and the link of the divine to a historic manifestation are mutually complementary" (cited in RICOEUR, "The Hermeneutics of Testimony," 148).

[232] While acknowledging that "human action makes sense because we may discern in some places adequation between rationality and reality," RICOEUR goes on to affirm that "there is something broken in the very heart of human action which prevents our partial experience of fulfilled achievements from equating the whole field of human action." In his opinion, "It is that breach, that brokenness, which is denied by the Hegelian claim to absolute knowledge and its bold extension from partial rationality to total rationality" ("Hope and the Structure of Philosophical Systems," 62-63). We might say that this same breach is also denied by the Job of the Dialogues, who demanded a trial based on the notion of judicial equity; in turn, the Job who "despise(s) yet repent(s)" in the Theologue re-establishes the duality of fulfilled achievement and unfulfilled claim.

Job's encounter with the divine thereby brings this circle to its close, and with it the tale will also conclude — the repentant Job has become a sage.

Chapter Five

JOB: THE "ICON" OF A SAGE

In order to complete the process of interpretation, according to the phenomenological hermeneutics of Ricoeur, an "appropriation" of the truth of a narrative is necessary. With a transposition from the sense of the written work to its reference, this last stage seeks to understand the "world of the text" so as to make possible a renewed understanding of the "world of the reader." Thus, in order to complete our interpretive itinerary with regard to Job's "repentance," we return once again to the theo-linguistic plot of the book as a whole.

Having considered the creative manner with which the poet has composed the tale (chapter two), and having individualized the key texts in which the narrative reaches its paradoxical resolution (chapters three and four), we can now attempt to delineate the possible horizon of meaning proposed in and by Job's final utterances. His words in response to Yahweh bespeak a transformation from rational discordance to existential concordance, a newfound state of being for Job which is given approbation by the events narrated in the Epilogue. From this twofold resolution, it may be suggested that the "world of the text" of the Book of Job concerns the acquisition of wisdom on the part of a sage.

In order to explicate this thesis, we will propose that the words of Job in the Theologue reflect a "contemplative consciousness" consonant with his mystical vision of Yahweh in the words from the storm. By virtue of this spiritual experience, Job does acquire wisdom, and the particularity of this narrative resolution marks the unique contribution of the Book of Job to the world of biblical wisdom literature. Read in light of the Ricoeur's notion of "iconic augmentation," the distinctive characterization of Job testifies to what it means to be a sage, and therein lies the potential for renewal in the world of theology today.

CONTEMPLATIVE CONSCIOUSNESS

Within this tale of theo-linguistics, the search for proper speech about God has passed from the language of a-critical faith in the Prologue to that of questioning controversy in the Dialogues. Yet only *after* the silence and repentance of Job in the Theologue does Yahweh affirm in the Epilogue that the protagonist has spoken "rightly" (Job 42:7). Consequently, the experience of Job narrated in chapters 38-41 serves as the locus of his sapiential transformation. In this context, Job's repentance attests to a new mode of awareness, a "contemplative consciousness" which results from his "mystical" vision of Yahweh in the words from the storm.

A "Mystical" Life-Story

To suggest that Job's final words be read in terms of mysticism tends to arouse suspicion since it entails a series of interpretive difficulties. In the first place, reference to mystical experience smacks of vagueness, irrationality and eccentricity; consequently, emphasis on the event of the Joban theophany, apart from the poetic content of the divine discourses, would not be susceptible to critical reflection.[1] Further, mysticism often implies a "oneness" of God and man that tends to obliterate individuality; in the case of Job this simply would not apply.[2] Finally, and perhaps most significant, a mystical interpretation threatens to demean the literary artistry of the book as a whole; recourse to such a "non-intellectual" solution belies the energic efforts of the poet in his advanced illumination of the cognitive confrontation

---

[1] WHARTON, "The Unanswerable Answer," 55: "What is described here is something altogether different from warm feelings of the pious heart, or the mystic's 'beatific vision,' or soulful intimations of transcendence."

[2] FOHRER, *Das Buch Hiob*, p. 535, n. 6: "So ist die Erfahrung auch nicht mystisches Einswerden; Gott bleibt Gott, Mensch bleibt Mensch."

between experience and tradition.[3] Nonetheless, despite this critical hesitancy, we maintain that the interpretation of Job's final words as the expression of a mystical experience can be justified as reflecting the trans-intellectual consciousness of a new world of meaning given in the context of his sapiential life-quest.

Among contemporary studies on the interpretation of religious experience, the contemplative dimension of human knowing is considered to pertain to the existential, rather than simply the intellectual, domain. In this context, the particular experience which qualifies as "mystical" has been defined as a "pure 'consciousness-of' something so powerfully meaningful and valuable to the person involved that that person is radically transformed by that experience"; through such an event the person involved comes to "a vivid experiential realization of that into which one fits as a cognizing, valuing, existing individual."[4] Reference to a mystical experience, therefore, does not represent a phenomenon detached from actual existence but connotes, instead, a new and enduring chapter in the story of one's life.[5] As such, what is intended by Job's "seeing" Yahweh is not necessarily out of character with a life in pursuit of wisdom. To the contrary, such an experience both corresponds to and completes the "spiritual journey" being narrated in this sacred tale.[6]

Recalling the narrative characterization provided by the prose framework, a superior spiritual experience would be fully consistent with Job's pious integrity. Presented in the Prologue as "blameless and upright, one who fears God and shuns evil" (1:1,8; 2:3), Job is

---

[3] TSEVAT, *The Meaning of the Book of Job*, 11: "Is it conceivable that the author invested this stupendous intellectual energy in the question only to seek, receive, and transmit the whole solution on a non-intellectual level?"

[4] S.B. KING, "Two Epistemological Models for the Interpretation of Mysticism," *JAAR* 56 (1988) 273, 275.

[5] J. KRISTO, "The Interpretation of Religious Experience: What Do Mystics Intend When They Talk about Their Experiences?" *JRel* 62 (1982) 22: "The story (of a person) is a story of broadening of horizons, and mystical experience is a moment in a personal story with a specific horizon."

[6] WILLIAMS, "Deciphering the Unspoken," 63; cf. W. VOGELS, "The Spiritual Growth of Job: A Psychological Approach to the Book of Job," *BTB* 11 (1981) 77-80.

depicted as an archetypal paragon of wisdom.[7] For one so legendary, intense religiosity is not at all extraneous to daily life: his is the custom of offering preemptive sacrifices in favor of his children (1:5), and even amid news of disaster he does not fail to worship (1:20-21). So, too, theological lucidity is part and parcel of Job's character, as he sees through the folly of his wife's suggestion that he curse the God who stands at the origin of his undeserved sufferings (2:9-10).

This depth of religious integrity, particularly as it is concerned with truthful speech,[8] carries Job through the Dialogues. There he repeatedly calls into question the inimical vision of God in his regard (7:17-19), but his lamentation pertains to the greater whole of a devoted yearning to encounter this apparently distant God. The notion of "seeing" God then becomes the ground of Job's hope as an abeyant expectation (cf. 16:18-22; 18:3; 19:25-27).[9] Ardently awaited by the reader as well, the appearance of God is geared to bring some resolution to this enigmatic narrative.

Nevertheless, Job's actual experience of "seeing" God is limited to the Theologue. There his quest for a divine-human dialogue is fulfilled, though not at all as he had foreseen it (cf. 9:16; 13:22; 14:15). Read against the literary background of Old Testament theophanies, Job's encounter with the voice from the storm pertains not to the forum of decisive judicial proceedings but instead to the realm of perceptive religious experiences.[10] As such, the manifestation of the divine presence becomes the point of origin for Job's novel learning.[11]

---

[7] WEISS, *The Story of Job's Beginning*, 25: "The four expressions are common terms in the doctrine of the Wisdom school: by defining Job as possessing these four characteristics, the story defines him as having those attributes which are desirable according to the Wisdom ideal."

[8] Cf. PENCHANSKY, *The Betrayal of God*, 44-51.

[9] LÉVÊQUE, *Job et son Dieu*, 449-497.

[10] Cf. VERGOTE, "Experience of the Divine, Experience of God," 79: "If there is religious experience, it occurs within the framework of the symbolic religious systems which present the supernatural being with such suggestive power that it acquires the quality of supreme reality."

[11] Cf. GUTIÉRREZ, *On Job*, 91: "Job has learned from the Lord that the language the prophets use in speaking of God must be supplemented by the language of contemplation and worship. The point of origin for both languages is not so much a doctrine as a presence."

Yet the fullness of this theophanic event resounds in the actual words of the divine discourse.   There a poetic panorama of cosmic forces offers Job a new perspective on life.   It thrusts him into a mysterious world of meaning and inculcates a unifying interconnectedness of things under the ultimate ordering power of the Creator.   In such a world, Job's language takes on a correspondingly new tone.

The Theo-Linguistic Resolution

By means of the theophanic revelation, Job is transported into a new world of meaning, a wondrous world in which encounter with mysteries to be contemplated supersedes the investigation of problems to be solved.[12]   In direct response to the poetic discourse of Yahweh, Job can take up once again his theological ruminations, purposely stifled since the apologetic oath which concludes the Dialogues (chap. 31).   Even more so, he resumes his unique ability to speak not only about but *to* God.[13]   Yet the words which Job adopts here differ dramatically from the language of doubt and interrogation prevalent in the Dialogues.   Replete with paradox, the sparsity of his speech yet depth of his response bespeak that passivity and totality which can characterize a mystical experience.[14]   In this respect, the interplay of Job's sudden silence and vivid vision and repentant renunciation becomes an indicator of the workings of a contemplative consciousness.

Job's initial response, in answer to the leading sapiential question posed by Yahweh in 40:2, is to invoke the power of silence (40:4-5).

---

[12] Cox, *Man's Anger and God's Silence*, 98: "By a simple stroke of the divine artist's brush Job stands revealed as one who is incapable of fathoming the mysteries of nature and of coping with the seeming chaos of creation.   But he is also one who is capable of *contemplating* this fact."   Cf. N.P. HARVEY, "Revelation and Contemplation," *NB* 72 (1991) 156: "What is at stake might be described as a choice between remaining problem-centered, which is a recipe for sterility, or opting for mystery-encountering."

[13] PATRICK, "Job's Address of God," 277: "The first thing of note is that Job *does* address God in these responses.   He had lost his ability to pray in the course of the dialog, but Yahweh's speaking revives it.   Job clearly takes Yahweh's addresses to him as reason to return to divine-human dialog.   The enmity between them has been overcome."

[14] Cf. M.A. MCPHERSON OLIVER, "Mystical Experience and the Literary Technique of Silence," *StMyst* 1,1 (1978) 5-20; J. WEISMAYER, "Was ist Mystik?   Zum Verständnis von Glaube und religiöser Erfahrung," *GeistL* 61 (1988) 348-358.

Yet, as we have suggested, this self-imposed silence is not simply the result of fateful fright; rather, it reflects a willingness to listen to the "visible words" of divine revelation in Yahweh's poetic creation theology.[15] With an openness to the divine that intimates sapiential sophistication, Job participates in an encounter with the bearer of truth and meaning, and in this watershed moment lies the genesis of his ultimate stance.

The understanding which grounds the concluding response of 42:2-6 comes to Job by way of a new mode of learning — "seeing" as distinct from "hearing." Characterized as something experiential, personal, and immediate, Job's "seeing" of God constitutes a particular manner of acquiring knowledge. Consistent with the tradition of spiritual encounters recorded in the Psalms, the theophanic dialogue engenders a new mode of understanding for Job, a means of insightfulness which brings his sapiential quest to its culmination.[16] By means of what may be called an "appreciative awareness," Job's knowledge of God and the world is enriched beyond that which reason alone makes possible.[17] In his apprehension of the transcendent, Job reaches a new epistemological consciousness;[18] by his contemplation of the

---

[15] Cf. T.E. FRETHEIM, *The Suffering of God:* An Old Testament Perspective (OBT, 14; Philadelphia 1984) 79: "God's Word is thereby embodied, made visible, enabling a knowing, a becoming, a convincing, and a living that would not otherwise be possible."

[16] J. LUYTEN, "Psalm 73 and Wisdom," *La Sagesse de l'Ancien Testament* (ed. M. GILBERT) (BETL, 51; Leuven 1979) 77: "The visit to the temple (in Ps 73:17) has evidently the same function as the theophany in *Job*, 38,1. Where reason halts, faith continues. The speaker of *Ps.*, 73 learns to recognize the real state of affairs through a deeper contact with God." Cf. M. SMITH, "'Seeing God' in the Psalms: The Background to the Beatific Vision in the Hebrew Bible," *CBQ* 50 (1988) 171-183.

[17] J.J. MUELLER, "Appreciative Awareness: The Feeling-Dimension in Religious Experience," *TS* 45 (1984) 62: "With this [appreciative] mode, categories at hand fail to exhaust the meaning of the datum, and what is being attended to in experience cannot be reduced to some structure already known and defined. This mode of consciousness entails an 'intellectual humility' to what one knows and clarifies, a 'wonder' toward reality, 'reverence,' or simply 'open awareness.' Whatever one prefers to call it, such an attitude is essential to the orientation of the mind."

[18] M. HUNTINGTON, "Mysticism and the Limits of Language," *Language in Religion* (eds. H. TONKIN and A. ARMSTRONG) (Lanham 1989) 38: "... the failure to experience transcendence is a direct consequence of the dominance of thought to the detriment of apprehension. ... On the epistemological level with which we are concerned, true knowledge is the immediate experience, the direct apprehension of reality."

mysterious, he enters a new existential relation.[19] And along with the personal knowledge gained from this visionary experience, the "transvaluation" of his life takes place.[20]

Based on the orientation provided by his contemplative consciousness, the change in Job comes to poetic expression in the metaphorical language of "repentance." Rooted in the phenomenon of inter-personal relations, this language serves Job as a means of trying to reverse the inadequacy of his wisdom-less pronouncements. Yet, the real change in stance effected here does not pertain to the ethos of penitential return, as commonly understood. Rather, as a result of having encountered his God, Job affirms his theological convictions in a statement whose tensional duality summarizes the wisdom thematic of the tale: "Therefore I despise yet repent (concerning) the dust and ash (of human existence as it appears in this chaotic world)." Cognitive dissonance is here displaced by existential consonance, and Job need speak no more.

That Job's newfound understanding be grounded on a mystical experience need not, however, be considered something non-intellectual and thereby inappropriate to the pursuit of wisdom. To the contrary, the phenomenon represented in Job's "seeing" is trans-intellectual, one that brings his sapiential discernment beyond mere reflection to its very summit. At this poetic height, the imaginative declarations of the divine discourse proffer a unique epistemological ambience, a new world of givenness. There, consciousness of the harmonious interrelationship of God, world, and self occurs not by way of the mediating filters of the reasoning process but via the optic fibers of the mind's inner eye. There, the extraordinariness of Job's experience radiates a certain lucidity which surpasses the exact logic of rhetorical argumenta-

---

[19] Cf. J. McKechnie, *Job: Moral Hero, Religious Egoist and Mystic* (New York 1927) 135: "Life is wider and wiser than reason. Life overleaps difficulties which reason cannot remove. When we relate ourselves to God with part of our being — as thinkers — He may seem impersonal; when we relate ourselves to Him with our whole being — as worshippers — He invariably beams upon us as personal. If then God is impersonal, there is no resisting the conclusion — paradoxical though it may be — that we can establish personal relations with the impersonal. Religious experience does more than prove the possibility of such relations; it proves that when man finds God such relations invariably come into being. Into Job's search for God the sustained passion of his being entered; it is certain that the God he found was a personal God."

[20] Crenshaw, "The Acquisition of Knowledge," 251.

tion. There, Job realizes with clarity his existential conviction, one which may not be considered an objective resolution but which nevertheless yields a certainty that is beyond deception. Sustained by the transcendent transformation effected by this theophanic encounter,[21] Job has been empowered to make a cognitive and volitional investment in the wisdom offered to him.[22] He has come to his sapiential destination, and with this mystically-based wisdom, his religion has reached its ultimate stage.[23]

WORLD OF WISDOM

In terms of the development of religious thought, most scholars readily assign the Book of Job to a place within the literary and theological world of "wisdom" literature.[24] A brief consideration of the intellectual perspective and thematic principles of this tradition will allow us to highlight the distinctiveness of Job's story in comparison with similar works in the Old Testament and from the Ancient Near East. We will then be in a position to suggest that the world proposed by the text of Job, particularly in the words of 40:4-5 and 42:2-6, is the world of wisdom, a world which can be fully appreciated only

---

[21] HARVEY, "Revelation and Contemplation," 157: "If revelation is the showing-forth or unveiling of the transcendent dimension of all reality then contemplation is the sustaining of that perspective, that sense indivisibly of the otherness of God and the glory of the universe."

[22] KRISTO, "The Interpretation of Religious Experience," 28: "There is an intimate interplay between these two modalities of human experience (i.e., between the 'insighting the truthfulness' of something for life and 'giving one's heart' to it). ... This is not an exclusive domain either of the intellect or of the will; it is the seeing of a person, which means that all available forces are engaged."

[23] According to G. SCHOLEM, *Major Trends in Jewish Mysticism* (Jerusalem 1941), the ultimate stage of monotheistic religion entails the experience of bridging the gap between the divine and the human "by evolving new means of communion and re-establishing unity between man and his Maker" (p. 10).

[24] Cf. R.N. WHYBRAY, *The Intellectual Tradition in the Old Testament* (BZAW, 135; Berlin 1974), 61-70, who excludes Job from the "wisdom" current. This author also cites others who do not classify the Book of Job as "wisdom": WESTERMANN and WEISER, who label it a "lamentation"; RICHTER, who emphasizes the "forensic" element; HUMBERT, who points to the "individual" character of the tale; and POPE, who claims that the book is *"sui generis."*

through the paradoxical interplay of rational engagement and mystical detachment.

The Literary-Theological Environment

While precise definitions of wisdom are lacking and exact emphases are debated,[25] the governing perspective of this tradition may be described, in simplified terms, as an intellectual listening. With a focus on human experience, on the concrete data observable in the everyday events of living beings in the world, questions are raised primarily with regard to the matter of human understanding rather than knowledge of God,[26] and the answer to such questions comes by way of human reflection rather than divine intervention. Developed most often by observation and analogy, the knowledge thereby acquired is based on reason and directed toward virtue.[27] In sum, learning derives from listening to the experience of life itself and leads to a renewed way of living that life.[28]

The specific character of Israelite wisdom adds a properly religious dimension to this intellectual listening. Devoid of standard reference to the events of salvation history, the biblical writings in this tradition strive to encode the reasoned experience of the sages, whatever their social location may be.[29] But this sapiential quest exhibits both a theological concern and a revelational content. Proceeding by way of the experience of the created world, it seeks the God encountered in that experience as the very source of wisdom; operating within the

---

[25] See the survey in J. CRENSHAW, *Old Testament Wisdom:* An Introduction (Atlanta 1971) 11-25.

[26] According to the thesis of J. CRENSHAW, "Popular Questioning of the Justice of God in Ancient Israel," *ZAW* 82 (1970) 382: "... the question of meaning is more basic than that of God, indeed that biblical man's point of departure was not God but self. In essence, the God question is secondary to self-understanding."

[27] CRENSHAW, "The Acquisition of Knowledge," 247: "But these teachers never forgot that wisdom (hearing) was a stage beyond knowledge (teaching) and that it meant far more than the accumulation of information. Wisdom, the capacity to use information for human good, includes virtue."

[28] R.E. MURPHY, "Israel's Wisdom: A Biblical Model of Salvation," *StMiss* 30 (1981) 39-42.

[29] See the socio-historical discussion in *The Sage in Israel and the Ancient Near East* (eds. J.G. GAMMIE and L.G. PERDUE) (Winona Lake 1990) 95-181.

realm of the rational, it nevertheless includes a faith dimension as it pursues human understanding.[30]

Within this decidedly intellectual perspective, certain themes emerge as principles of wisdom. Primary among these is the notion of "order" and its corollary in "conflict."[31] Observable in nature, the order of the world is postulated as being guaranteed by the presence and activity of the divine,[32] and it is within this realm of "order" that questions regarding justice and injustice arise. Consequently, wisdom becomes the search for truth and meaning in light of the human experiences of prosperity and suffering; its ongoing aim is the promotion of life amid the confines of human finitude.[33] Based on that listening which derives from rational reflection on experience, wisdom entails and enables an active and productive participation in the order of the created world. At the same time, however, wisdom recognizes the limits of its quest. Despite the presupposition of order and propriety,[34] wisdom acknowledges ambiguity and mystery as integral to the

---

[30] For A. DE PURY, "Sagesse et révélation dans l'Ancien Testament," *RTP* 27 (1977) 1-50, wisdom involves the realm of the rational, to the exclusion of any faith relationship; cf. J.J. COLLINS, "The Biblical Precedent for Natural Theology," *JAAR Supplement* 45 (March 1977) 44: "Revelation in the wisdom books is a religious experience but not (or only exceptionally) a direct encounter with a personal God. It is found rather in the depth dimension of the common human experience of the world and of life." However, R. MURPHY rightly argues that wisdom "is more than an 'experience of the world and of life.' It is an experience of the Lord through the world and life" ("Israel's Wisdom," p. 9, n. 7); thus he concludes, in *The Tree of Life:* An Exposition of Biblical Wisdom Literature (Anchor Bible Reference Library; Garden City 1990), that "(w)hatever knowledge ... [humans] have of God is the lifeline to the free and faithful submission that they can make to him" (p. 124).

[31] See L.G. PERDUE, "Cosmology and the Social Order in the Wisdom Tradition," in *The Sage in Israel and the Ancient Near East*, 457-478.

[32] See J.L. CRENSHAW, "In Search of Divine Presence," *RevExp* 74 (1977) 353-369.

[33] R.E. MURPHY, "The Theological Contribution of Israel's Wisdom Literature," *Listening* 19 (1984) 34-39; cf. CRENSHAW, *Old Testament Wisdom*, 19: "thematically, wisdom comprises self-evident intuitions about mastering life for human betterment, groping for life's secrets with regard to innocent suffering, grappling with finitude, and quest for truth concealed in the created order and manifested in Dame Wisdom."

[34] In her recent dissertation, *Control of Reality in Israelite Wisdom* (Duke University, Chapel Hill 1988), E. HUWILER argues that the sages sought not the principle of "order" but perceptional correspondences and distinctions between things and events.

experience of human life and, consequently, as an epistemological datum in the sapiential endeavor.[35]

In the Israelite tradition, these thematic principles assume specifically religious dimensions. The postulate of meaningful order in the cosmos is vested with the cloak of creation theology; co-extensive with the eternity of the creator, the primal order is inserted into the world by Yahweh, and from this foundational position it continues to appeal to persons of reason.[36] Its presence is praised as contiguous with the workings of worldly retribution, yet in its ineffable awesomeness, due to which it cannot be completely known, it remains the object of reverential "fear."[37]

A Unique Contribution

The place of the Book of Job within this tradition may be considered in terms of both general affinities and specific literary parallels. Clearly the intellectual perspective common to the wisdom writings predominates in this biblical tale. By means of exhaustive dialogues, the author gives voice to the observations of human experience and rational reflection upon this experience in comparison with the expectations of tradition; the intellectual "listening" that does or does not take place (cf. 13:6,17; 16:2-3; 21:2-3) thereby moves the "action" of the narrative.[38] Yet this is a specifically religious narrative. Though not bound to the sacral conventions of Israelite history, the Book of Job does establish faith at the basis of reason and centers on the presence of God (assumed, questioned, and narrated) in the human experience of life in the world.

Similarly, the principles valued in the wisdom tradition are in some way present as themes in the Book of Job. What occasions the dialogic reflection is the very search for order in the midst of existential conflict. The suffering of Job becomes the setting for the sapiential

---

[35] O'CONNOR, *The Wisdom Literature*, 19-20.

[36] R.E. MURPHY, "What and Where Is Wisdom?" *CurTM* 4 (1977) 283-287.

[37] Cf. R.E. MURPHY, "Religious Dimensions of Israelite Wisdom," *Ancient Israelite Religion* (FS. Frank Moore Cross; eds. P.D. MILLER, et al.) (Philadelphia 1987) 456: "Although wisdom seems to be taken up with the ordinary, everyday events, it retains its basic relationship to God, and the fear of the Lord is an essential ingredient in this achievement."

[38] Cf. FOHRER, "Dialog und Kommunikation," 135-146.

question of divine justice, and the speeches which constitute the bulk of the story focus on proper human understanding and action in this situation.[39] Yet here, too, mystery is paramount. From the heavenly challenge (unknown on earth), through the probing questions (unanswered by the interlocutors), to the divine nature-poetry (unrelated as it seems), the element of wonder pervades the dramatic movement. Correspondingly, Job's struggle for truth in the midst of ambiguity incorporates the religious dimension of the "fear of the Lord" as the tale proceeds from a "sacrificial" fear in the Prologue, through a gradual loss of fear in the Dialogues, to the return of fear as "awe" in the Theologue (for which "silence" and "repentance" are appropriate characteristics) and the benefits of such religious fear (both spiritual and material) in the Epilogue.

Beyond this correspondence of intellectual perspective and thematic content, the Book of Job gives evidence of a literary affinity with both Old Testament and Ancient Near Eastern texts in the wisdom tradition. In addition to verbal correspondences with other biblical texts,[40] the Book of Job shares a similar structure with the stories of Abraham and Joseph.[41] Specific parallels can be discerned in the sayings on retribution in Proverbs[42] and in the form of lament in the Psalms.[43] In particular, references to "wisdom" and its themes abound in the Book of Job,[44] thereby generating resonance with similar works of the Old Testament.

Nonetheless, the specific form under which the quest for wisdom is narrated in the Book of Job causes it to surpass any Old Testament parallels. In its properly narrative character, as the tale of a heroic

---

[39] PERDUE, *Wisdom in Revolt*, 269: "With its central metaphor of conflict, the book of Job is a narrative journey of a character whose life is a quest for the knowledge of God and the why of human existence. ... In this dramatic rendering of Job's journey, the story becomes the verbalization of the metaphor of struggle." Similarly, COX speaks of "an attitude of contestation" as "essential to the dramatic nature of the *Book of Job* ..." (*Man's Anger and God's Silence*, 126).

[40] These are charted in HARTLEY, *The Book of Job*, 11-12.

[41] R.G. ALBERTSON, "Job and Ancient Near East Wisdom Literature," *Scripture in Context, II:* More Essays on the Comparative Method (eds. W.H. HALLO, J.C. MOYER, and L.G. PERDUE) (Winona Lake 1983) 216-218.

[42] Cf. WHYBRAY, *The Intellectual Tradition*, 61.

[43] Cf. J.S. CUSTER, *The Poetics of Complaint at the Limits of Theology* (PUG dissertation, Roma 1987).

[44] These are given in MURPHY, *The Tree of Life*, 33-35.

human figure placed before the divine, the Book of Job resembles more closely the literary tradition of the Ancient Near East. Its genre, characterization and theme disclose a certain affinity with a wide range of Ancient Near Eastern works,[45] but two texts in particular deserve mention due to the similarity of resolution in the tale.

The first, commonly known as "The Babylonian Theodicy," follows a dialogue form in its treatment of the question of human misery and ends with the invocation of the divinity in the hope of eventual mercy:

> I have gone about the square of my city unobtrusively,
> My voice was not raised, my speech was kept low.
> I did not raise my head, but looked at the ground.
> May the god who has abandoned me give help,
> May the goddess who has (forsaken me) show mercy.[46]

The second text, designated "A Version of the Just Sufferer" (*Ludlul bēl nēmeqi*), also shows a similarity of thought and expression, but its pattern is significantly closer to that of the Book of Job in as much as it also concludes with the affirmation of the protagonist in words attributed to the divinity:

> Thy démarche is worthy of a man. Thy heart is innocent.
> The years are fulfilled, the days have redeemed thy suffering.
> Hadst thou not been called to life, how wouldst thou
>   have come to the end of this serious illness?
> Thou has known anguish, fear in its full extent.
> Until the end hast thou borne thy heavy load.
> The way was blocked; it is open to thee.
> The road is levelled; grace is granted to thee.
> In the future forget not thy god,
> Thy creator when thou hast received thy health.[47]

---

[45] See the conclusion of M. WEINFELD, "Job and Its Mesopotamian Parallels — A Typological Analysis," in *Text and Context* (ed. W. CLAASSEN) (JSOTSup, 48; Sheffield 1988) 225: "What can be stated is that philosophical discussions about individual retribution were common in the ancient Near East in the first millennium BCE and it is even possible that the Arameans (compare the Aramean background of Job) were a dominant factor in the diffusion of this type of literature."

[46] Translation by W.G. LAMBERT, *Babylonian Wisdom Literature* (Oxford 1960) 89.

[47] Quoted in J. GRAY, "The Book of Job in the Context of Near Eastern Literature," *ZAW* 82 (1970) 259.

Here, as in the Book of Job, the direct intervention of God, with the inclusion of a divine decree in favor of the protagonist, affirms the significance of the human character and sanctions the wisdom process adopted by him.[48]

However, notwithstanding these affinities to Old Testament and Ancient Near Eastern literature, the Book of Job remains a unique work in the wisdom tradition.   From a literary standpoint, the distinctiveness of the Joban narrative appears in its extended use of dialogue to treat a single theme and in the exaggerations with which the book is characterized.[49] From a thematic perspective, the intellectual quest in this biblical tale gives evidence of an unparalleled courage and audacity as the assumption of cosmic order is challenged by the conflict of experiential chaos.[50]

But perhaps most significant is the uniqueness of the Joban tale relative to its resolution of the sapiential question, for in the narration of the divine discourse and Job's response to it, one finds the implicit assertion that new knowledge is acquired, that Job has come to apprehend what was otherwise unfathomable.   Unlike the human protagonist in the "Babylonian Theodicy," who ultimately accepts his plight with an invocation of divine mercy, Job displays an emotional depth in his intellectual yearning. As J. Gray points out:

> The Mesopotamian sage, with academic detachment acquiesced in the situation; the theologian in Job agonized over the paradox of the suffering of the innocent and the Order of God .... The traditional view that suffering implied sin and alienation from God was exploded in the conclusion of Job, and when the sufferer in Job rose above this traditional fatalism he found fresh hope in the living fellowship of God with its infinite possibilities of fresh revelation of the nature of God and man's experience of His grace.

---

[48] GRAY, "The Book of Job in the Context of Near Eastern Literature," 260: "'Thy démarche is worthy of man' in this Mesopotamian text, which has so much in common with the Book of Job, may indicate that the Divine approval of Job's statements about God in 42,7 does not refer to his re-iteration of faith in the theodicy which orthodoxy asserted, but in his refusal to blink the embarrassing facts which seemed to call it in question in contrast to the dishonest assent of the friends in the Dialogue."

[49] Summarized in ALBERTSON, "Job and Ancient Near East Wisdom Literature," 227.

[50] Cf. ALONSO SCHÖKEL, *Giobbe*, 87, and PERDUE, "Cosmology and Social Order," 460.

And, unlike the figure in the "Just Sufferer," Gray notes that Job

> is not explicitly declared innocent, though his relative innocence is
> implied in the fact that, as the theophany and Divine declaration of
> themselves indicate, he is not alienated from God's notice and
> fellowship, with a prospect depending on his response to the fresh
> impact of God on his life and ultimately on God's continued grace.[51]

That response is Job's "despising yet repenting," which, as we have
suggested, derives from his newfound contemplative consciousness.

It is this heightened level of awareness, borne by Job's mystical
experience of "seeing" God in the revelatory words from the storm,
that marks the unique contribution of the Book of Job to the world of
wisdom. In comparison with other sapiential writings, the resolution
of the Joban narrative by means of this spiritual encounter is both
unusual and distinctive.[52] In marked contrast to the process of
rational reflection which characterizes the wisdom enterprise and which
has suffused the inter-human dialogues in the Book of Job, the event of
the theophany portends a new mode of awareness for the protagonist.
In the symbolic power of the storm, Yahweh participates in the dialogic
action of the tale in an admittedly extraordinary fashion, though this
need not be considered arbitrary or unrealistic.[53] Instead, the advent
of the divine signals real presence[54] and dynamic transcendence,[55]

---

[51] GRAY, "The Book of Job in the Context of Near Eastern Literature," 258, 260.

[52] Cf. CRENSHAW, "The Acquisition of Knowledge," 251: "From one perspective,
such claims (of immediate encounter with the Transcendent One) do not belong in
wisdom literature, where a premium is placed on verifiability. ... The ending to the
book of Job, for example, is a response that derives from traditions which are more at
home in prophecy and sacred narrative than in wisdom."

[53] Cf. PATRICK, *The Rendering of God in the Old Testament*, 74: "First, he
(Yahweh) is an explicit or implicit party to the action from the beginning to end, so his
action is not unexpected. Second, his acts are suitable to the dramatic sequence, and
the resolution follows inevitably from the entire course of events."

[54] T. METTINGER, *In Search of God:* The Meaning and Message of the Everlasting
Names (Philadelphia 1988) 186: "In short, when we read that God speaks to Job 'out
of the whirlwind,' we are to understand that the hidden god emerges from concealment
and reveals himself. God manifests his presence, and this in such a way that it cannot
be questioned. In other words, the absence and silence of God are not the last word of
the Book of Job. Ultimately, the book deals with the *Deus praesens*, the near and
present God who speaks out forthrightly in a particular situation."

the mutuality of which lies at the heart of the narrative resolution. In the words of the divine discourse, the wisdom which had heretofore been unattainable is offered with poetic originality, and as a result, the "pathos of human sufficiency" in the sapiential process of understanding reality here collapses.[56] Yet it is upon this mystical experience that the ethos of true wisdom is constructed.

SAPIENTIAL TESTIMONY

By attributing to the repentant Job the acquisition of wisdom, the biblical text opens upon the world of theology. With its narrative focus on the question of theo-linguistics, this literary work proposes a paradigm of wisdom's attempt to delve into the mystery of human life by way of those limit-situations which jolt the meaning of earthly existence. By way of his responses to the divine speeches which corroborate that very mystery, the final words of Job express a theological integrity as his "despising yet repenting" remains true to his inherited faith, human reason, and spiritual experience. Consequently, our reading of the narrative, aided by the phenomenological hermeneutics of Ricoeur, suggests that the protagonist of this compelling story is not merely an ancient folk-hero or a paragon of existential thought. Rather, as one whose life-story embodies the process of gaining wisdom, Job can rightfully be called a sage, and the book bearing his name can take its place as a scriptural icon.

---

[55] P.D. HANSON *Dynamic Transcendence:* The Correlation of Confessional Heritage and Contemporary Experience in a Biblical Model of Divine Activity (Philadelphia 1978) 21: "God accordingly is not seen as a static Being over against life, to which life against its very nature must conform. God is rather seen as dynamic Reality at the heart of all reality, encountered in life in its manifold forms, and yet transcendent as that upon which all that is and will be is utterly dependent."

[56] J.L. CRENSHAW, "The Wisdom Literature," *The Hebrew Bible and Its Modern Interpreters* (eds. D.A. KNIGHT and G.M. TUCKER) (Philadelphia 1985) 373: "The pathos of the wisdom literature arose from a consuming passion to maintain this belief in human sufficiency in the face of unjust suffering and divine despotism. Little by little this distinctive viewpoint collapsed — first with the emergence of a heavenly messenger, Dame Wisdom, then with theophany as the resolution of a grievous spiritual problem, and finally with Ben Sira's wholesale embracing of sacral traditions which breathed the atmosphere of God's gracious dealings with a chosen race."

The Wisdom Phenomenon

In terms of a phenomenological hermeneutics, the description of the Book of Job as theo-linguistic discourse remains necessarily bound to the "wisdom" form of the tale. As Ricoeur notes, the basic theme of biblical wisdom concerns the meaningfulness of life: "... its meditation bears upon the human condition in its togetherness. It is addressed directly to the sense and non-sense of existence. It is a struggle for sense in spite of non-sense."[57] Specifically, the search for meaning inherent to the wisdom quest takes place within the arena of the human situation, especially where this involves the perennial tension arising from the interrogation of man's place before the divine: "At its limit wisdom discourse encounters a hidden God who takes for a mask the anonymous and inhuman course of things."[58] In the tale of Job, this sapiential questioning spurs the development of the inter-human Dialogues, which are themselves generated by the inexplicable situation in which Job finds himself at the end of the Prologue.

As part of this sapiential quest, revelation assumes an epistemo-logical character in that it provides a "horizon of meaning" for one's possible way of being and living in the world. As a properly sapiential phenomenon, however, the search for sense incorporates the realm of revelation not so much as an authoritative psychological inspiration but as a dialogic means of participating in the greater mystery of worldly existence.[59] Read in this light, the divine revelation of the Yahweh-speeches confronts the human limitation of Job's understanding, and from this juxtaposition results Job's sapiential challenge: sharing in the quest of the sages, he faces the choice of how to appreciate human existence and the corresponding task of witnessing to his choice by means of speech.[60]

---

[57] RICOEUR, "Nommer Dieu," 356.

[58] RICOEUR, "Nommer Dieu," 356. Cf. RICOEUR, "Temps biblique," 32-34.

[59] RICOEUR, "Toward a Hermeneutic of the Idea of Revelation," 87-88: "The prophet claims divine inspiration as guaranteeing what he says. The sage does nothing of the sort. He does not declare that his speech is the speech of another. But he does know that wisdom precedes him and that in a way it is through participation in wisdom that someone may be said to be wise."

[60] Cf. P. RICOEUR, "Interrogation philosophique et engagement," in LEROUX, *Pourquoi la philosophie*, 17-21.

This choice Job does make, as attested by the originary affirmation uttered in his final words. Due to his mystical experience of "seeing" God in the revelatory words from the storm, Job has come to understand the divine design more in terms of potential than as a fixed plan. As Ricoeur suggests, "(w)hat is revealed is the possibility of hope in spite of .... This possibility may still be expressed in the terms of a design, but of an unassignable design, a design which is God's secret."[61] Having entered into this secret by way of his contemplative consciousness,[62] Job chooses to locate himself anew in the world, which he does by way of "repentance." In so doing he "presupposes an unsuspected meaning which cannot be transcribed by speech or *logos* a human being may have at his disposal."[63] Yet the apprehension of this meaning or sense initiates Job's personal participation in wisdom.

By his last spoken words, Job discloses his complete theological integrity as he responds definitively to the challenge which has given impetus to the tale. In the shift from the language of a-critical faith to that of doubt and interrogation, the wisdom quest begins as Job seeks to reconcile his inherited notion of the divine-human relation with the experiential reality of his present situation. Yet this quest does not end with the self-defensive stance of chapters 29-31; no "answer" has been given to Job by way of rational reflection alone. Only when he moves beyond the "rationality of iconoclastic discourse" toward that intelligibility which comes via the "second hearing" of the Yahweh-speeches does Job gain the insight sufficient for a meaningful appreciation of his existence.[64]

Thus, the transposition from reasoned reflection to theophanic revelation provides Job with a new basis for his speech about God. His contemplative consciousness makes of this mystical event a "culminating experience," one in which he has been able "to find the inappreciable" and thereby overturn, as it were, the distressing crisis which had previously brought him to his sapiential limit.[65] Based on this experi-

---

[61] RICOEUR, "Toward a Hermeneutic of the Idea of Revelation," 87.

[62] Cf. MCKECHNIE, *Job*, 127-128: "Job has risen above complaints, he has risen above comparisons because he has achieved a new consciousness, the consciousness of the universal. He 'mingles with the universe,' loses himself to find himself in the vast ocean of life. He is a nature-mystic."

[63] RICOEUR, "Toward a Hermeneutic of the Idea of Revelation," 87.

[64] Cf. RICOEUR, "Manifestation et proclamation," 74.

[65] RICOEUR, "Manifestation et proclamation," 70.

ence, Job utters that paradoxical declaration which forms the grand finale to his theo-linguistic development. "Despising yet repenting," Job gives voice to his own wisdom — what Ricoeur might call a "*docta ignorantia*"[66] — and the phenomenon represented by this conclusive speech characterizes him as a figure of theological integrity and enables him to be affirmed as the sole right-speaker among the human interlocutors.

This linguistic characterization, in turn, discloses the essential message of the book and gives to this sapiential tale a heuristic force. In the progression from faith to reason and from reason to contemplation, the narrative schema highlights a methodological search for wisdom. And here the fictional power of the story emerges, for its poetic expression creates a character in whom the essential features of this sapiential process are to be discovered.[67]

An Iconic Augmentation

The heuristic force of this tale plays on the successive speeches of the protagonist. In this respect, the narrative portrayal of Job can be likened to the artistic notion of an "iconic augmentation," whereby the message of the book is communicated through the figurative depiction of the main character.[68] Understood thus, the structure provides the medium and the speeches become the instrument through which relevant traits of reality are re-described in the narrative.

---

[66] P. RICOEUR, "Response" (to Karl Rahner's Lecture: On the Incomprehensibility of God), in *Celebrating the Medieval Heritage:* A Colloquy on the Thought of Aquinas and Bonaventure (ed. D. TRACY) (Chicago 1978) 128: "Language is raised to *ignorantia* to the extent that the horizon of the unexpressed, of the unsaid, is revealed as constitutive of the experience of language itself. But this *ignorantia* is *docta*, to the extent that it is not a capitulation of language but an untiring and everlasting struggle with the problematic of language — a struggle to bring language to the threshold of silence."

[67] RICOEUR, "Appropriation," 187: "For poetry proceeds to the essential, whereas history remains content with the anecdotal. Such is the significant link between fiction, figuration and recognition of the essential."

[68] According to Paul Henle, from whom Ricoeur borrows this notion, "We are led [by figurative discourse] to think of something by a consideration of something like it, and this is what constitutes the iconic mode of signifying" (cited by RICOEUR in "The Metaphorical Process," 147). Cf. RICOEUR, *The Rule of Metaphor*, 198-199.

Put simply, the abstract thought of the text can be grasped in the imaginary life of the character.[69] Employing the literary power to elaborate upon reality by way of a given characterization,[70] the truthfulness of the narrative pertains to a different epistemological order. To repeat Ricoeur's explanation of "the paradox of iconic augmentation":

> The more imagination deviates from that which is called reality in ordinary language and vision, the more it approaches the heart of the reality which is no longer the world of manipulable objects, but the world into which we have been thrown by birth and within which we try to orient ourselves by projecting our innermost possibilities upon it, in order that we *dwell* there, in the strongest sense of that word.[71]

It is this projective power which displays itself in the poetic language of the protagonist. By forming a "matrix of new semantic pertinence" or a "schematization of metaphorical attribution,"[72] such language gives to the narrative figure the ability to transcend the limits of ordinary discourse and thereby create new meaning. From this poetic display the literary icon emerges.

Applied to the Book of Job, the notion of iconic augmentation highlights the properly religious truth of this fictional narrative as it portends meaning in the realm of theological discourse. Without attempting to document historically the travails of an actual person, the biblical narrative recounts a sapiential odyssey.[73] In this literary journey, the adventures of the protagonist center on conflicting modes of knowledge and speech. The dialogic action is propelled from

---

[69] RICOEUR, "The Metaphorical Process," 148: "... each time the new intended connection is grasped as what the icon describes or depicts."

[70] In *The Rule of Metaphor*, Ricoeur claims that "the iconic representation harbours the power to elaborate, to extend the parallel structure" of metaphorical expressions (p. 189).

[71] RICOEUR, "The Function of Fiction in Shaping Reality," 139.

[72] RICOEUR, "The Function of Fiction in Shaping Reality," 132.

[73] LÉVÊQUE, *Job et son Dieu*, 623: "... à travers ses plaintes et ses outrances, Job vit une authentique expérience de sagesse, car il essaie bel et bien de trouver le secret de l'action de Dieu, l'ordre mystérieux qui traverse le désordre du mal; il tente, lui aussi, de maîtriser l'existence, une existence qui s'est faite tragique. Le contexte humain a changé, et avec lui les modes d'expression, mais l'aventure spirituelle du sage se poursuit en s'approfondissant."

indifferent worship through embittered disputation to repentant silence, and this multiplicity of linguistic representations serves to "figure" the various ways by which one can approach the very real question of the meaningfulness of human existence in the world.

These successive figures portray a clash of religious epistemologies, for the speech of the protagonist in each section of the book derives from a different source of knowledge. The Job of the Prologue, who refuses to submit to the maledictory "folly" suggested by his wife (2:9-10), speaks from the faith of the covenant tradition; this Job stands tall as a properly religious figure, fundamentally distinct from the suffering purveyors of pure existentialism.[74] The Job of the Dialogues, who contests the validity of his Friends' appeal to universal experience, ancient tradition, and supernatural inspiration,[75] speaks from personal reflection upon the reality of his own life; this Job rises above the others as a truly philosophical figure, one whose conviction is authenticated by the reasoning process.[76] Finally, the Job of the Theologue, who maintains his rationally based position yet renounces the need for rigorous conceptual clarity, speaks from the contemplative experience of his encounter with Yahweh; this Job is elevated as a thoroughly sapiential figure, one whose intellectual prowess is complemented by an appreciative consciousness.

Specifically, it is the narrative twist inherent in Job's final utterance — *Therefore I despise yet repent of dust and ash* (42:6) — which discloses the paradoxical motif and message of the book relative to "the unfolding of wisdom."[77] On the one hand, the main character takes up the hermeneutic of engagement valued in the wisdom tradition. The Job who no longer acquiesces in the apparent surety of an unchallenged

---

[74] Cf. R. GORDIS, "Biblical Wisdom and Modern Existentialism," *ConsJ* 21,4 (1967) 1-10.

[75] R. ALBERTZ, "The Sage and Pious Wisdom in the Book of Job: The Friends' Perspective," in *The Sage in Israel and the Ancient Near East*, 251-252.

[76] COX, *Man's Anger and God's Silence*, 89: "In what, then lies the value of the first part of the *Book of Job*, the poetic Dialogue? ... Perhaps what is new is the intellectual process itself, the path Job took to reach his conclusions: the process of pure reason. At the end of the Dialogue one thing is certain: it is Job alone who has come out of the conflict with an enhanced dignity."

[77] The thesis that the Book of Job "discuss(es) wisdom by means of wisdom" is strongly supported by T. AIURA, "Wisdom Motif in the Joban Poem," *Kwansei Gakuin University Annual Studies* 15 (1966) 1-20.

faith,[78] who repels the temptation to abdicate reason and reflection in favor of contrite consolation,[79] who promotes at all costs the value of intellectual integrity and existential honesty[80] — this Job *despises* the non-sense of life and thereby takes his rightful place as a leading figure in the world of wisdom.

On the other hand, this same Job ultimately *repents*. Reason alone has not brought wisdom to Job,[81] yet by means of a spiritual apprehension — mysterious but real, wondrous but authentic, unusual but unquestioned — his character is transfigured. In this way, the movement from question to answer which directs Job's intellectual itinerary extends beyond both the a-critical faith underlying his existential angst and the experiential reasoning whose deductions only confirm his conundrums, to reach its resolution in the intelligibility which is founded on a contemplative awareness of the divine. Only with this illumined apprehension does Job become the subject of wisdom.[82]

---

[78] N.C. HABEL, "'Of Things Beyond Me': Wisdom in the Book of Job," *CurTM* 10 (1983) 153: "Central to Job's change of attitude is that he no longer sought understanding through past piety or traditional mediated vehicles for knowing God." The later claim by this same author that Job "admits he does not possess wisdom" and that "(h)e did not find wisdom but he found God" is based on the interpretation of 42:3 as ignorant submission, an interpretation whose appropriateness we have challenged above.

[79] GORDIS, "Biblical Wisdom and Modern Existentialism," 10: "It is the outlook of the Biblical Wisdom teachers who point the way to a world-view which can sustain man's spirit without demanding the abdication of his mind, that man counts in this mysterious universe, that life has meaning and can be endowed with joy — this conviction is possible for the Biblical sages, who look upon the world clear-eyed and unafraid, and refuse to accept cant or convention."

[80] MOORE, "The Integrity of Job," 31: "If the poet's paradigm is less faithful to God, it is more faithful to human experience. Existential honesty receives a deity's rebuke, but it also receives a poet's sympathy— even God thinks enough to pay a visit to that kind of integrity."

[81] Cf. A. BARUCQ, "Dieu chez les sages d'Israël," *La notion biblique de Dieu:* Le Dieu de la Bible et le Dieu des philosophes (ed. J. COPPENS) (BETL, 41; Leuven 1976) 186: "Sur l'image de Yahweh qui, sorti de la tempête, converse sereinement avec son accusateur se referme le recueil des dialogues et c'est fort bien ainsi. Pour le sage il devait en résulter qu'il n'y a pas de sagesse, de cette sagesse qui mène à Dieu, que de la seule raison."

[82] S. TERRIEN, *The Elusive Presence: The Heart of Biblical Theology* (Religious Perspectives, 26; San Francisco 1983) 373: "In spite of darkness, presence induced illumination." In his "Le sujet convoqué: à l'école des récits de vocation prophétique," *RICP* 28 (1988) 90-93, RICOEUR speaks of a similar epistemological phenomenon, which he describes as "consulting interior truth."

And herein lies the corrective message of the Book of Job. Whereas "wisdom" traditionally encompasses the pragmatic truths of immanent earthly concerns,[83] its treatment in the Book of Job lays claim to the presence of the transcendent[84] and, consequently, to the need for mysticism.[85] Extending beyond the rational pursuit of an experiential world order and likewise exceeding the pious principles of sacred tradition, wisdom for Job involves a way of life that necessarily includes a contemplative dimension.[86] It may be likened to what Michalson once called a "penultimate mysticism," for the experience narrated of Job represents

an articulation of self-consciousness *in via* as one's life bruises itself upon the conditions of the world and raises the question about the ultimate significance of it all. It is an engagement with life so thoroughgoing that in the process either one is left exhausted and

---

[83] D. COX, *Proverbs*, with an Introduction to Sapiential Books (OTM, 17; Wilmington 1982) 13: "While it is tied to, and for the most part remains loyal to, the biblical faith, Wisdom literature emphasizes one particular aspect — mankind in its secular, terrestrial existence, as the human person confronts the material world, human history and existence, and wrests meaning and value from them at the everyday level."

[84] Cf. WHARTON, "The Unanswerable Answer," 63: "Job affirms the human in the face of the absurd on a level of freedom and responsibility that even the most sanguine humanist must concede still lies out there as a frontier to be explored rather than an achievement to be boasted of. ... A kind of 'transcendence' then re-enters, through the back door of the ruined cathedral of allegedly bankrupt religions, a transcendence capable of restoring to human beings, in some measure, their lost capacity for wonder and awe. ... At such a moment of disclosure, even the highest imaginable humanity can bend the knee in adoration, not in servile abnegation of human dignity, but as the ultimate expression of it."

[85] Cf. D. WINSTON, "The Sage as Mystic in the Wisdom of Solomon," in *The Sage in Israel and the Ancient Near East*, 392: "The significance of prayer for the attainment of wisdom lies in the sage's firm conviction that all human accomplishments are in reality only the obverse side of effective divine action, and that the fundamental error that must be avoided above all is the self-conceit of one who thinks that human power is completely autonomous."

[86] A similar claim is expressed in the language of "process" thought by SOUTHWICK, "Job: An Exemplar for Every Age," 390: "Our relationship with God is open-ended. Potentiality for this ever-growing covenant is inherent within us; Wisdom teases our awareness of our potentialities into consciousness, and God participates with us as we energize our potentialities into positive modes of newness."

unsatisfied, or he is met by a source of authenticity from beyond himself.[87]

When that source of authenticity is revealed in the Theologue, it confers legitimacy on the theological method employed by Job.[88] Yet, at the same time, it also critiques the sufficiency of human reason in the quest for understanding.[89] When, in the Epilogue, Job is affirmed as having spoken "rightly" (42:7,8), the icon fully emerges: at once believing, thinking, and "seeing," Job has overcome the dialectic of reason and tradition by virtue of his experiential knowledge of God.[90]

With such an experience, the life story of Job may be likened to that of a prophet. As Samuel Terrien claims:

> When at last Yahweh spoke to him out of the whirlwind and offered him the opportunity to engage in the debate so long desired, Job desisted, for he had learned the immense difference between sapiential hearsay and prophetic seeing (42:6). The God from whom he had expected vindication of his honor and therefore justification had been bequeathed to him by the tradition of the wise. His new knowledge reflected a sensual experience of divinity. The sage became a prophet.[91]

However, whereas this interpretation rightly emphasizes the epistemological difference provided by Job's experience of the theophany, the claim that Job "became a prophet" seems misdirected. Job's encounter

---

[87] C. MICHALSON, "Existentialism Is a Mysticism," *Theology Today* 12 (1955-56) 359.

[88] COX, *Man's Anger and God's Silence*, 130: "Had Yahweh not spoken on his own behalf the Dialogue, standing alone, would represent a forceful existential statement. By intervening, God confers legitimacy on the method adopted by Job in the first and most passionate part of the book, whose great contribution is the fact that it brings theology out of its prison by opening it up to doubt about its sufficiency."

[89] LÉVÊQUE, *Job et son Dieu*, 691: "Il a fallu la théophanie et sa grâce de révélation pour que Job consentît enfin à rejoindre Yahweh au-delà de toute image effrayante ou sécurisante; et jusqu'à ce moment de vérité, la critique a rongé la vie spirituelle qu'elle avait seulement mission d'assainir."

[90] RICOEUR, *The Rule of Metaphor*, 189: "The essential role of the icon is to contain an internal duality that at the same time is overcome."

[91] S. TERRIEN, "Job as a Sage," in GAMMIE and PERDUE, *The Sage in Israel and the Ancient Near East*, 242.

does parallel the dissymetrical dialogue through which Yahweh confronts a human being, but it takes place at the *end* of Job's life story, after which only silence follows. As such, it does not appear as a vocational transformation intended to establish the identity of the person in view of a subsequent prophetic mission; rather, it substantiates the figure of Job as one who has attained a degree of personal knowledge that makes of him a "mediator of wisdom."

In this sense, Job's character may more aptly be described as "spiritual master." If, as Dermot Cox postulates, "(t)he *hakam* was one who, by God's gift, by learning and by prayer, might rise to a perception (*yd'*) of God and intimacy with him while still involved in everyday life and secular affairs,"[92] then Job seems to be the very epitome of the wise man. He who manages to "see" God in the voice from the storm, who emerges from this divine-human dialogue willing to "repent," and who comes to be affirmed and restored by divine decree — this is the biblical character who embodies the basic paradox of the wisdom experience: "on the one hand, wisdom is something acquired by discipline and docility, but on the other hand, it is a gift of God."[93]

---

[92] D. COX, "Learning and the Way to God: The Spiritual Master in the Wisdom Literature of Israel," *StMiss* 36 (1987) 23.

[93] R. MURPHY, *The Tree of Life*, 114-115.

CONCLUSION:

The Integrity of Biblical Theology

The development of this study has taken its cue from an assertion made by Paul Ricoeur in his 1984 plenary address to the American Academy of Religion, namely, that with regard to interpretations of the Book of Job, "because of the enigmatic and perhaps even deliberately ambiguous character of its conclusion ... speculation is left to pursue more than one direction."[1] The speculation we have pursued has focused on the meaning of the responses of Job to the speeches of Yahweh, and the direction we have followed has been the "approach" to interpretation championed by Ricoeur himself.[2] At once phenomenological, hermeneutical, and reflexive, the Ricoeurian approach is a perspectival one.[3] Working by way of the dialectic of explanation and

---

[1] RICOEUR, "Evil: A Challenge to Philosophy and Theology," *JAAR* 53 (1985) 638.

[2] P. RICOEUR, "Contribution d'une réflexion sur le langage à une théologie de la parole," in LÉON-DUFOUR, *Exégèse et herméneutique*, 302: "l'herméneutique devient quelque chose de plus que la *méthodologie* de l'exégèse, i.e. un discours de second ordre appliqué aux règles de lecture du texte; elle concerne la constitution de l'objet théologique comme 'procès de parole' ...."

[3] P. RICOEUR, "Du conflit à la convergence des méthodes en exégèse biblique," in LÉON-DUFOUR, *Exégèse et herméneutique*, 51: "Ce caractère perspectiviste de l'interprétation n'exclut pas toute exigence méthodologique, mais au contraire la situe avec précision. C'est parce que le sens doit être parié, présumé, que des procédures de validation sont requises pour soumettre à une logique de la probabilité, comparable à la logique de la vérification empirique, la solidité de nos présomptions de sens. C'est sur ce trajet de la validation que l'herméneutique recoupe, et, éventuellement incorpore à titre d'étape méthodologique, l'approche historico-critique et l'approche structurale."

understanding, we have sought to comprehend the meaningfulness of Job's paradoxical "repentance" by studying the internal dynamic at work in the text and by postulating the world of wisdom as the external projection of this literary and biblical classic.[4]

Thus, our interpretive quest began with a consideration of the phenomenon of *narrativity* as it may be applied to the Book of Job. Based on the discordance emplotted in the various sections of the tale, and particularly on the paradoxical conclusion in which Yahweh declares that Job alone has spoken "rightly" (Job 42:7,8), we have suggested that a prevailing theme in this biblical book is the question of "theo-linguistics" or how to know and speak correctly about God given our human situation. The answer to this question, it would seem, is posed in the variety of narrative "figures" by which Job is characterized in the book.

This theo-linguistic focus, in turn, occasioned a more detailed analysis of the *poetics* of Job's speech in the Theologue. Transported into a new world of meaning by the "symbolic" event of Yahweh's theophanic manifestation and proclamation, Job utters two brief, though climactic, responses to the voice from the storm. Read in a "metaphorical" light, his silence and subsequent repentance bespeak a newfound awareness of his place in the cosmic scene: maintaining his own intellectual integrity, Job *despises* the senselessness of human existence as he knows it; *yet*, bastioned by the wisdom gained through his encounter with his God, he *repents* of the need for absolute rational certainty with regard to the meaning of this existence.

The significance of Job's twofold affirmation led us, finally, to a reconsideration of the message which the Book of Job offers for possible *appropriation*. Having situated this story within the literary and theological "world of wisdom," we developed the thesis that the figure of Job ultimately acts as a literary "icon." Augmented to exemplary proportions, the fictional character of Job leads us on a sapiential

---

[4] Cf. RICOEUR, "On Interpretation," 193-194: "Once it is freed from the primacy of subjectivity, what may be the first task of hermeneutics? It is, in my opinion, to seek in the text itself, one the one hand, the internal dynamic which governs the structuring of the work and, on the other hand, the power that the work possesses to project itself outside itself and to give birth to a world which would truly be the 'thing' referred to by the text. This internal dynamic and external projection constitute what I call the work of the text. It is the task of hermeneutics to reconstruct this twofold work."

"journey" that becomes paradigmatic for all theology.[5] By way of the interplay of intellectual reasoning and contemplative consciousness, this biblical hero represents to us what it means to be a sage.

Thus, in our effort to validate the interpretive "guess" that the repentant Job stands out as an icon for theology, we have brought together in this study both the philosophical principles of hermeneutics and a philological analysis of the Hebrew text. Without suggesting that this be *the* uniquely conclusive interpretation, we nevertheless offer it as adequately probable given the hermeneutical indices suggested by Ricoeur's philosophical theory.[6] The question remains, however, as to what may be culled from this hermeneutical enterprise as first-fruits relative to the ongoing work of biblical theology. What does the icon of Job, interpreted by way of Ricoeur's hermeneutics, say to the contemporary world of theological readers?

In a somewhat indirect fashion, our adoption of the Ricoeurian approach to interpretation highlights the contemporary need for biblical theology to fight "against a reduction of understanding to empathy and a reduction of explanation to an abstract combinatory system."[7] In our search for the sense immanent to the enigmatic text of Job's responses, we have assumed a particular reference point in philosophical hermeneutics, especially as it appreciates the phenomena of fictional narratives and poetic language. Such recourse to "hermeneutics," as differentiated from more narrowly-defined types of "criticism," offers

---

[5] POLZIN, *Biblical Structuralism*, 74: "By means of its remarkable resources [the Book of Job] takes the reader on a journey, the beginning of which may be described as equilibrium without insight and whose conclusion is appropriately equilibrium with insight. The genius of this journey is that insight is conferred not by the avoidance of contradiction and inconsistency but precisely by the courageous integration of contradiction and resolution. In other words the story is paradigmatic."

[6] P. RICOEUR, "Esquisse de conclusion," in LÉON-DUFOUR, *Exégèse et herméneutique*, 295: "Si en outre l'interprétation est elle-même un processus du texte, qui constitue le vouloir-dire du texte, notre interprétation est d'une certaine façon liée par celle du texte. C'est pourquoi l'interprétation n'est ni une ni multiple. Elle n'est pas une, car il y a toujours plusieurs possibilités de lire le même texte; mais elle n'est pas non plus multiple, au sens d'un infini indénombrable." For a discussion of the criteria of valid interpretation amenable to Ricoeur's hermeneutical theory, see S. SCHNEIDERS, *The Revelatory Text: Interpreting the New Testament as Sacred Scripture* (San Francisco 1992) 157-179 (esp. 164-167).

[7] RICOEUR, "On Interpretation," 194-195.

to biblical theology a wider array of interpretive possibilities and a greater potential for meaningful dialogue.[8]

In a more direct manner, the actual interpretation of Job's words which we have proposed here presents a possible corollary to the process involved in the work of biblical theology. Like the "rebellious" Job of the Dialogues, who could no longer tacitly submit to the pre-critical understanding of his life-situation, so the interpreter cannot remain unquestioning before the biblical text. Without the use of analytical and systematic tools of exegesis, biblical theology risks the promotion of a fundamentalistic naiveté. Yet, like the "repentant" Job of the Theologue, who comes to existentially sufficient understanding only through his encounter with the divine, so the interpreter of biblical texts cannot remain an objectively detached scholar. Without the fruit of a spiritual consciousness of the God about whom Scripture speaks, biblical theology risks the sterility of a purely academic exercise.

According to our interpretation, the Book of Job canonizes the wisdom process by portraying the main character as a sapiential icon, as the embodiment of what it means to be a sage. The mystical awareness which substantiates his repentant response functions as a necessary complement to his customary worship and experiential logic, and it is the mutuality of these theological approaches that comes to be affirmed by divine decree in the Epilogue as the rightful expression of his integrity. As such, the theophanic conclusion to this biblical tale need not be relegated to the passive undoing of human thought, nor derogated as a poignant sign of the futility of theological discussion, nor castigated as the failed outcome of the quest for wisdom.[9]

---

[8] Cf. SCHNEIDERS, *The Revelatory Text*, 177: "The reason that critical exegesis is insufficient as a total approach to the text and that interpretation in the full sense of the term must terminate in appropriation is precisely that the ultimate question is not simply, What does the text say? but, What is the meaning of the text for the believing community? ... Appropriation of the meaning of the text, the transformative achievement of interpretation, is neither a mastery of the text by the reader (an extraction of its meaning by the application of method) nor a mastery of the reader by the text (a blind submission to what the text says) but an ongoing dialogue with the text about its subject matter."

[9] Respectively, WILCOX, *The Bitterness of Job*, 218; LARUE, "The Book of Job on the Futility of Theological Discussion," 79; and DELL, *The Book of Job as Sceptical Literature*, 78.

Rather, the message of this biblical narrative, as explicated according to the principles of Ricoeur's hermeneutics, forces us ultimately "to rework our conventional concept of truth, that is to say to cease to limit this concept to logical coherence and empirical verification alone, so that the truth claim related to the transfiguring action of fiction can be taken into account."[10] To account for, and testify to, the transformative power of Sacred Scripture is precisely the task of biblical theology. And in this interpretive domain, the truth which the repentant Job claims is singularly important: *whereas criticism is needed, mysticism is essential* — for only by seeing does Job repent.

---

[10] RICOEUR, "On Interpretation," 187.

BIBLIOGRAPHIES

Studies on Philosophical Hermeneutics

BOLING, Robert G. (ed.). *Symposium: Paul Ricoeur and Biblical Hermeneutics. BR* 24-25 (1979-80).

BOURGEOIS, Patrick L. "Paul Ricoeur's Hermeneutical Phenomenology." *PT* 16 (1972) 20-27.

BROWN, Frank Burch. "Transfiguration: Poetic Metaphor and Theological Reflection." *JRel* 62 (1982) 39-56.

CROSSAN, John Dominic (ed.). *The Book of Job and Ricoeur's Hermeneutics* [*Semeia*, 19]. Missoula: Scholars Press, 1977.

CROSSAN, John Dominic (ed.). *Paul Ricoeur on Biblical Hermeneutics* [*Semeia*, 4]. Missoula: Scholars Press, 1975.

DORNISCH, Loretta. *Faith and Philosophy in the Writings of Paul Ricoeur* [Problems in Contemporary Philosophy, 29]. New York: Edwin Mellen Press, 1991.

GERAETS, Th.-F. (ed.). *A la recherche du sens* [FS. Paul Ricoeur]. *RUO* 55,4 (1985).

GERHART, Mary. "Paul Ricoeur." In *A Handbook of Christian Theologians.* Edited by Martin E. MARTY and Dean G. PEERMAN. Nashville: Abingdon, 1984, pp. 608-624.

GERHART, Mary. "Paul Ricoeur's Hermeneutical Theory as Resource for Theological Reflection." *Thomist* 39 (1975) 496-527.

GERHART, Mary. *The Question of Belief in Literary Criticism.* An Introduction to the Hermeneutical Theory of Paul Ricoeur. Stuttgart 1979.

GIUSTINIANI, Pasquale. "Paul Ricoeur: ermeneutica e teologia." *Asprenas* 36 (1989) 494-507.

IHDE, Don. *Hermeneutic Phenomenology:* The Philosophy of Paul Ricoeur [Studies in Existential Philosophy]. Evanston: Northwestern University Press, 1971.

JEANROND, Werner G. *Text and Interpretation as Categories of Theological Thinking.* New York: Crossroad, 1988.

JOY, Morny. "Hermeneutics and *Mimesis.*" *SR* 19 (1990) 73-86.

KELLNER, Hans. "'As Real As It Gets ...' Ricoeur and Narrativity." *PT* 34 (1990) 229-242.

KEMP, T. Peter (ed.). *The Narrative Path:* The Later Works of Paul Ricoeur. *PSC* 14,2 (1988).

KLEMM, David E. *The Hermeneutical Theory of Paul Ricoeur:* A Constructive Analysis. Cranbury 1983.

KLEMM, David E. and William SCHWEIKER (eds.). *Meanings in Texts and Actions:* Questioning Paul Ricoeur. Charlottesville: University Press of Virginia, 1993.

LAWRENCE, George E. "Conference on Religious Studies and the Humanities: Theories of Interpretation. First Session: Paul Ricoeur." *Criterion* 17,2 (1978) 20-23.

LECHNER, Robert (ed.). *A Presentation of THE RULE OF METAPHOR by Paul Ricoeur* [*PT*, Supplement to vol. 21]. Toronto: University of Toronto Press, 1977.

LEROUX, G. (ed.). *Pourquoi la philosophie?* Montréal 1968.

LOWE, Walter J. "The Coherence of Paul Ricoeur." *JRel* 61 (1981) 384-402.

MIGLIASSO, Secondo. "Dal simbolo al linguaggio simbolico: l'interèsse di una svolta nella teoria ermeneutica di Paul Ricoeur per un'ermeneutica biblica creativa." *RivB* 29 (1981) 187-203.

MOLONEY, Raymond. "Stages in Ricoeur's Hermeneutics." *ITQ* 58 (1992) 118-128.

MUDGE, Lewis S. (ed.). *Paul Ricoeur: Essays on Biblical Interpretation.* London: SPCK, 1981.

MUKENGEBANTU, Paul. "L'unité de l'oeuvre philosophique de Paul Ricoeur." *LTP* 46 (1990) 209-222.

NAKJAVANI, Erik. "Phenomenology and Theory of Literature: An Interview with Paul Ricoeur." *Modern Language Notes* 96,5 (December 1981) 1084-1090.

NKERAMIHIGO, Theoneste. *L'homme et la transcendance selon Paul Ricoeur.* Essai de poétique dans la philosophie de Paul Ricoeur. Paris 1984.

PELLAUER, David. "Paul Ricoeur on the Specificity of Religious Language." *JRel* 61 (1981) 264-284.

PELLAUER, David. "Silence and Phenomenology of Religious Experience." *PT* 27 (1983) 138-142.

PELLAUER, David. "*Time and Narrative* and Theological Reflection." *PT* 31 (1987) 262-286.

PEREPPADAN, Jose. "The Contributions of Paul Ricoeur to Biblical Hermeneutics." *Jeevadhara* 12 (1982) 156-163.

PRAMMER, Franz. *Die philosophische Hermeneutik Paul Ricoeurs in ihrer Bedeutung für eine theologische Sprachtheorie* [Innsbrucker theologische studien, 22]. Innsbruck 1988.

RASMUSSEN, D.M. *Mythic-Symbolic Language and Philosophical Anthropology:* A Constructive Interpretation of the Thought of Paul Ricoeur. The Hague: Nijhoff, 1971.

REAGAN, Charles (ed.). *Studies in the Philosophy of Paul Ricoeur.* Athens: Ohio University Press, 1978.

REAGAN, Charles and David STEWART (eds.). *The Philosophy of Paul Ricoeur:* An Anthology of His Work [Beacon paperback, 567]. Boston: Beacon Books, 1978.

RICOEUR, Paul. "La Bible et l'imagination." *RHPR* 62 (1982) 339-360.

RICOEUR, Paul. "The Biblical Worldview and Philosophy." *NICM Journal* 6,3 (1981) 91-111.

RICOEUR, Paul. "Can Fictional Narratives Be True?" In *The Phenomenology of Man and of the Human Condition*. Individualisation of Nature and the Human Being, I: Plotting the Territory for Interdisciplinary Communications [AnHuss, 14]. Edited by A.-T. TYMIENIECKA. Dordrecht: Reidel, 1983, pp. 3-19.

RICOEUR, Paul. "Le conflit des herméneutiques: épistémologie des interprétations." *CISymb* 1,1 (1963) 152-184.

RICOEUR, Paul. *Le conflit des interprétations:* Essais d'herméneutique [L'ordre philosophique]. Paris: Seuil, 1969.

RICOEUR, Paul. "Contingence et rationalité dans le récit." *PhänF* 18 (1986) 11-29.

RICOEUR, Paul. "The Creativity of Language." In *Dialogues with Contemporary Continental Thinkers*. Edited by R. KEARNEY. Manchester 1984, pp. 17-36.

RICOEUR, Paul. "La crise: un phénomène spécifiquement moderne?" *RTP* 120 (1988) 1-19.

RICOEUR, Paul. "Culpabilité tragique et culpabilité biblique." *RHPR* 33 (1953) 285-307.

RICOEUR, Paul. *Du texte à l'action*. Essais d'herméneutique, II [Collection Esprit]. Paris: Seuil, 1986.

RICOEUR, Paul. "Éloge de la lecture et de l'écriture." *ETR* 64 (1989) 395-405.

RICOEUR, Paul. "Entre herméneutique et sémiotique." In *Nouveaux actes sémiotiques*. Limoges, 1990, pp. 3-19.

RICOEUR, Paul. "Entre philosophie et théologie: la Regle d'Or en question." *RHPR* 69 (1989) 3-9.

RICOEUR, Paul. "Entre temps et récit: concorde/discorde." In *Recherches sur la philosophie et le langage.* Cahier du groupe de recherches sur la philosophie et le langage de l'université de Grenoble. Edited by R. PIETRA. Grenoble 1982, pp. 3-14.

RICOEUR, Paul. "Epilogue: The 'Sacred' Text and the Community." In *The Critical Study of Sacred Texts* [Berkeley Religious Studies]. Edited by W.D. O'FLAHERTY. Berkeley 1979, pp. 271-276.

RICOEUR, Paul. "Événement et sens." *AF* 41,2 (1971) 15-34.

RICOEUR, Paul. "Événement et sens dans le discours." In *Paul Ricoeur ou la liberté selon l'espérance* [Philosophes de tous les temps, 72]. Edited by M. PHILIBERT. Paris: Seghers, 1971, pp. 177-187.

RICOEUR, Paul. "Evil, a Challenge to Philosophy and Theology." *JAAR* 53 (1985) 635-650.

RICOEUR, Paul. "Faith and Action: A Christian Point of View." *Criterion* 2,3 (1963) 10-15.

RICOEUR, Paul. *Fallible Man.* New York: Fordham University Press, ² 1986.

RICOEUR, Paul. "Fides Quarens Intellectum: antécédents bibliques?" *AF* 68 (1990) 19-42.

RICOEUR, Paul. "La fonction narrative et l'expérience humaine du temps." *AF* 50,1 (1980) 343-367.

RICOEUR, Paul. *Freud and Philosophy:* An Essay on Interpretation. New Haven: Yale University Press, 1970.

RICOEUR, Paul. "From Proclamation to Narrative." *JRel* 64 (1984) 501-512.

RICOEUR, Paul. "The Function of Fiction in Shaping Reality." *MW* 12,2 (1979) 123-141.

RICOEUR, Paul. "Herméneutique philosophique et herméneutique biblique." In *Exégèse: Problèmes de methode et exercises de lecture* (Genèse 22 et Luc 15). Edited by F. BOVON et G. ROUILLER. Paris 1975, pp. 216-228.

RICOEUR, Paul. *History and Truth.* Evanston: Northwestern University Press, ² 1965.

RICOEUR, Paul. "Hope and the Structure of Philosophical Systems." In *Philosophy and Christian Theology* [PACPA]. Edited by G.F. MCLEAN and F. DOUGHERTY. Washington, DC: Catholic University of America, 1970, pp. 55-69.

RICOEUR, Paul. "The Human Experience of Time and Narrative." *RP* 9 (1979) 17-34.

RICOEUR, Paul. "L'identité narrative." In *La narration:* quand le récit devient communication [Lieux théologiques, 12]. Edited by P. BÜHLER and J.-F. HABERMACHER. Généve: Labor et Fides, 1988, pp. 287-300.

RICOEUR, Paul. "Imagination in Discourse and Action." In *The Human Being in Action:* The Irreducible Element in Man, part II - Investigations at the Intersection of Philosophy and Psychiatry [AnHuss, 7]. Edited by A.-T. TYMIENIECKA. Dordrecht: Reidel, 1978, pp. 3-22.

RICOEUR, Paul. *Les incidences théologiques des recherches actuelles concernant le langage.* Paris: Institut d'Études Oecuméniques, 1969.

RICOEUR, Paul. *Interpretation Theory:* Discourse and the Surplus of Meaning. Fort Worth: Texas Christian University, 1976.

RICOEUR, Paul. "The Language of Faith." *USQR* 28 (1973) 213-224.

RICOEUR, Paul. "Life: A Story in Search of a Narrator." In *Facts and Values:* Philosophical Perspectives from Western and Non-Western Traditions. Edited by M.C. DOESER and J.N. KRAAY. Dordrecht: Nijhoff, 1986, pp. 121-132.

RICOEUR, Paul. "'Logique herméneutique'?" In *Contemporary Philosophy: A New Survey*, vol. I: Philosophy of Language, Philosophical Logic. Edited by G. FLOISTAD. The Hague: Nijhoff, 1981, pp. 179-223.

RICOEUR, Paul. *Main Trends in Philosophy* [Main Trends in the Social and Human Sciences, 4]. New York: Holmes and Meier, 1979.

RICOEUR, Paul. "Manifestation et proclamation." *AF* 44,2-3 (1974) 57-76.

RICOEUR, Paul. "Mimesis and Representation." *Annals of Scholarship:* Metastudies of the Humanities and Social Sciences 2,3 (1981) 15-32.

RICOEUR, Paul. "Mimèsis, référence et refiguration dans *Temps et Récit.*" *ÉPhén* 11 (1990) 29-40.

RICOEUR, Paul. "Myth as the Bearer of Possible Worlds." In *Dialogues with Contemporary Continental Thinkers.* Edited by R. KEARNEY. Manchester 1984, pp. 36-45.

RICOEUR, Paul. "Narrative and Hermeneutics." In *Essays on Aesthetics* [FS. M.C. Beardsley]. Edited by J. FISHER. Philadelphia: Temple University, 1983, pp. 149-160.

RICOEUR, Paul. "Narrative Time." *CritInq* 7 (1980) 169-190.

RICOEUR, Paul. "Narrativité, phénoménologie, et herméneutique." In *Encyclopédie philosophique universelle*, I: L'univers philosophique. Edited by A. JACOB. Paris 1989, pp. 63-71.

RICOEUR, Paul. "On Interpretation." In *Philosophy in France Today.* Edited by A. MONTEFIORE. London: Cambridge University Press, 1983, pp. 175-197.

RICOEUR, Paul. "Parole et symbole." *RevScRel* 49 (1975) 142-161.

RICOEUR, Paul. "Phénoménologie et herméneutique." *MW* 7 (1974) 223-253.

RICOEUR, Paul. "Philosophie et langage." *RPFE* 103 (1978) 449-463.

RICOEUR, Paul. "La philosophie et la specificité du langage religieux." *RHPR* 55 (1975) 13-26.

RICOEUR, Paul. "Philosophy and Religious Language." *JRel* 54 (1974) 71-85.

RICOEUR, Paul. "Pluralismo e convizione." *Protestantismo* 42 (1987) 129-139.

RICOEUR, Paul. "Poétique et symbolique." In *Initiation à la pratique de la théologie*, I: Introduction. Edited by B. LAURENT and F. REFOULE. Paris: Cerf, 1982, pp. 37-61.

RICOEUR, Paul. "The Power of the Word: Science and Poetry." *PT* 29 (1985) 59-70.

RICOEUR, Paul. "Religion, Atheism, Faith." In *The Religious Significance of Atheism* [The 18th Series of Bampton Lectures, 1966]. Edited by Alistair MACINTYRE. New York: Columbia University, 1969, pp. 57-98.

RICOEUR, Paul. "Response to Karl Rahner's Lecture: On the Incomprehensibility of God." In *Celebrating the Medieval Heritage:* A Colloquy on the Thought of Aquinas and Bonaventure [*JRel* supplement, 58]. Edited by D. TRACY. Chicago 1978, pp. 126-131.

RICOEUR, Paul. "Response to Josef Blank ('According to Scriptures': The New Testament Origins and Structure of Theological Hermeneutics)." In *Paradigm Change in Theology:* A Symposium for the Future. Edited by Hans KÜNG and David TRACY. New York: Crossroad, 1991, pp. 283-286.

RICOEUR, Paul. "Rhétorique - poétique - herméneutique." In *De la métaphysique à la rhétorique* [FS. Ch. Perelman]. Edited by M. MEYER. Brussels 1986, pp. 143-155.

RICOEUR, Paul. *The Rule of Metaphor:* Multi-Disciplinary Studies of the Creation of Meaning in Language. Toronto: University of Toronto Press, 1977.

RICOEUR, Paul. "Le scandale du mal." *Esprit* 7-8 (1988) 57-63.

RICOEUR, Paul. "The Status of *Vorstellung* in Hegel's Philosophy of Religion." In *Meaning, Truth and God*. Edited by L.S. ROUNER. Notre Dame 1982, pp. 70-88.

RICOEUR, Paul. "Le sujet convoqué: à l'école des récits de vocation prophétique." *RICP* 28 (1988) 83-99.

RICOEUR, Paul. "Sur la phénoménologie." *Esprit* 2 (1953) 821-839.

RICOEUR, Paul. "The Symbol ... Food for Thought." *PT* 4 (1960) 196-207.

RICOEUR, Paul. *The Symbolism of Evil* [Religious Perspectives, 17]. New York: Harper and Row, 1967.

RICOEUR, Paul. "Le symbolisme et l'explication structurale." *CISymb* 2,4 (1964) 81-96.

RICOEUR, Paul. "Tasks of the Ecclesial Community in the Modern World." In *Theology of Renewal, II:* Renewal of Religious Structures [Proceedings of the Congress on the Theology of the Renewal of the Church, Centenary of Canada 1867-1967]. Edited by L.K. SHOOK. New York: Herder & Herder, 1968, pp. 242-254.

RICOEUR, Paul. "Temps biblique." *AF* 53,1 (1985) 23-35.

RICOEUR, Paul. *Time and Narrative*, 3 vols. Chicago: University of Chicago Press, 1984-88.

RICOEUR, Paul. "The Text as Dynamic Identity." In *The Identity of the Literary Text*. Edited by M.J. Valdés and O. MILLER. Toronto: University of Toronto Press, 1985, pp. 175-186.

RICOEUR, Paul. "That Fiction 'Remakes' Reality." *Journal of the Blaisdell Institute* 12,1 (1978) 44-62.

ROGERS, W.E. "Ricoeur and the Privileging of Texts: Scripture and Literature." *RelLit* 18 (1986) 1-26.

SACKS, Sheldon (ed.). *On Metaphor*. Chicago: University of Chicago Press, 1979.

STEVENS, Bernard. "Herméneutique philosophique et herméneutique biblique dans l'oeuvre de Paul Ricoeur." *RTL* 20 (1989) 178-193.

STEVENS, Bernard. "L'unité de l'oeuvre de Paul Ricoeur saisie selon la perspective de son ouvrage *Temps et récit I*." *TF* 47 (1985) 111-117.

STEWART, D. "Paul Ricoeur and the Phenomenological Movement." *PT* 12 (1968) 227-235.

THOMPSON, John B. (ed.). *Paul Ricoeur: Hermeneutics and the Human Sciences*. Essays on Language, Action and Interpretation. Cambridge: Cambridge University Press, 1981.

TIFFENEAU, Dorian (ed.). *La narrativité* [Phénoménologie et herméneutique]. Paris: CNRS, 1980.

VALDÉS, Mario J. (ed.). *A Ricoeur Reader:* Reflection and Imagination. Toronto: University of Toronto Press, 1991.

VAN DEN HENGEL, J. "Faith and Ideology in the Philosophy of Paul Ricoeur." *EgT* 14 (1983) 63-89.

VAN NOPPEN, J.-P (ed.). *Theolinguistics* [Studiereeks Tijdschrift Vrije Universteit Brussel, n.s. 8]. Brusselles 1981.

VANHOOZER, Kevin J. *Biblical Narrative in the Philosophy of Paul Ricoeur: A Study in Hermeneutics and Theology.* Cambridge: Cambridge University Press, 1990.

WALLACE, Mark I. "Can God Be Named without Being Known? The Problem of Revelation in Thiemann, Ogden, and Ricoeur." *JAAR* 59 (1991) 281-308.

WALLACE, Mark I. *The Second Naiveté:* Barth, Ricoeur, and the New Yale Theology [Studies in American Biblical Hermeneutics,6]. Macon, GA: Mercer University Press, 1990.

WELLS, H. "Theology and Christian Philosophy: Their Relation in the Thought of Paul Ricoeur." *SR* 5,1 (1975) 45-56.

WETHERBEE PHELPS, Louise (ed.). *Ricoeur and Rhetoric. PreText* 4, 3-4 (1983).

WUELLNER, Wilhelm (ed.). *Philosophical Hermeneutics and Theological Hermeneutics:* Ideology, Utopia, and Faith [Protocol of the 17th Colloquy]. Berkeley: Center for Hermeneutical Studies in Hellenistic and Modern Culture, 1975.

Studies on the Book of Job

AHRONI, R. "An Examination of the Literary Genre of the Book of Job." *Tarbiz* 49 (1979-80) 1-13.

AIURA, T. "Wisdom Motif in the Joban Poem." *Kwansei Gakuin University Annual Studies* 15 (1966) 1-20.

ALBERTSON, R.G. "Job and Ancient Near East Wisdom Literature." In *Scripture in Context, II:* More Essays on the Comparative Method. Edited by W.H. HALLO, J.C. MOYER, and L.G. PERDUE. Winona Lake: Eisenbrauns, 1983, pp. 213-230.

ALBERTZ, Rainer. "Der sozialgeschichtliche Hintergrund des Hiobbuches und der 'Babylonische Theodizee'." In *Die Botschaft und die Boten* [FS. Hans Walter Wolff]. Edited by J. JEREMIAS and L. PERLITT. Neukerchen-Vluyn, 1981, pp. 349-372.

ALEXANDER, Jon. "Job Considered as a Conversion Account." *SpTod* 42 (1990) 126-139.

ALONSO SCHÖKEL, Luis and J.J. SICRE DIAZ. *Giobbe:* commento teologico e letterario. Roma: Borla, 1985.

ALTER, Robert. "The Voice from the Whirlwind." *Commentary* 77 (1984) 33-41.

ANDERSON, Francis I. *Job:* An Introduction and Commentary [TynOTC]. Leicester: Inter-Varsity Press, 1976.

ARARAT, Nisan. "Concerning Job's 'Fear of God'." *BM* 29 (1983-84) 263-278.

ATKINSON, David. *The Message of Job* [The Bible Speaks Today]. Leicester: Inter-Varsity Press, 1991.

BACHAR, S. "God's Answer to Job." *BM* 25 (1979) 25-29.

BARR, James. "The Book of Job and Its Modern Interpreters." *BJRL* 54 (1971) 28-46.

BATTEN, L.W. "The Epilogue of the Book of Job." *ATR* 15 (1933) 125-128.

BENNETT, T. Miles. *When Human Wisdom Fails:* An Exposition of the Book of Job. Grand Rapids: Baker, 1971.

BERGANT, Dianne. *Job, Ecclesiastes* [OTM, 18]. Wilmington: Michael Glazier, 1982.

BERGANT, Dianne. "Might Job Have Been a Feminist?" *TBT* 28 (1990) 342-346.

BERGANT, Dianne. "Things Too Wonderful for Me (Job 42:3)." In *Scripture and Prayer* [FS. Carroll Stuhlmueller]. Edited by Carolyn OSIEK and Donald SENIOR. Wilmington: Michael Glazier, 1988, pp. 62-75.

BERRY, D.L. "Scripture and Imaginative Literature: Focus on Job." *JGenEd* 19 (1967) 119-131.

BEZUIDENHOUT, L.C. "Struktuur en strekking van Job 38:39 - 39:30." *HTS* 43 (1987) 709-722.

BLOMMERDE, Anton. *Northwest Semitic Grammar and Job* [BibOr, 22]. Roma: PIB, 1969.

BLOOM, H. (ed.). *The Book of Job* [Modern Critical Interpretations]. New York: Chelsea House, 1988.

BONNARD, P.E. "Job ou l'homme enfin exstasié." *LumVie* 13 (1964) 15-33.

BONORA, Antonio. *Giobbe: il tormento di credere*. Il problema e lo scandolo del dolore. Padova: Gregoriana Libreria Editrice, 1990.

BOWES, Paula J. "The Structure of Job." *TBT* 20 (1982) 329-333.

BRANDON, S.G.F. "The Book of Job: Its Significance for the History of Religions." *HistTod* 2 (1961) 547-554.

BREITBART, Sidney. "The Problem of Job: The Question Still Remains." *JBQ* 20 (1991-92) 105-110.

BRENNER, Athalya. "God's Answer to Job." *VT* 31 (1981) 129-137.

BRENNER, Athalya. "'Job the Pious': The Characterization of Job in the Narrative Framework of the Book." *JSOT* 43 (1989) 37-52.

BUTTENWIESER, Moses. *The Book of Job*. New York: MacMillan, 1925.

BURROWS, Millar. "The Voice from the Whirlwind." *JBL* 47 (1928) 117-132.

CAMPION, P. G. "The Transformation of Job." *TBT* 30 (1992) 208-212.

CAQUOT, A. "Le Léviathan de Job 40,25 — 41,26." *RB* 99 (1992) 40-69.

CERESKO, Anthony R. "Gustavo Gutiérrez, *On Job*: Some Questions of Method." *ITS* 29 (1992) 223-233.

CERESKO, Anthony R. *Job 29-31 in the Light of Northwest Semitic:* A Translation and Philological Commentary [BibOr, 36]. Roma: PIB, 1980.

CERESKO, Anthony. "The Option for the Poor in the Book of Job." *ITS* 26 (1989) 105-121.

CIUBA, E. "Job and the God Question." *TBT* 54 (1971) 376-385.

CLINES, David J.A. "The Arguments of Job's Three Friends." In *Art and Meaning:* Rhetoric in Biblical Literature [JSOTSup, 19]. Edited by David J.A. CLINES, David M. GUNN, and Alan J. HAUSER. Sheffield: Almond Press, 1982, pp. 199-214.

CLINES, David J.A. "Deconstructing the Book of Job." *What Does Eve Do to Help?* and Other Readerly Questions to the Old Testament [JSOTSup, 94]. Sheffield: Almond Press, 1990, pp. 106-123.

CLINES, David J.A. "False Naivety in the Prologue to Job." *HAR* 9 (1985) 127-136.

CLINES, David J.A. "Job." In *The Books of the Bible*, I: The Old Testament/The Hebrew Bible. Edited by B.W. ANDERSON. New York 1989, pp. 181-201.

CLINES, David J.A. *Job 1-20* [WBC, 17]. Waco, TX: Word Books, 1989.

COLLINS, Brendan. "Wisdom in Jung's *Answer to Job*." *BTB* 21 (1991) 97-101.

COOPER, Alan. "Narrative Theory and the Book of Job." *SR* 11 (1982) 35-44.

COOPER, Alan. "Reading and Misreading the Prologue to Job." *JSOT* 46 (1990) 67-79.

COX, Dermot. "The Book of Job as 'Bipolar *Mašal*': Structure and Interpretation." *Anton* 62 (1987) 12-25.

COX, Dermot. "The Desire for Oblivion in Job 3." *SBFLA* 23 (1973) 37-49.

COX, Dermot. *Man's Anger and God's Silence: The Book of Job*. Middlegreen: St. Paul Publications, 1991.

COX, Dermot. "A Rational Inquiry into God: Chapters 4-27 of the Book of Job." *Greg* 67 (1986) 621-658.

COX, Dermot. "Reason in Revolt: The Poetic Dialogues in the Book of Job." *SBFLA* 24 (1974) 317-328.

COX, Dermot. "Structure and Function of the Final Challenge: Job 29-31." *PIBA* 5 (1981) 55-71.

COX, Dermot. *The Triumph of Impotence:* Job and the Tradition of the Absurd [AnGreg, 212]. Roma: PUG, 1978.

CRAIGIE, P.C. "Biblical Wisdom in the Modern World, III: Job." *Crux* 16 (1980) 7-10.

CRENSHAW, James L. "When Form and Content Clash: The theology of Job 38:1 - 40:5." In *Creation in the Biblical Traditions* [CBQMS, 24]. Edited by Richard J. CLIFFORD and John J. COLLINS. Washington, DC: Catholic Biblical Association of America, 1992, pp. 70-84.

CRÜSEMANN, Frank. "Hiob und Kohelet: Ein Beitrag zum Verständnis des Hiobbuches." In *Werden und Wirken des Alten Testaments* [FS. C. Westermann]. Edited by R. ALBERTZ, H.-P. MÜLLER, H.W. WOLFF, and W. ZIMMERLI. Göttingen: Vandenhoeck und Ruprecht, 1980, pp. 373-393.

CURTIS, John Briggs. "On Job's Response to Yahweh." *JBL* 98 (1979) 497-511.

DAILEY, Thomas F. "The Aesthetics of Repentance: Re-Reading the Phenomenon of Job." *BTB* 23 (1993) 64-70.

DAILEY, Thomas F. "And Yet He Repents — On Job 42,6." *ZAW* 105 (1993) 205-209.

DAILEY, Thomas F. "The Book of Job: A Theo-Novella." Paper delivered at the SBL International meeting, Leuven 1994.

DAILEY, Thomas F. "The Book of Job as Optimistic Wisdom." forthcoming in the *Journal of Theta Alpha Kappa* 18,1 (1994).

DAILEY, Thomas F. "Job — the 'Icon' of a Sage." Paper delivered at the AAR/SBL annual meeting, San Francisco 1992 (*Abstracts*, p. 285).

DAILEY, Thomas F. "Seeing He Repents: Contemplative Consciousness and the Wisdom of Job." forthcoming in the *ABR* 45 (1994).

DAILEY, Thomas F. "Theophanic Bluster: Job and the Wind of Change." *SR* 22 (1993) 187-195.

DAILEY, Thomas F. "The Wisdom of Divine Disputation? On Job 40:1-5." forthcoming in the *JSOT* 48 (1994).

DAILEY, Thomas F. "'Wondrously far from me'— The Wisdom of Job 42,2-3." *BZ* 36 (1992) 261-264.

DAVIS, E.F. "Job and Jacob: The Integrity of Faith." In *Reading Between Texts:* Intertextuality and the Hebrew Bible [Literary Currents in Biblical Interpretation]. Edited by Danna Nolan FEWELL. Louisville: Westminster/John Knox, 1992, pp. 203-224.

DE BOER, P.A.H. "Does Job Retract? Job xlii,6." *Selected Studies in Old Testament Exegesis* [OTS, 27]. Edited by C. VAN DUIN. Leiden: Brill, 1991, pp. 179-195.

DELL, Katherine J. *The Book of Job as Sceptical Literature* [BZAW, 197]. Berlin: Walter de Gruyter, 1991.

DE WILDE, Amos. *Das Buch Hiob:* eingeleitet, übersetzt und erlautert [OTS, 22]. Leiden: Brill, 1981.

DE WILDE, A. "Jobs slotwoord." *NedTTs* 32 (1978) 265-269.

DHORME, Edouard Paul. *A Commentary on the Book of Job.* London: Thomas Nelson, 1967.

DICK, Michael B. "Job 31, the Oath of Innocence, and the Sage." *ZAW* 95 (1983) 31-53.

DIEWERT, David. "Job xxxvi 5 and the Root *m's* II." *VT* 39 (1989) 71-77.

DiLELLA, Alexander. "An Existential Interpretation of Job." *BTB* 15 (1985) 49-55.

DITTRICH, William F. "An Experience of Developing Relationship: The Book of Job." *TBT* 29 (1991) 169-174.

DRIVER, Samuel R. and George B. GRAY. *A Critical and Exegetical Commentary on the Book of Job* [ICC]. Edinburgh: T&T Clark, 1921.

DUQUOC, C. and C. FLORISTAN (eds.). *Job and the Silence of God* [*Concilium*, 169]. Edinburgh: T&T Clark, 1983.

EATON, J.H. *Job* [OT Guides, 5]. Sheffield: Academic Press, 1985.

EERDMANS, B.D. *Studies in Job*. Leiden 1939.

FEDRIZZI, Pio. *Giobbe* [La Sacra Bibbia]. Torino: Marietti, 1972.

FESTORAZZI, Franco. "Giobbe e Qohelet: crisi della sapienza." In *Problemi e prospettive di scienze bibliche*. Edited by Rinaldo FABRIS. Brescia: Queriniana, 1981, pp. 233-258.

FISCH, Harold. "Job: Tragedy Is Not Enough." *Poetry with a Purpose:* Biblical Poetics and Interpretation [Indiana Studies in Biblical Literature]. Bloomington: Indiana University Press, 1988, pp. 26-42.

FOHRER, Georg. *Das Buch Hiob* [KAT, 16]. Gütersloh: Mohn, 1963.

FOHRER, Georg. *Studien zum Buche Hiob* (1956-1979) [BZAW, 159]. Berlin: Walter de Gruyter, ² 1983.

FONTAINE, Carole. "Folkstale Structure in the Book of Job: A Formalist Reading." In *Directions in Biblical Hebrew Poetry* [JSOTSup, 40]. Edited by E.R. FOLLIS. Sheffield: Almond Press, 1987, pp. 205-232.

FORD, L.S. "The Whirlwind Addresses Job." *SLJT* 24 (1980-81) 217-221.

FORREST, Robert. "The Two Faces of Job: Imagery and Integrity in the Prologue." In *Ascribe to the Lord* [FS. P.C. Craigie; JSOTSup, 67]. Edited by L. ESLINGER and G. TAYLOR. Sheffield: Almond Press, 1988, pp. 385-398.

FORREST, Robert. "An Inquiry into Yahweh's Commendation of Job." *SR* 9 (1979) 159-168.

FRANÇOIS, Frère. "Une louange au-delà du désespoir. Méditation sur Job 38-42." *VSpir* 136 (1982) 47-65.

FREEDMAN, David N. "Is It Possible to Understand the Book of Job?" *BRev* 4,3 (1988) 26-33.

FREUND, Yosef. "'For You Have Not Spoken Correctly of Me As Has My Servant Job' (Job 42:7)." *BM* 34 (1989-90) 124-130.

FULLERTON, Kember. "On the Text and Significance of Job 40:2." *AJSL* 49 (1932-33) 197-211.

FULLERTON, Kember. "The Original Conclusion to the Book of Job." *ZAW* 42 (1924) 116-135.

GAMMIE, John G. "Behemoth and Leviathan: On the Didactic and Theological Significance of Job 40:15-41:26." In *Israelite Wisdom* [FS. Samuel Terrien]. Edited by J.G. GAMMIE, et al. New York: Union Theological Seminary 1978, pp. 217-231.

GAVALER, Campion P. "The Transformation of Job." *TBT* 30,4 (1992) 208-212.

GIBSON, John C.L. "The Book of Job and the Care of Souls." *SJT* 42 (1989) 303-317.

GIBSON, John C.L. *Job* [Daily Study Bible]. Edinburgh: St. Andrew Press, 1985.

GINSBERG, H.L. "Job the Patient and Job the Impatient." In *Congress Volume* [VTSup, 17]. Edited by J.A. EMERTON. Leiden: Brill, 1969, pp. 88-111.

GIRARD, René. "'The Ancient Trail Trodden by the Wicked': Job as Scapegoat." *Semeia* 33 (1985) 13-41.

GLATZER, Nahum N. "The Book of Job and Its Interpreters." *Biblical Motifs:* Origins and Transformations [Philip W. Lown Institute of Advanced Judaic Studies, Studies & Texts, 3]. Cambridge 1966, pp. 197-220.

GLATZER, Nahum N. (ed.). *The Dimensions of Job:* A Study and Selected Readings. New York: Schocken, 1969.

GOOD, Edwin M. *In Turns of Tempest:* A Reading of Job, with a Translation. Stanford: Stanford University Press, 1991.

GOOD, Edwin M. "Job." In *Harper's Bible Commentary*. Edited by James L. MAYS. San Francisco: Harper and Row, 1988, pp. 407-432.

GOOD, Edwin M. "Job and the Literary Task: a response." *Soundings* 56 (1973) 470-484.

GORDIS, Robert. *The Book of God and Man:* A Study of Job. Chicago: University of Chicago Press, 1965.

GORDIS, Robert. *The Book of Job:* Commentary, New Translation and Special Studies. New York: KTAV, 1978.

GORDIS, Robert. "Job and Ecology (and the Significance of Job 40:14)." *HAR* 9 (1985) 189-202.

GORDIS, Robert. "The Lord Out of the Whirlwind: The Climax and Meaning of 'Job'." *Judaism* 13 (1964) 48-63.

GORDIS, Robert. "The Temptation of Job — Tradition versus Experience in Religion." *Judaism* 4 (1955) 195-208.

GOWAN, Donald E. "God's Answer to Job: How Is It an Answer?" *HBT* 8,2 (1986) 85-102.

GOWAN, Donald E. "Reading Job as a 'Wisdom Script'." *JSOT* 55 (1992) 85-96.

GRABBE, Lester L. *Comparative Philology and the Text of Job:* A Study in Methodology [SBLDS, 34]. Missoula: Scholars Press, 1977.

GRAMLICH, Miriam Louise. "Job — Before and After." *TBT* 94 (February 1978) 1494-1502.

GRAY, J. "The Book of Job in the Context of Near Eastern Literature." *ZAW* 82 (1970) 251-269.

GREEN, Barbara. "Recasting a Classic: A Reconsideration of Meaning in the Book of Job." *NB* 74 (1993) 213-222.

GREENBERG, Moshe. "Job." In *The Literary Guide to the Bible.* Edited by R. ALTER and F. KERMODE. Cambridge, MA: Harvard University Press, 1987, pp. 283-304.

GREENBERG, Moshe and Jonas C. GREENFIELD and Nahum M. SARNA. *The Book of Job:* A New Translation according to the Traditional Hebrew Text, with Introductions. Philadelphia 1980.

GUILLAUME, A. *Studies in the Book of Job*, with a New Translation [*Annual of the Leeds University Oriental Society* Supplement, 2]. Leiden 1968.

GUINAN, Michael D. *Job* [Collegeville Bible Commentary, OT #19]. Collegeville: Liturgical Press, 1986.

GUTIÉRREZ, Gustavo. *On Job:* God-Talk and the Suffering of the Innocent. Maryknoll, NY: Orbis Books, 1987.

HABEL, Norman. *The Book of Job: A Commentary* [OTL]. Philadelphia: Westminster, 1985.

HABEL, Norman. "'Naked I Came ...'; Humanness in the Book of Job." In *Die Botschaft und die Boten* [FS. H. Walter Wolff]. Edited by J. JEREMIAS und L. PERLITT. Neukerchen-Vluyn, 1981, pp. 373-392.

HABEL, Norman. "The Narrative Art of Job: Applying the Principles of Robert Alter." *JSOT* 27 (1983) 101-111.

HABEL, Norman. "'Of Things Beyond Me': Wisdom in the Book of Job." *CurTM* 10 (1983) 142-154.

HABEL, Norman. "'Only the jackal is my friend': On Friends and Redeemers in Job." *Int* 31 (1977) 227-236.

HARRIS, Scott L. "Wisdom or Creation? A New Interpretation of Job." *VT* 33 (1983) 419-427.

HARROP, G.C. "But Now Mine Eye Seeth Thee." *CJT* 12,2 (1966) 80-84.

HARTLEY, John E. *The Book of Job* [NICOT]. Grand Rapids: Wm. B. Eerdmans, 1988.

HERMISSON, Hans-Jürgen. "Notizen zu Hiob." *ZTK* 86 (1989) 125-139.

HESSE, Franz. *Hiob* [ZBAT, 14]. Zürich: Theologischer Verlag, 1978.

HOFFMAN, Yair. "Ancient Near Eastern Literary Conventions and the Restoration of the Book of Job." *ZAW* 103 (1991) 399-411.

HOFFMAN, Yair. "Irony in the Book of Job." *Immanuel* 17 (1983-84) 7-21.

HOFFMAN, Yair. "The Relation between the Prologue and the Speech Cycles in Job: A Reconsideration." *VT* 31 (1981) 160-170.

HOLBERT, John C. "The Rehabilitation of the Sinner: The Function of Job 29-31." *ZAW* 95 (1983) 229-237.

HOLLAND, J.A. "On the Form of the Book of Job." *AusJBA* 1 (1972) 160-177.

HOUTMAN, C. "Zu Hiob 2:12." *ZAW* 90 (1978) 269-272.

HUBERMAN-SCHOLNICK, Sylvia. "The Meaning of *mišpat* in the Book of Job." *JBL* 101 (1982) 521-529.

HUBERMANN SCHOLNICK, Sylvia. "Poetry in the Courtroom: Job 38-41." In *Directions in Biblical Hebrew Poetry* [JSOTSup, 40]. Edited by E.R. FOLLIS. Sheffield: Almond Press, 1987, pp. 185-204.

HULME, William E. *Dialogue in Despair:* Pastoral Commentary on the Book of Job. Nashville: Abingdon, 1968.

HUNTER, Alistair G. "Could Not the Universe Have Come into Existence 200 Yards to the Left? A Thematic Study of Job." In *Text and Pretext* (FS. Robert Davidson; JSOTSup, 138). Edited by Robert P. CARROLL. Sheffield: JSOT Press, 1992, pp. 140-159.

JANZEN, J. Gerald. *Job* [Interpreter's Bible Commentary]. Atlanta: John Knox, 1985.

JANZEN, J. Gerald. "The Place of the Book of Job in the History of Israel's Religion." In *Ancient Israelite Religion* [FS. Frank Moore Cross]. Edited by P.D. MILLER, et al. Philadelphia 1987, pp. 523-537.

KAPLAN, L.J. "Maimonides, Dale Patrick and Job 42:6." *VT* 28 (1978) 356-358.

KEEL, Othmar. *Jahwes Entgegnung an Ijob:* Eine Deutung von Ijob 38-41 vor dem Hintergrund der zeitgenössischen Bildkunst [FRLANT, 121]. Göttingen: Vandenhoeck, 1978.

KEEL, Othmar. "Zwei kleine Beitrage zum Verstandnis der Gottesreden im Buch Ijob." *VT* 31 (1981) 220-225.

KESSLER, Rainer. "'Ich weiss, dass mein Erlöser lebet.' Sozialgeschichtlicher Hintergrund und theologische Bedeutung der Löser-Vorstellung in Hiob 19,25." *ZTK* 89 (1992) 139-158.

KINET, Dirk. "Der Vorwurf an Gott. Neuere Literartur zum Ijobbuch." *BKir* 36 (1981) 255-259.

KINNER WILSON, J.V. "A Return to the Problems of Behemoth and Leviathan." *VT* 25 (1975) 1-14.

KISSANE, Edward. *The Book of Job,* Translated from a Critically Revised Hebrew Text with Commentary. New York: Sheed and Ward, 1946.

KNIGHT, Harold. "Job, Considered as a Contribution to Hebrew Theology." *SJT* 9 (1956) 63-76.

KUBINA, Veronica. *Die Gottesreden im Buch Hiob:* Ein Beitrag zur Diskussion um die Einheit von Hiob 38,1 - 42,6 [Freiburger theologischer studien, 115]. Freiburg: Herder, 1979.

KUHL, Curt. "Neuere Literarkritik des Buches Hiob." *TRu* 21 (1953) 163-205, 257-313.

KUHL, Curt. "Vom Hiobbuche und seinen Problemen." *TRu* 22 (1954) 261-316.

KUTSCH, Ernst. "Jiob und seine Freunde. Zu Problemen der Rahmenerzählung des Hiobbuches." In *Zur Aktualität des Alten Testaments* (FS Georg Sauer). Edited by Siegfried JREUZER and Kurt LÜTHI. Frankfurt am Main: Lang, 1992, pp. 73-83.

KUYPER, L.J. "The Repentance of Job." *VT* 9 (1959) 91-94.

LACOQUE, A. "Est-ce gratuitement que Job craint Dieu?" In *Mélanges André Neher*. Edited by E. AMADO-VALENSI, *et al.* Paris 1975, pp. 175-179.

LANG, Bernhard. "Ein Kranker sieht seinen Gott (Hiob 38-41)." In *Wie Wird man Prophet in Israel?* Aufsätze zum AT. Düsseldorf 1980, pp. 137-148.

LARCHER, C. *Le livre de Job* [Bible de Jerusalem]. Paris: Cerf, 1957.

LARUE, Gerald. "The Book of Job on the Futility of Theological Discussion." *The Personalist* 45 (1964) 72-79.

LASINE, Stuart. "Bird's-Eye and Worm's-Eye Views of Justice in the Book of Job." *JSOT* 42 (1988) 29-53.

LAURIN, Robert. "The Theological Structure of Job." *ZAW* 84 (1972) 86-89.

LEVENSON, J.D. *The Book of Job in Its Time and in the Twentieth Century*. London 1972.

LÉVÊQUE, Jean. *Job et son Dieu:* Essai d'exégèse et de théologie biblique, 2 volumes [ÉBib]. Paris: Gabalda, 1970.

LÉVÊQUE, Jean. *Job:* le livre et le message [*Cahiers Évangile*, 53]. Paris 1985.

LÉVÊQUE, Jean. "Souffrance et métamorphose de Job." *Communio* 2,3 (May 1977) 6-16.

LICHTENSTEIN, Aaron. "Irony in the Book of Job." *DD* 13 (1984) 41-42.

LICHTENSTEIN, Aaron. "Toward a Literary Understanding of the Book of Job." *HebSt* 20/21 (1979-80) 34-35.

LILLIE, W. "The Religious Significance of the Theophany in the Book of Job." *ExpTim* 68 (1957) 355-358.

LOADER, J.A. "Job — Answer or Enigma?" *OTE* 2 (1984) 1-38.

LONG, T.G. "Job: Second Thoughts in the Land of Uz." *TTod* 75 (1988) 5-20.

MAAG, Victor. *Hiob:* Wandlung und Verarbeitung des Problems in Novelle, Dialogdichtung und Spätfassungen [FRLANT, 128]. Göttingen 1982.

MACKENZIE, R.A.F. "The Purpose of the Yahweh Speeches in the Book of Job." *Bib* 40 (1959) 435-445.

MACKENZIE, R.A.F. "The Transformation of Job." *BTB* 9 (1979) 51-57.

MACKENZIE, R.A.F. and R.E. MURPHY. "Job." In *New Jerome Biblical Commentary*. Edited by R.E. BROWN, J.A. FITZMYER, and R.E. MURPHY. Englewood Cliffs: Prentice-Hall, 1990, pp. 466-488.

MALCHOW, Bruce. "Nature from God's Perspective, Job 38-39." *Dialog* 21 (1982) 130-133.

MARTINI, Carlo Maria. *Avete perseverato con me nelle mie prove:* riflessioni su Giobbe. Casala Monferrato: Piemme, 1990.

MCDONAGH, Kathleen. "Job and Jeremiah: Their Approach to God." *TBT* 18 (1980) 331-335.

MCKEATING, Henry. "The Central Issue of the Book of Job." *ExpTim* 82 (1970) 244-247.

MCKECHNIE, James. *Job:* Moral Hero, Religious Egoist and Mystic. New York: Doran, 1927.

MCKENNA, D.L. *Job* [Communicator's Commentary]. Waco: Word Books, 1986.

MEIER, Sam. "Job i-ii: A Reflection of Genesis i-iii." *VT* 39 (1989) 183-193.

MEIRON, Menahem. "Does the Lord's Response Provide an answer to Job's Argument?" *BM* 37 (1992-92) 241-244.

METTINGER, Tryggve. "Job and His God." *In Search of God:* The Meaning and Message of the Everlasting Names. Philadelphia 1988, pp. 175-200.

MICHEL, W.L. *Job in the Light of Northwest Semitic*, vol I: Prologue and First Cycle of Speeches (Job 1:1 — 14:22) [BibOr, 42]. Roma: PIB, 1987.

MILLER, James E. "Structure and Meaning of the Animal Discourse in the Theophany of Job (38,3 - 39,30)." *ZAW* 103 (1991) 418-421.

MILLER, Ward S. "The Structure and Meaning of Job." *ConJ* 15 (1989) 103-120.

MITCHELL, Stephen. *The Book of Job:* Translated with an Introduction. San Francisco 1987.

MITCHELL, Stephen. *Into the Whirlwind:* A Translation of the Book of Job. Garden City: Doubleday, 1979.

MOORE, Michael S. "Job's Texts of Terror." *CBQ* 55 (1993) 662-675.

MOORE, Rick D. "The Integrity of Job." *CBQ* 45 (1983) 17-31.

MORROW, W. "Consolation, Rejection, and Repentance in Job 42:6." *JBL* 105 (1986) 211-225.

MUENCHOW, C. "Dust and Dirt in Job 42:6." *JBL* 108 (1989) 597-611.

MÜLLER, Hans-Peter. "Altes und Neues zum Buch Hiob." *EvT* 37 (1977) 284-304.

MÜLLER, Hans-Peter. "Gottes Antwort an Ijob und das Recht religiöser Wahrheit". *BZ* 32 (1988) 210-231.

MÜLLER, Hans-Peter. *Das Hiobproblem:* Seine Stellung und Entstehung im Alten Orient und im AT [Erträge Forschung, 84]. Darmstadt 1978.

MÜLLER, Hans-Peter. "Die sogennante Straussenperikope in den Gottesreden des Hiobbuches." *ZAW* 100 (1988) 90-105.

MÜLLER, Hans-Peter. "Theodizee? Anschlusserörterungen zum Buch Hiob." *ZTK* 89 (1992) 249-279.

MURPHY, Roland E. *The Psalms, Job* [OT Witness for Preaching]. Philadelphia 1977.

NAKAZAWA, Koki. "On the Dénouement of the Joban Poem." *Kirisutokyo Gaku* 19 (1977) 1-17.

NASH, J. "Images of Job." *RRel* 42 (1983) 28-33.

NEHER, André. "L'homme biblique, Job." *L'existence juive.* Paris 1962, pp. 63-72.

NEIMAN, D. *The Book of Job:* A Presentation of the Book with Selected Portions Translated from the Original Hebrew Text. Jerusalem: Massada, 1972.

NEL, P.J. "Cosmos and Chaos: A Reappraisal of the Divine Discourses in the Book of Job." *OTE* 4 (1991) 206-226.

NERI, P. "Nota: Chiave di lettura del libro di Giobbe." *BeO* 164 (1990) 102.

NEWELL, B. L. "Job: Repentant or Rebellious?" *WTJ* 46 (1984) 298-316.

NEWSOM, Carol A. "Cultural Politics and the Reading of Job." *BInt* 1 (1993) 119-138.

O'CONNOR, Daniel J. "The Comforting of Job." *ITQ* 53 (1987) 245-257.

O'CONNOR, Daniel J. "The Cunning Hand: Repetitions in Job 42:7,8." *ITQ* 57 (1991) 14-25.

O'CONNOR, Daniel J. "The Futility of Myth-Making in Theodicy: Job 38-41." *PIBA* 9 (1985) 81-99.

O'CONNOR, Daniel J. "The Hybris of Job." *ITQ* 55 (1989) 125-141.

O'CONNOR, Daniel J. "Job's Final Word - 'I Am Consoled' (42:6b)." *ITQ* 50 (1983-84) 181-197.

O'CONNOR, Daniel J. "Reverence or Irreverence in Job." *ITQ* 51 (1985) 85-104.

O'CONNOR, Daniel J. "Theodicy in the Whirlwind." *ITQ* 54 (1988) 161-174.

OBERFORCHER, Robert. "Abraham, Jeremia, Ijob: Typen des von Gott beanspruchten Menschen." *BLit* 52 (1979) 183-191.

PARSONS, Gregory W. "Literary Features of the Book of Job." *BSac* 138 (1981) 213-229.

PARSONS, Gregory W. "The Structure and Purpose of the Book of Job." *BSac* 138 (1981) 139-157.

PATRICK, Dale. *Arguing with God:* The Angry Prayers of Job. St. Louis: Bethany Press, 1977.

PATRICK, Dale. "Job's Address of God." *ZAW* 91 (1979) 268-282.

PATRICK, Dale, "The Translation of Job XLII 6." *VT* 26 (1976) 369-371.

PEAKE, A.S. "Job: The Problem of the Book." In *Theodicy in the Old Testament* [Issues in Religion and Theology, 4]. Edited by James L. CRENSHAW. Philadelphia: Fortress Press, 1983, pp. 100-108.

PENCHANSKY, David. *The Betrayal of God:* Ideological Conflict in Job [Literary Currents in Biblical Interpretation]. Louisville: Westminster/John Knox Press, 1990.

PERDUE, Leo G. *Wisdom in Revolt:* Metaphorical Theology in the Book of Job [JSOTSup, 112]. Sheffield: Almond Press, 1991.

PERDUE, Leo G. and W. Clark GILPIN (eds.). *The Voice from the Whirlwind:* Interpreting the Book of Job. Nashville: Abingdon Press, 1992.

PIFANO, P. "Nel grido di Giobbe il grido dell'uomo contemporaneo." *Asprenas* 31 (1984) 497-524.

PIXLEY, J.V. "Jób, ou o diálogo sobre a razâo teológica." *CuadT* 3 (1973) 57-80.

POLZIN, Robert. "The Framework of the Book of Job." *Int* 28 (1974) 182-200.

POLZIN, Robert and David ROBERTSON (eds.). *Studies in the Book of Job* [*Semeia*, 7]. Missoula: Scholars Press, 1977.

POPE, Marvin H. "Job, book of." *IDB*, 2: 911-924.

POPE, Marvin H. *Job:* Introduction, Translation, and Notes [AB, 15]. Garden City: Doubleday, ³1973.

PORTER, Stanley E. "The Message of the Book of Job: Job 42:7b as Key to Interpretation?" *EvQ* 63 (1991) 291-304.

PREUß, Horst Dietrich. "Jahwes Antwort an Hiob und die sogennannte Hiobliteratur des alten Vorderen Orients." In *Beiträge zur alttestamentlichen Theologie* [FS. W. Zimmerli]. Edited by H. DONNER, R. HANHART and R. SMEND. Göttingen: Vandenhoeck, 1977, pp. 323-343.

PRIEST, John. "Job and *J.B.*: The Goodness of God or the Godness of Good." *Hor* 12,2 (1985) 265-283.

PYPER, Hugh. "The Reader in Pain: Job as Text and Pretext." In *Text and Pretext* (FS. Robert Davidson; JSOTSup, 138). Edited by Robert P. CARROLL. Sheffield: JSOT Press, 1992, pp. 234-255.

RAVASI, Gianfranco. "Giobbe: male fisico e male morale." *ParSpV* 19 (1989) 83-94.

RAVASI, Gianfranco. *Giobbe:* il silenzio di Dio. Roma: Paoline, 1984.

RAVASI, Gianfranco. *Giobbe,* traduzione e commento. Roma: Borla, ³1991.

REDDY, Mummadi Prakasa. "The Book of Job — A Reconstruction." *ZAW* 90 (1978) 59-94.

REYBURN, William. *A Handbook on the Book of Job.* New York: United Bible Societies, 1992.

RILEY, William. "The Book of Job and the Terrible Truth about God." *ScrC* 18 (1988) 322-326.

ROBERTS, J.J.M. "Job and the Israelite Religious Tradition." *ZAW* 89 (1977) 107-114.

ROBERTS, J.J.M. "Job's Summons to Yahweh: The Exploitation of a Legal Metaphor." *ResQ* 16 (1973) 159-165.

ROBERTSON, David. "The Book of Job." *The Old Testament and the Literary Critic.* Philadelphia 1977, pp. 33-54.

RODD, Cyril. *The Book of Job* [Narrative Bible Commentary]. Philadelphia 1990.

ROWLEY, H.H. "The Book of Job and Its Meaning." *From Moses to Qumran:* Studies in the Old Testament. London 1963, pp. 141-183.

ROWLEY, H.H. *Job* [NCent; rev. ed.]. London: Marshall, Morgan & Scott, 1986.

ROWOLD, Henry. "*Mi hu'? Li hu?* Leviathan and Job in Job 41:2-3." *JBL* 105 (1986) 104-109.

ROWOLD, Henry. "Yahweh's Challenge to Rival: The Form and Function of the Yahweh Speech in Job 38-39." *CBQ* 47 (1985) 199-211.

RUPRECHT, E. "Das Nilpferd im Hiobbuch. Beobachtungen zu der soggennante zweiten Gottesrede." *VT* 21 (1971) 209-231.

SAFIRE, William. *The First Dissident:* The Book of Job in Today's Politics. New York: Random House, 1992.

SANDERS, P.S. (ed.). *Twentieth Century Interpretations of the Book of Job.* A Collection of Critical Essays. Englewood Cliffs: Prentice-Hall, 1968.

SARRAZIN, Bernard. "Du rire dans la Bible? La théophanie de Job comme parodie." *RevScRel* 76 (1988) 39-56.

SAWICKI, M. "Technological Imagery in the Yahweh Speeches. What Did Job See?" *TBT* 91 (1977) 1304-1310.

SCAFELLA, Frank. "A Reading of Job." *JSOT* 14 (1979) 63-67.

SCHLOBIN, Roger C. "Prototypic Horror: The Genre of the Book of Job." In *Fantasy and the Bible [Semeia #60]*. Edited by G. ACHELE and T. PIPPIN. Atlanta: Scholars Press, 1992, pp. 23-38.

SCHREINER, Susan E. "'Where Shall Wisdom Be Found?' Gregory's Interpretation of Job." *ABR* 39 (1988) 321-342.

SCHULZ, Karl A. *Where Is God When You Need Him?* Sharing Stories of Suffering with Job and Jesus: From Easy Answers to Hard Questions. New York: Alba House, 1991.

SCHWIENHORST-SCHÖNBERGER, Ludger and Georg STEINS. "Zur Entstehung, Gestalt und Bedeutung der Ijob-Erzählung (Ijob 1f; 42)." *BZ* 33 (1989) 1-24.

SEITZ, C.R. "Job: Full Structure, Movement and Interpretation." *Int* 43 (1989) 5-17.

SEVERINO CROATTO, J. "El libro de Job como clave hermeneutica de la teologia." *RevistB* 43 (1981) 33-45.

SHELLEY, John C. "Job 42:1-6 — God's Bet and Job's Repentance." *RevExp* 89 (1992) 541-546.

SIA, Santiago. "Reflections on Job's Question." *SpTod* 37 (1985) 234-242.

SIMUNDSON, Daniel J. "Job and His Ministers." In *All Things New* (FS. Roy A. Harrisville; Word and World Supplement Series, 1). Edited by Arland J. HULTGREN, et al. St. Paul: Word and World, 1992, pp. 33-42.

SIMUNDSON, Daniel J. *The Message of Job:* A Theological Commentary [Augsburg Old Testament Series]. Minneapolis: Augsburg/Fortress, 1986.

SMICK, Elmer B. "Architectonics, Structural Poems, and Rhetorical Devices in the Book of Job." In *A Tribute to Gleason Archer*. Edited by W. KAISER and R. YOUNGBLOOD. Chicago 1986, pp. 87-104.

SMICK, Elmer B. "Semiological Interpretation of the Book of Job." *WTJ* 46 (1986) 135-149.

SMITH, Gary V. "Is There a Place for Job's Wisdom in Old Testament Theology?" *TrinJ* 13 (1992) 3-20.

SNAITH, N.H. *The Book of Job:* Its Origin and Purpose [SBT, n.s., 11]. London 1968.

SNELL, P. "A Journey of Faith." *TBT* 20 (1982) 334-337.

SOUTHWICK, Jay. "Job: An Exemplar for All Ages." *Encounter* 45 (1984) 373-391.

STEINBERG, Milton. "Job Answers God: Being the Religious Perplexities of an Obscure Pharisee." *JRel* 12,2 (1932) 159-176.

STIER, Fridolin. *Das Buch Ijjob*. München: Kosel, 1954.

STOCKHAMMER, S.E. "Job's Problem." In *Faith and Reason:* Essays in Judaism. Edited by Robert GORDIS. New York 1973, pp. 54-60.

STOCKTON, E. "Literary Development of the Book of Job." *AusCR* 49 (1972) 137-143.

STRONG, David. "The Promise of Technology Versus God's Promise in Job." *TTod* 48 (1991) 170-181.

SWANEPOEL, M.G. "Job 12 — An(other) Anticipation of the Voice from the Whirlwind?" *OTE* 4 (1991) 192-205.

TAYLOR, David Bruce. *Job: A Rational Exposition*. Braunton Devon: Merlin Books, 1990.

TERRIEN, Samuel. *Job* [CAT]. Neuchâtel 1963.

TERRIEN, Samuel. "Job — Introduction and Exegesis." *IB*, 3:877-1198.

TERRIEN, Samuel. "The Yahweh Speeches and Job's Responses." *RevExp* 68 (1971) 497-509.

THELEN, Mary Frances. "*J.B.*, Job, and the Biblical Doctrine of Man." *JBR* 27 (1959) 201-205.

THOMPSON, Kenneth. "Out of the Whirlwind: The Sense of Alienation in the Book of Job." *Int* 14 (1960) 51-63.

TILLEY, Terrence. "Considering Job: Does Job Fear God for Naught?" *The Evils of Theodicy*. Washington, DC: Georgetown University Press, 1991, pp. 89-112.

TILLEY, Terrence. "God and the Silencing of Job." *ModT* 5 (1989) 257-270.

TORTOLONE, Gian Michele. "L'enigma di Giobbe. Destino dell'uomo e silenzio di Dio." *Asprenas* 36 (1989) 22-38.

TSEVAT, Matitiahu. *The Meaning of the Book of Job and Other Biblical Studies*. Essays on the Literature and Religion of the Hebrew Bible. New York 1980.

TSMUDI, Yosef. "God's Answer to Job." *BM* 34 (1988-89) 302-311.

TUR-SINAI, N.H. (H. Torczyner). *The Book of Job: A New Commentary*. Jerusalem: Kiryath Sepher, 1957.

URBROCK, William J. "Job as Drama: Tragedy or Comedy?" *CurTM* 8 (1981) 35-40.

VAN OORSCHOT, Jürgen. *Gott als Grenze:* eine literar- und redaktions-geschichtliche Studie zu den Gottesreden des Hiobbuches [BZAW, 170]. Berlin: Walter de Gruyter, 1987.

VAN SELMS, A. *Job:* A Practical Commentary [Text and Interpretation]. Grand Rapids: Eerdmans, 1985.

VAWTER, Bruce. *Job and Jonah:* Questioning the Hidden God. New York: Paulist Press, 1983.

VERMEYLEN, J. "'Connais-tu les lois des cieux?' Une lecture de Job 38-41." *Le Foi et le Temps* 20 (1990) 197-210.

VERMEYLEN, J. *Job, ses amis et son Dieu:* le légende de Job et ses relectures postexiliques [StBib, 2]. Leiden: Brill, 1986.

VINTON, Patricia. "Radical Aloneness: Job and Jeremiah." *TBT* 99 (1978) 1843-1849.

VISCHER, Wilhelm. "God's Truth and Man's Lie — A Study in the Message of the Book of Job." *Int* 15 (1961) 131-146.

VOGELS, Walter. "The Analysis of a Book: The Book of Job." *Reading and Preaching the Bible:* A New Semiotic Approach [Background Books, 4]. Wilmington: Michael Glazier, 1986, pp. 80-106.

VOGELS, Walter. "The Inner Development of Job. One More Look at Psychology and the Book of Job." *ScEs* 35 (1983) 227-230.

VOGELS, Walter. "Job a parlé correctement -- une approche structurale du livre de Job." *NRT* 102 (1980) 835-852.

VOGELS, Walter. "The Spiritual Growth of Job: A Psychological Approach to the Book of Job." *BTB* 11 (1981) 77-80.

VON RAD, Gerhard. "Hiob xxxviii und die altägyptische Weisheit." In *Wisdom in Israel and in the Ancient Near East* [FS. H.H. Rowley; VTSup, 3]. Edited by M. NOTH and D. WINTON-THOMAS. Leiden: Brill, 1955, pp. 293-301.

VON ROHR SAUER, Alfred. "Salvation by Grace: The Heart of Job's Theology." *ConTM* 37 (1966) 259-270.

WAGNER, Siegfried. "Theologischer Versuch über Ijob 42,7-9." In *Alttestamentliche Glaube und Biblische Theologie* (FS. Horst Dietrich Preuß). Edited by Jutta JAUSMANN and Hans-Jürgen ZOBEL. Stuttgart: Kohlhammer, 1992, pp. 216-224.

WARNER, Martin. "Job versus His Comforters: Rival Paradigms of Wisdom." *Philosophical Finesse:* Studies in the Art of Rational Persuasion. Oxford: Clarendon Press, 1989, pp. 105-151.

WEBSTER, Edwin. "Strophic Patterns in Job 29-42." *JSOT* 30 (1984) 95-109.

WEIGART, Mazal. "God's Reply to Job." *DD* 3,1 (1974) 25-29.

WEINFELD, M. "Job and Its Mesopotamian Parallels — A Typological Analysis." In *Text and Context* [JSOTSup, 48]. Edited by W. CLAASSEN. Sheffield: JSOT Press, 1988, pp. 217-226.

WEISER, A. *Das Buch Hiob* [ATD, 13]. Göttingen ⁵1968.

WEISS, Meir. *The Story of Job's Beginning, Job 1-2:* A Literary Analysis. Jerusalem: Magnes Press, 1983.

WESTERMANN, Claus. *The Structure of the Book of Job:* A Form-Critical Analysis. Philadelphia: Fortress Press, 1981.

WHARTON, J.A. "The Unanswerable Answer: An Interpretation of Job." In *Texts and Testaments:* Critical Essays in the Bible and Early Church Fathers [FS. S.D. Currie]. Edited by W.E. MARCH. San Antonio: Trinity University Press, 1980, pp. 37-70.

WHYBRAY, R.N. *Two Jewish Theologies:* Job and Ecclesiastes. Hull 1980.

WILCOX, John T. *The Bitterness of Job:* A Philosophical Reading. Ann Arbor: University of Michigan Press, 1989.

WILLIAMS, James G. "Deciphering the Unspoken: The Theophany of Job." *HUCA* 49 (1978) 59-72.

WILLIAMS, James G. "Job's Vision: The Dialectic of Person and Presence." *HAR* 8 (1984) 259-272.

WILLIAMS, James G. "'You have not spoken truth of me' - Mystery and Irony in Job." *ZAW* 83 (1971) 231-255.

WINTON-THOMAS, Daniel. "Types of Wisdom in the Book of Job." *IJT* 20 (1971) 157-165.

WOLFERS, David. "Bulrush and Bramble." *JBQ* 19 (1990-91) 170-175.

WOLFERS, David. "Is Job After All Jewish?" *DD* 14 (1985) 39-44.

WOLFERS, David. "The Lord's Second Speech in the Book of Job." *VT* 40 (1990) 474-499.

WOLTERS, A. "A Child of Dust and Ashes? (Job 42,6b)." *ZAW* 102 (1990) 116-119.

WÜRTHWEIN, Ernst. "Gott und Mensch in Dialog und Gottesreden des Buches Hiob." *Wort und Existenz*, Studien zum AT. Göttingen: Vandenhoeck, 1970, pp. 217-295.

ZERAFA, P. *The Wisdom of God in the Book of Job*. Rome 1978.

ZIMMERMAN, Frank. "Supplementary Observations on Job 40:2." *AJSL* 51 (1934-35) 46-47.

ZUCK, Roy B. (ed.). *Sitting with Job:* Selected Studies on the Book of Job. Grand Rapids: Baker, 1992.

ZUCKERMAN, B. "Job, book of." *IDBSup*, 479-481.

ZUCKERMAN, B. *Job the Silent:* A Study in Historical Counterpoint. New York: Oxford University Press, 1989.

Other Useful Studies

ALONSO SCHÖKEL, Luis. *A Manual of Hebrew Poetics* [SubsBib, 11]. Roma: PIB, 1988.

ALTER, Robert. *The Art of Biblical Narrative*. New York: Basic Books, 1981.

ALTER, Robert. *The Art of Biblical Poetry*. New York: Basic Books, 1985.

AMMASSARI, Antonio. "'Vedere Dio.' Un tema arcaico di religiosità nella Bibbia e in Omero." *BeO* 18 (1976) 87-93.

AMMASSARI, Antonio. "La ricerca di Dio nella Bibbia." *BeO* 23 (1981) 11-17.

BALANTINE, Samuel E. *Prayer in the Hebrew Bible:* The Drama of Divine-Human Dialogue [OBT]. Minneapolis: Fortress Press, 1993.

BARRÉ, Michael L. "'Fear of God' and the World View of Wisdom." *BTB* 11 (1981) 41-43.

BARUCQ, A. "Dieu chez les Sages d'Israël." In *La notion biblique de Dieu:* Le Dieu de la Bible et le Dieu des philosophes [BETL, 41]. Edited by Joseph COPPENS. Leuven: Leuven University Press, 1976, pp. 169-189.

BEGG, Christopher T. "Access to Heavenly Treasures: The Traditionsgeschichte of a Motif". *BN* 44 (1988) 15-20.

BERGANT, Dianne. *What Are They Saying about Wisdom Literature?* New York: Paulist Press, 1984.

BLANCY, A. "Icônes et symboles." *Foi et Vie* 91 (1992) 21-46.

BONNARD, P.E. *La Sagesse en personne*, annoncée et venue [Lectio Divina, 44]. Paris 1966.

BOWKER, John. *The Religious Imagination and the Sense of God.* Oxford: Clarendon Press, 1978.

BRUEGGEMANN, Walter. "A Neglected Sapiential Word Pair." *ZAW* 89 (1977) 234-258.

CERESKO, Anthony R. *Psalmists and Sages:* Studies in Old Testament Poetry and Religion [*ITS* Supplements, 2]. Bangalore: St. Peter's Pontifical Institute, 1994.

CHILDS, Brevard S. "Die theologische Bedeutung der Endform eines Textes." *TQ* 167 (1987) 242-251.

CLEMENTS, Ronald E. *Wisdom for a Changing World:* Wisdom in Old Testament Theology [Berkeley Lectures, 2]. Berkeley: BIBAL Press, 1990.

COATS, George W. (ed.). *Saga, Legend, Tale, Novella, Fable:* Narrative Forms in Old Testament Literature [JSOTSup, 35]. Sheffield: Almond Press, 1985.

COLEMAN, Robert O. "Repentance in the Old Testament." *BibIll* 12 (Summer 1986) 30-31.

COUROYER, B. "'Mettre sa main sur sa bouche' en Égypte et dans la Bible." *RB* 68 (1960) 197-209.

COX, Dermot. "Human Dignity in Old Testament Wisdom." *StMiss* 39 (1990) 1-19.

COX, Dermot. "Learning and the Way to God: The Spiritual Master in the Wisdom Literature of Israel." *StMiss* 36 (1987) 1-23.

Cox, Dermot. *Proverbs,* with an Introduction to the Sapiential Books [OTM, 17]. Wilmington: Michael Glazier, 1982.

CRENSHAW, James L. "The Acquisition of Knowledge in Israelite Wisdom Literature." *WW* 7 (1987) 245-252.

CRENSHAW, James L. "In Search of Divine Presence." *RevExp* 74 (1977) 353-369.

CRENSHAW, James L. *Old Testament Wisdom:* An Introduction. Atlanta: John Knox Press, 1981.

CRENSHAW, James L. "Popular Questioning of the Justice of God in Ancient Israel." *ZAW* 82 (1970) 380-395.

CRENSHAW, James L. (ed.). *Studies in Ancient Israelite Wisdom.* New York 1976.

CRENSHAW, James L. *A Whirlpool of Torment:* Israelite Traditions of God as an Oppressive Presence [OBT, 12]. Philadelphia: Fortress Press, 1984.

CRENSHAW, James L. "Wisdom and Authority: Sapiential Rhetoric and Its Warrants." In *Congress Volume* [VTSup, 32]. Edited by J.A. EMERTON. Leiden: Brill, 1981, pp. 10-29.

CRENSHAW, James L. "The Wisdom Literature." In *The Hebrew Bible and Its Modern Interpreters.* Edited by Douglas A. KNIGHT and Gene M. TUCKER. Philadelphia: Fortress Press, 1985, pp. 369-407.

CROSSAN, John Dominic. "Waking the Bible: Biblical Hermeneutic and Literary Imagination." *Int* 32 (1978) 269-285.

CUSTER, John S. *The Poetics of Complaint at the Limits of Theology.* Dissertation, PUG. Roma 1987.

DAILEY, Thomas F. "In Praise of God's Word: Biblical Studies Since Vatican II." In *The Church in the Nineties:* Its Legacy, Its Future. Edited by Pierre HEGY. Collegeville: Liturgical Press, 1993, pp. 50-62.

DAVIDSON, Robert. *The Courage to Doubt:* Exploring an Old Testament Theme. Philadelphia 1988.

DAVIES, G. Henton. "Theophany." *IDB,* 4:619-620.

DE PURY, Albert. "Sagesse et révélation dans l'Ancien Testament." *RTP* 110 (1977) 1-50.

DE NICHOLAS, Antonio and Evanghelos MOUTSOPOULOS (eds.). *God: Experience or Origin?* New York 1985.

DONALD, Trevor. "The Semantic Field of 'Folly' in Proverbs, Job, Psalms, and Ecclesiastes." *VT* 13 (1963) 285-292.

EATON, John. *The Contemplative Face of Old Testament Wisdom in the Context of World Religions.* London: SPCK, 1989.

FOHRER, Georg. "Methoden und Moden in der alttestamentlichen Wissenschaft." *ZAW* 100 (supplement 1988) 243-254.

FOHRER, Georg. "Theophanie." In *Calwer Bibellexicon.* Edited by Karl GUTRON, Reinhold KÜRKLICH, and Theodor SCHLATTER. Stuttgart: Calwer Verlag, 1959, col. 1310-1313.

FRETHEIM, Terrence E. "The Color of God: Israel's God-Talk and Life Experience." *WW* 6 (1986) 259-263.

FRETHEIM, Terrence E. "The Repentance of God: A Key to Evaluating Old Testament God-Talk." *HBT* 10,1 (1988) 47-70.

FRETHEIM, Terrence E. *The Suffering of God:* An Old Testament Perspective [OBT, 14]. Philadelphia: Fortress Press, 1984.

GAMMIE, John G. *Holiness in Israel* [OBT, 13]. Minneapolis: Fortress Press, 1989.

GAMMIE, John G. and Leo G. PERDUE (eds.). *The Sage in Israel and the Ancient Near East.* Winona Lake: Eisenbrauns, 1990.

GELLIN, A. "'Voir Dieu' dans l'Ancien Testament." *BVC* 23 (1958) 3-12.

GILBERT, Maurice (ed.). *La Sagesse de l'Ancien Testament* [BETL, 51]. Leuven: Leuven University Press, 1979.

GOLDINGAY, John. "Modes of Theological Reflection in the Bible." *Theology* 94 (1991) 181-188.

GOLDINGAY, John. "The 'Salvation History' Perspective and the 'Wisdom' Perspective within the Context of Biblical Theology." *EvQ* 51 (1979) 194-207.

GORDIS, Robert. "Biblical Wisdom and Modern Existentialism." *ConsJ* 21,4 (1967) 1-10.

HABEL, Norman C. "Appeal to Ancient Tradition as a Literary Form." *ZAW* 88 (1976) 253-272.

HANSON, Paul D. *Dynamic Transcendence:* The Correlation of Confessional Heritage and Contemporary Experience in a Biblical Model of Divine Activity. Philadelphia 1978.

HARVEY, Nicholas Peter. "Revelation and Contemplation." *NB* 72 (1991) 152-160.

HERANZ RODRIGUEZ, Juan C. "Dimensión teologica de la experiencia. Los libros Sapienciales." *SalTer* 62 (1974) 887-893.

HOHENSTEIN, Herbert E. "Oh Blessed Rage." *CurTM* 10 (1983) 162-168.

HUMPHREYS, W. Lee. *The Tragic Vision and the Hebrew Tradition* [OBT, 18]. Philadelphia: Fortress Press, 1985.

HUNTINGTON, Michael. "Mysticism and the Limits of Language." In *Language in Religion* [Papers of the Center for Research and Documentation in World Language Problems, 1]. Edited by Humphrey TONKIN and Allison ARMSTRONG. Lanham, MD: University Press of America, 1989, pp. 35-43.

JEREMIAS, Jörg. *Theophanie:* Die Geschichte einer alttestamentlichen Gattung [WMANT, 10]. Neukircher-Vluyn 1965.

JEREMIAS, Jörg. "Theophany in the OT." *IDBSup*, 896-898.

JOSSUA, Jean-Pierre." "About the Word 'Revelation'." *NB* 72 (1991) 124-130.

JOÜON, Paul and T. MUROAKA. *A Grammar of Biblical Hebrew*, 2 volumes [SubsBib, 14]. Roma: PIB, 1991.

KAISER, W.C. "Wisdom Theology and the Centre of Old Testament Theology." *EvQ* 56 (1978) 132-146.

KATZ, Steven. *Mysticism and Philosophical Analysis*. New York: Oxford University Press, 1978.

KING, Sallie B. "Two Epistemological Models for the Interpretation of Mysticism." *JAAR* 56 (1988) 257-279.

KREEFT, Peter. *Three Philosophies of Life:* Qoheleth, Job, and the Song of Songs. San Francisco: Ignatius Press, 1989.

KRISTO, Jure. "The Interpretation of Religious Experience: What Do Mystics Intend When They Talk about Their Experiences?" *JRel* 62 (1982) 21-38.

LÉON-DUFOUR, Xavier (ed.). *Exégèse et herméneutique* [Parole de Dieu, 6]. Paris: Éditions du Seuil, 1971.

LÉVÊQUE, Jean. "Le contrepoint théologique apporté par la reflexion sapientielle." In *Questions disputées d'Ancien Testament.* Méthode et théologie [BETL, 33]. Edited by C. BREKELMANS. Leuven: Leuven University press, 1974, pp. 183-202.

McFAGUE, Sallie. *Metaphorical Theology:* Models of God in Religious Language. Philadelphia: Fortress Press, 1982.

McPHERSON OLIVER, Mary Anne. "Mystical Experience and the Literary Technique of Silence." *StMyst* 1,1 (1978) 5-20.

MEYER, Ben F. "A Tricky Business: Ascribing New Meaning to Old Texts." *Greg* 71 (1990) 743-761.

MICHALSON, C. "Existentialism Is a Mysticism." *TTod* 12 (1955-56) 355-368.

MICHAUD, Robert. *La littérature de sagesse, histoire et théologie.* Tome I: Proverbes et Job [Lire la Bible, 65]. Paris: Cerf, 1984.

MICKELSEN, A.B. "The Metaphorical Language of Theology: Its Experiential Basis, Biblical and Contemporary." In *Current Issues in Biblical and Patristic Interpretation* [FS. M.C. Tenney]. Edited by G.F. HAWTHORNE. Grand Rapids 1975, 346-354.

MILGROM, J. "Repentance in the Old Testament." *IDBSup*, 736-738.

MOWINCKEL, S. "Ecstatic Experience and Rational Elaboration in Old Testament Prophecy." *Acta Orientalia* 13 (1935) 264-291.

MUELLER, J.J. "Appreciative Awareness: The Feeling Dimension in Religious Experience." *TS* 45 (1984) 57-79.

MUILENBURG, James. "The Speech of Theophany." *HDB* 28 (1963-64) 35-47.

MURPHY, Roland E. "Hebrew Wisdom." *JAOS* 101 (1981) 21-34.

MURPHY, Roland E. "Israel's Wisdom: A Biblical Model of Salvation." *StMiss* 30 (1981) 1-43.

MURPHY, Roland E. "Religious Dimensions of Israelite Wisdom." In *Ancient Israelite Religion* [FS. Frank Moore Cross]. Edited by P.D. MILLER. Philadelphia 1987, pp. 449-458.

MURPHY, Roland E. "The Theological Contributions of Israel's Wisdom Literature." *Listening* 19 (1984) 30-40.

MURPHY, Roland E. *The Tree of Life:* An Exposition of Biblical Wisdom Literature [Anchor Bible Reference Library]. Garden City: Doubleday, 1990.

MURPHY, Roland E. "What and Where Is Wisdom?" *CurTM* 4 (1977) 283-287.

MURPHY, Roland E. *Wisdom Literature:* Job, Proverbs, Ruth, Canticle, Ecclesiastes, and Esther [FOTL, 11]. Grand Rapids: Eerdmans, 1981.

MURPHY, Roland E. "Wisdom Literature and Biblical Theology." *BTB* 24/1 (1994) 4-7.

MURPHY, Roland E. "Wisdom — Theses and Hypotheses." In *Israelite Wisdom* [FS. S. Terrien]. Edited by John G. GAMMIE et al. New York 1978, pp. 35-42.

NEARY, Michael. "The Importance of Lament in the God/Man Relationship in Ancient Israel." *ITQ* 52 (1986) 180-192.

NICCACCI, Alviero. "La teologia sapienziale nel quadro dell'Antico Testamento. A proposito di alcuni studi recenti." *SBFLA* 34 (1984) 7-24.

O'CONNOR, Kathleen M. *The Wisdom Literature* [Message of Biblical Spirituality, 5]. Wilmington: Michael Glazier, 1988.

PARUNAK, H. van Dyke. "A Semantic Survey of נחם." *Bib* 56 (1975) 512-532.

PATRICK, Dale. "How Should the Biblical Theologian Go About Constructing a Theological Model?" *Encounter* 47 (1986) 361-369.

PATRICK, Dale. *The Rendering of God in the Old Testament* [OBT, 10]. Philadelphia: Fortress Press, 1981.

PATRICK, Dale and Allen SCULT. *Rhetoric and Biblical Interpretation* [JSOTSup, 82]. Sheffield: Almond Press, 1990.

PERDUE, Leo G., Bernard Brandon SCOTT, and William Johnston WISEMANN (eds.). *In Search of Wisdom* [FS. John G. GAMMIE]. Louisville: Westminster/John Knox Press, 1993.

PFEIFFER, Robert H. "Wisdom and Vision in the Old Testament." *ZAW* 52 (1934) 93-101.

PHILLIPS, Anthony. "*Nebelah* - a Term for Serious Disorderly and Unruly Conduct." *VT* 25 (1975) 237-242.

PLANK, K.A. "Raging Wisdom: A Banner of Defiance Unfurled." *Judaism* 36 (1987) 323-330.

POLZIN, Robert. *Biblical Structuralism:* Method and Subjectivity in the Study of Ancient Texts [SBLSS]. Philadelphia: Fortress Press, 1977.

PONTIFICAL BIBLICAL COMMISSION. "The Interpretation of the Bible in the Church." *Origins* 23/29 (6 January 1994) 487, 499-524.

PREUß, Horst Dietrich. *Einführung in die alttestamentliche Weisheitsliteratur* [Urban-Taschenbücher, 383]. Stuttgart: Kohlhammer, 1987.

PRIEST, J. "Humanism, Skepticism, and Pessimism in Israel." *JAAR* 36 (1968) 311-326.

QUANBECK, W.A. "Repentance." *IDB*, 4:33-34.

SANDMEL, S. "The Enjoyment of Scripture: An Esthetic Approach." *Judaism* 22 (1973) 455-467.

SCHMID, H.H. *Wesen und Geschichte der Weisheit:* Eine Untersuchung zur altorientalischen und israelitischen Weisheitsliteratur [BZAW, 101]. Berlin: Walter de Gruyter, 1966.

SCHNEIDERS, Sandra. "Freedom: Response and Responsibility -The Vocation of the Biblical Scholar in the Church." *In Wither Creativity, Freedom, Suffering?* Humanity, Cosmos, God [Proceedings of the Theology Institute of Villanova University]. Edited by Francis A. EIGO. Villanova 1981, pp. 25-52.

SCHNEIDERS, Sandra M. "From Exegesis to Hermeneutics: The Problem of the Contemporary Meaning of Scripture." *Hor* 8,1 (1981) 23-39.

SCHNEIDERS, Sandra M. *The Revelatory Text:* Interpreting the New Testament as Sacred Scripture. San Francisco: HarperCollins, 1991.

SCOBIE, Charles H. "The Place of Wisdom in Biblical Theology." *BTB* 14 (1984) 43-48.

SHEPPHARD, Gerald T. *Wisdom as a Hermeneutical Construct:* A Study in the Sapientializing of the Old Testament [BZAW, 151]. Berlin: Walter de Gruyter, 1980.

SIMIAN-YOFRE, Horacio. " ‫נחם‬." *TWAT*, 5:366-384.

SKEHAN. Patrick W. *Studies in Israelite Poetry and Wisdom* [CBQMS, 1]. Washington, DC: Catholic University of America, 1971.

SMART, Ninian. "Interpretation and Mystical Experience." *RelSt* 1 (1965) 75-87.

SMITH, Mark S. "'Seeing God' in the Psalms: The Background to the Beatific Vision in the Hebrew Bible." *CBQ* 50 (1988) 171-183.

SOARS PABHU, George M. "The Prophet as Theologian: Biblical Prophetism as a Paradigm for Doing Theology." *AsiaJT* 2,1 (1988) 3-11.

ŠPIDLÍK, Thomas and Pierre MIQUEL. "Icône." In the *Dictionnaire de spiritualité*, ascetique et mystique, doctrine et histoire. Edited by A. RAYEZ, et al. Paris 1974, volume 7/2, col. 1224-1239.

STERNBERG, Meir. *The Poetics of Biblical Narrative:* Ideological Literature and the Drama of Reading. Bloomington: Indiana University Press, 1987.

STOEBE, H.J. " **נחם**." *THAT*, 2:59-66.

TERRIEN, Samuel. *The Elusive Presence:* The Heart of Biblical Theology [Religious Perspectives, 26]. San Francisco: Harper and Row, 1983.

TERRIEN, Samuel. "The Play of Wisdom, Turning Point in Biblical Theology." *HBT* 3 (1981) 125-153.

THEISSEN, Gerd. "L'herméneutique biblique et la recherche de la vérité religieuse." *RTP* 122 (1990) 485-503.

TRACY, David. "Religious Language as Limit-Language." *TDig* 22 (1974) 291-307.

VANHOOZER, Kevin. "A Lamp in the Labyrinth: The Hermeneutics of 'Aesthetic' Theology." *TrinJ* 8 (1987) 25-56.

VON RAD, Gerhard. *Wisdom in Israel.* London: SPCK, 1972.

WAGNER, S. " **מאס** *ma'as*." *TWAT*, 4:618-633.

WALSH, Jerome T. "Despair as a Theological Virtue in the Spirituality of Ecclesiastes." *BTB* 12 (1982) 46-49.

WEISMAYER, Josef. "Was ist Mystik? Zum Verständnis von Glaube und religiöser Erfahrung." *GeistL* 61,5 (1988) 348-358.

WHYBRAY, R.N. *The Intellectual Tradition in the Old Testament* [BZAW, 135]. Berlin: Walter de Gruyter, 1974.

WICKS, Jared. "Biblical Criticism Criticized." *Greg* 72 (1991) 117-128.

WIFALL, Walter. "Models of God in the Old Testament." *BTB* 9 (1979) 179-186.

WILLIAMS, Rowan. "Theological Integrity." *NB* 71 (1991) 140-151.

ZIMMERLI, W. "The Place and Limit of Wisdom in the Framework of the Old Testament Theology." *SJT* 17 (1964) 146-158.

INDEX OF AUTHORS

THOMAS F. DAILEY, O.S.F.S.

Having been granted degrees in Sacred Theology from the Pontifical Gregorian University (Rome), the author currently holds the position of Assistant Professor in the Department of Philosophy & Theology at Allentown College of St. Francis de Sales (Center Valley, PA).

He is a member of several professional organizations: the Catholic Biblical Assocation of America, the Society of Biblical Literature, the College Theology Society, and the Fellowship of Catholic Scholars.

He has published articles on the Book of Job in such scholarly journals as the *Zeitschrift für die alttestamentliche Wissenschaft*, the *Biblische Zeitschrift*, the *Biblical Theology Bulletin*, the *American Benedictine Review*, the *Journal for the Study of the Old Testament*, and *Studies in Religion/Sciences Religieuses*. He has published other articles on biblical theology in *Interpretation*, *The Bible Today*, the *Irish Theological Quarterly*, and *Studia Mystica*.

He has also contributed a chapter on biblical studies in an edited work entitled *The Church in the Nineties: Its Legacy, Its Future* (Liturgical Press, 1993).